Music and Globalization
Critical Encounters

Edited by Bob W. White

Indiana University Press
Bloomington and Indianapolis

This book is a publication of

Indiana University Press
601 North Morton Street
Bloomington, Indiana 47404-3797 USA

iupress.indiana.edu

Telephone orders   800-842-6796
Fax orders   812-855-7931

Manufactured in the United States of America

Library of Congress Cataloging-in-Publication Data

Music and globalization : critical encounters / edited by Bob W. White.
      p. cm. — (Tracking globalization)
   Includes bibliographical references and index.
      ISBN 978-0-253-35712-0 (cloth : alk. paper) — ISBN 978-0-253-22365-4 (pbk. : alk. paper) — ISBN 978-0-253-00541-0 (e-book) 1. World music—History and criticism. 2. Music and globalization. I. White, Bob W., [date]
   ML3545.M89 2012
   780.9—dc23
                                                                                    2011031949

1 2 3 4 5 17 16 15 14 13 12

Contents

Preface and Acknowledgments

This volume grows out of the work of Critical World, a virtual research laboratory that uses ethnographic research to explore the relationship between popular culture and globalization. A Web-based experiment in project-oriented teaching and research (www.criticalworld.net), Critical World provides resources for critical engagement with the products of global culture and creates the opportunity for debate about the role of globalization in our everyday lives. Professors, researchers, students, and artists from various cultural backgrounds and disciplinary perspectives participate in the project. Bringing them together is a common concern about the history and consequences of globalization and a shared interest in popular culture's potential to reveal something about the worlds that we inhabit. Critical World consists of a series of multimedia modules intended for use in university teaching and research permitting users to combine video, sound, images, and text in novel ways. In addition to providing basic information about the project, the website also allows visitors to correspond directly with the project's author, either to give feedback or make suggestions about potential contributions to the project.

The Critical World Project recieved financial support from the Social Sciences and Humanities Research Council of Canada (SSHRC). The project was launched officially in 2004 during a three-day international workshop made possible with the assistance of the SSHRC Research Workshops and Conferences program as well as the Department of Anthropology and the Faculty of Arts and Sciences at the University of Montreal, the Canada Research Chair in Comparative Memory (Laval University), l'Agence universitaire de la Francophonie (Bureau Amérique du nord), and the Center for Research on Intermediality (University of Montreal). A number of the analyses presented in this volume were originally formulated in presentations at the workshop. This workshop would not have been possible without the participation of Prof. Bogumil Jewsiewicki of Laval University in Québec.

Critical World has benefited from the guidance of a steering committee that has been critical to the project's success: Steven Feld, Timothy Taylor, Denis-Constant Martin, Louise Meintjes, and Jocelyne Guilbault. Many thanks to the students, research assistants, and professionals who gave life to the project through their hard work and creative ideas, especially Nelson Arruda, Alexandrine Boudreault-Fournier, Sophie Le-Phat Ho, Charles Prémont, Marc Lemieux, Camille Brochu, Yara El-Ghadban, Marc-Antoine Lapierre, Sebastien Ouellette, Kiven Strohm, Ribio Nzeza, Estelle Prébolin, and Benjamin Trépanier. I would also like to recognize Charles Hamel for his patient and thorough approach to programming, François Beaudet for his ongoing technical support, and Lesley Braun and Julie Dénommée who helped with the final formatting of the manuscript. I would especially like to acknowledge Marcel Savard, co-founder of Critical World and coordinator for the first and longest phase of the project. As my primary collaborator on this project, Marcel deserves a great deal of credit for making this vision into a reality, and I am profoundly grateful for his intellectual and artistic contribution. I would like to dedicate this volume to Lucie, for getting me through.

Bob W. White
Montréal
September 2011

Music and Globalization

Introduction:
Rethinking Globalization through Music
Bob W. White

World music—the umbrella category under which various types of traditional and non-Western music are produced for Western consumption—has been waiting to happen for a long time. At least since the invention of new technologies of reproduction at the turn of the twentieth century and the realization soon after that records, far from being simply a means of selling phonographs, were in fact themselves a lucrative and renewable resource. Relatively little is known about the marketing strategies of the first international record companies, but clearly these companies distinguished early on between "exotic" music for affluent European and North American audiences and music—perhaps no less exotic—intended for people elsewhere who wanted to hear the sounds of their own culture (White 2002). Yet today, listening to the various forms of music being marketed under the label "world music," something appears to be different about this historical moment. From our current perspective, world music gives the impression of opening our ears to a vast realm of cultural and political possibilities but at the same time seems to usher in vaguely familiar forms of cultural expansionism and exploitation. If world music has indeed become the soundtrack for globalization, then music is not merely a manifestation of global processes and dynamics but is the very terrain on which globalization is articulated.

To begin, we must consider whether there is something distinctive about music—and not just world music—that enhances our understanding of globalization. The chapters in this volume suggest that music is particularly mobile and therefore easily commodified; indeed, nothing seems more characteristic of global capitalism than its capacity to transform culture into a commodity. But music is also

1

important to our understanding of globalization, because the nature of music is primarily social. Music is generally intended to be heard and often takes the form of a group activity, especially when one considers the way that communities of taste emerge and organize around particular styles and artists. Nonetheless, and despite all the feel-good promotional language about music being a "universal language," musical practice is everywhere deeply embedded in culture and history, an observation that ethnomusicologists have been making for decades. This means that a complex understanding of the performance and promotion of music can provide a wealth of information about how people from different cultures and class backgrounds engage with one another and attempt to work through what it means to be simultaneously "of the world" and "in the world." The phenomenon of world music, at least in terms of marketing, has only existed for about twenty years. But this is only a recent manifestation of a much older historical process, and the social science literature on globalization tends to focus more on *the culture of globalization* than on *cultures in a time of globalization*.

World Music and Globalization

The recent phenomenon of world music provides a window on human experience and social life during an era of globalization, but as a broadly diverse form of human expression music has always been global. The invention of new recording and reproduction technologies at the end of the nineteenth century created certain possibilities for music, regarding composition as well as distribution (Gronow 1998). In various places around the globe, the first half of the twentieth century was a period of great mobility for popular music (Jones 2001; Vianna 1999; White 2002). Afro-Cuban music in the interwar period, already a mixture of styles and sounds that emerged from the transatlantic slave trade, was able to take advantage of a lively commercial and cultural corridor between Havana and New York (Moore 1997). Several decades later the Western popular music soundscape saw the emergence of a series of exotic musical appropriations that were influenced not only by the war but also by the spectacular evolution of the tourism industry (Hayward 1999; Keightley 2004). In the 1970s Bob Marley's music made him an internationally recognized star and made reggae music an international standard of global popular music (Konaté 1987). The music that we call world music is the product of several waves of exchange, movement, and appropriation. Understanding its emergence as a commercial and musical phenomenon improves our ability to understand the links between consumer capitalism (Taylor 2007), new regimes of technology (Sterne 2003), and the evolution of the modern nation-state (Wade 2000).

The term "world music," as a label used for marketing and promotion, is a relatively recent creation. The idea of world music gained considerable momentum following a series of meetings in England, in 1987, attended by music industry specialists including journalists, producers, and promoters of independent music, all seeking to improve their strategies for promoting musicians from non-Western countries. The solution they arrived at was to group the various artists under the world music label and organize a promotional campaign targeting record stores, most of which still did not know how to classify the various styles and artists:

> We had a very simple, small ambition. It was all geared to record shops, that was the only thing we were thinking about. In America, King Sunny Ade [from Nigeria] was being filed under reggae. That was the only place shops could think of to put him. In Britain they didn't know where to put this music—I think Ade was just lost in the alphabet, next to Abba. In 1985 Paul Simon did Graceland and that burst everything wide open, because he created an interest in South African music. People were going into shops saying: "I want some of that stuff" and there wasn't anywhere for them to look. (Charlie Gillet, cited in Denselow 2004)

The details of these meetings (often referred to as the "Empress of Russia" meetings, after the restaurant-bar where they took place) are published on the website for the musical magazine *fRoots*.[1] The editors of this site have carefully presented meeting minutes, agendas, and comments from the editor-in-chief, who was present at the meetings. An interview with one of the attendees gives the impression that the use of the term "world music" at these meetings somehow predated the phenomenon:

> People started to make what they thought was world music. Ian Anderson at Rogue Records put out a wonderful cassette made in Senegal by Baaba Maal, which was pure world music as all of us thought about it. Baaba Maal was subsequently signed to Island Records, and began to make what he and his producers conceived as "world music." It was a hotchpotch, a hybrid, a fusion—but it would not have existed before we came up with this term. (Charlie Gillet, cited in Denselow 2004)

With no intention of minimizing the historic nature of these meetings, I suggest that this reading is inaccurate given what we currently know about the history of globalization and music. Not only was the term "world music" used earlier in the music industry (for example, at Peter Gabriel's WOMAD festival, first held in 1982), but it also has a long intellectual history within the painted halls and ivory towers of the academy.

Steven Feld (2001) situates the origins of the term within North American music conservatories of the 1960s, which were criticized for their programs' ethnocentrism, as they had focused solely on Western musical canons. The growing division between musicology and ethnomusicology in the 1970s ran counter to the historical analysis of Western classical music (termed "music") to the study of non-European traditions (termed "world music" or "music of the world"), but, according to Feld, the pluralist intentions underlying this division had the unfortunate consequence of further widening the ideological gap between these two domains. The term "world music," however, did not become problematic until the 1980s, when a number of artists and promoters, influenced by ethnomusicologists' recordings of "traditional" music, began to use the term more systematically to refer to musical traditions outside the Western industrialized nations.

The most outspoken critics of world music argue that it is little more than a marketing tool (Brennan 2001; Byrne 1999; Goodwin and Gore 1990). According to this reasoning, the term has no meaning, as it is generally used to designate a hodge-podge of non-Western music with no concern for the formal or historical characteristics of the genre. Nonetheless, some have attempted to define world music as a commercial category or in terms of geography or a cultural region. Others describe it in more abstract terms, such as Veit Erlmann's (1996) view of world music as an expression of a "global imagination." According to Julien Mallet, we have yet to come up with a satisfactory definition:

> What emerges from these examples is that definitions oscillate between an empirical classification that, when rigorous, causes the notion to implode, and an attempt to delimit a concept that will only have meaning for sociologists and anthropologists who specialize in the study of music. Needless to say, these attempts at definition are fundamentally flawed. (2002, 841–842; my translation)

Much like "world music," "globalization" is a concept often loosely defined and ideologically motivated. But given all that we have invested in the notion of globalization and all that is at stake—intellectually and otherwise—we cannot simply write it off as imprecise or, even worse, as meaningless. Regardless of its amorphous, protean qualities, globalization, in a certain sense, is indeed *out there*. Although "globalization" is difficult to define, "we cannot easily discard the word, in part because, just like modernity, it seems to point to phenomena not easily covered by other words" (Trouillot 2003, 47). Instead of fretting over the word, we need to focus on what globalization does or, more precisely, what people do with globalization.

Despite the complex and dynamic nature of the processes of globalization, much of what is said about it has become rather predictable; for example, globalization is the expansion of commercial networks, the blurring of cultural and national boundaries, and the compression of space and time. Most definitions begin with a description of globalization as a globalized-globalizing world overflowing with spectacular combinations of material culture, juxtapositions of place, and confusions of scale. Illustrations include American fast-food restaurants in formerly communist economies, indigenous people from the Amazon basin in full traditional garb using a video camera, and cell phones in the African bush. This snapshot approach to the study of globalization is troublesome, because it plays on a series of "surprising" juxtapositions that place the material culture of Western modernity in the same semiotic frame as the West's imagined Others (for example, capitalism vs. communism, tradition vs. modernity, big vs. small). As a rhetorical device, these images can be quite effective, but from an analytical point of view they tell us more about Western categories of knowledge than about the "world of globalization" (Inda and Rosaldo 2008). Indeed, the rhetorical device of juxtaposition has been a central feature in much of the anthropological literature on the topic of globalization, and this trend suggests that our theoretical frames are limited by a tendency to think about complex problems in the simplified terms of opposition (cf. Tsing 2000). Commentators on globalization can easily be divided into cheerleaders and naysayers, and this is also true of the scholarly literature.[2]

Anna Tsing (2000) argues that we should be just as interested in the phenomenon of globalization as we are in "endorsements of the importance of globalization," which she refers to as "globalism." According to Tsing, globalization's charisma—its ability to "excite and inspire"—should not cause us to shy away from the critical study of this phenomenon but should serve instead as a source of critical reflection and, as others have argued, theoretical renewal (Mazzarella 2004, 348). In her reading of David Harvey's contribution to the field of globalization studies, Tsing argues that globalist anthropology has uncritically reproduced Harvey's notion of "time-space compression" as proof that we have entered a new era in which cultural diversity is increasingly in danger of being organized (Hannerz 1996) and difference increasingly commodified (Erlmann 1996). Although technological changes in transportation and telecommunication have certainly altered our way of moving and communicating, it is far from clear that these changes are experienced in a universal fashion (Bauman 1998).[3] If we can establish that the way in which people experience time and space has changed, what are the advantages, either intellectually or politically, of documenting this type of change? The critical study of global encounters through music points in rather different directions; not only does it show that knowledge about the world is made possible through various types of encounters but also that the outcomes of these encounters are highly constrained by actors and institutions outside, or beyond the control of, individual artists or consumers.

Global Encounters through Music

The last thirty years have witnessed an impressive amount of scholarship about the production and performance of music in cultural settings outside the industrialized nations of the West. In this rapidly growing field of research, important advances have been made in terms of historical analysis (Jones 2001; Moore 1997;

Shain 2002), increased emphasis on the relationship between music and politics (Averill 1997; Meintjes 1990; White 2008), and greater attention to national and regional identity (Guilbault 1993; Askew 2002), race (Wade 2000; Meintjes 2003), and experience (Rice 2003; Taylor 1998). A quick glance at the U.S.-based journal *Ethnomusicology*—the flagship publication for ethnomusicological research in North America—brings to light the extent to which research on non-Western music has evolved in recent years. Not only has there been a greater emphasis on various forms of contemporary and popular music (such as hip-hop, jazz, rock, and state-sponsored folk or neo-traditional music, all genres for ethnomusicology), but much recent scholarship is exploring these globalizing forms of musical practice in surprising places (for example, rock music in Trinidad, hip-hop in Japan, and underground punk in Jakarta). Although recent research in anthropology and ethnomusicology has been increasingly concerned with the relationship between various types of local and global musical forms, including stylistic borrowing or appropriation, relatively little scholarship has focused on the actual encounters— the chance meetings, coordinated misunderstandings, and ongoing collaborations— that bring people of different musical or cultural backgrounds together or the ways that these encounters condition musical practice and knowledge about the world.

The notion of "global encounter" refers to situations in which individuals from radically different traditions or worldviews come into contact and interact with one another based on limited information about one another's values, resources, and intentions. An encounter can be limited in its frequency or duration but can also be characterized by constancy and repetition. Under certain historical circumstances, actors may sense that something is totally new or unique about the encounter, as in the staging mechanism of certain forms of tourism (MacCannell 1976) or in the colonial encounter described by Talal Asad (1973; cf. Bastos and Feld, this volume). Even in the field of anthropology, which has a long history of examining various forms of cultural borrowing or blending, analyses have been more concerned with the result of encounters than the encounters themselves. Indeed, the idea of encounters in cross-cultural settings, in which various types of actors and agents are called upon to negotiate power differentials and different versions of reality, has rarely been the object of systematic inquiry. As this volume will show, the encounters that emerge through music in the context of globalization are multifaceted and require complex conceptual tools to explain how musical practice produces not only difference but also various forms of locality and value (see Noveck, this volume).

Communication across cultures can be articulated through the language of violence and brutality, especially in places where the ghosts of colonialism and slavery still hover (Browning, Bastos, this volume); in the words of Daniel Noveck's informants: "They treat us like animals." Encounters occur on the terrain (or at least on the terms) of the powerful, who mostly ignore the privilege that allows them to play by rules of their choosing. As White demonstrates, many of the encounters in the history of globalizing music are characterized by projection, fear, prejudice, and miscommunication, but face-to-face encounters are subject to the same modalities of misunderstanding (2011).

People come to encounters with their own baggage or "tradition"[4] and, under the right circumstances, a certain coordination can occur despite differences in knowledge and goals, as in the encounter discussed in this volume by Rafael Bastos: "Sting was experiencing a period of questioning and engagement regarding global issues and social justice, which was emblematic of Raoni's quest. The same may be said of Raoni in relation to Sting. . . . And so their encounter, though appearing to be casual, was marked by mutual condemnation." Fundamentally skeptical about the nature of the "we" created in these situations of contact, Bastos asks difficult questions about the globalization literature itself, which, he argues, tends to reduce the colonial encounter to a form of communicative exchange through the articulation of a "recalibrated culturalism." His discussion of the encounter between Sting and Raoni is more about an encounter of two universes than two individuals, and his analysis offers an important lesson for future research because of its ability to render the cultural complexity that lies behind this meeting, namely the political jockeying that informs Raoni's participation in Sting's project, a backstory to which Sting is mostly oblivious.

Focusing on ethnographic detail, but also performing the daunting task of zooming out to look at the overarching determinants of ideology and political economy, the chapters in this volume attempt to give new weight to the concept of globalization, one that is firmly grounded but also floating above the observational fray. If, as Timothy Taylor suggests in his contribution to the volume, *music* from non-Western musical cultures is indeed becoming progressively fragmented and absorbed into commercial practice in the West in the form of *sounds,* how can social scientific research separate the musical sounds from the political noise? And from local artists' perspective, how is one to "navigate that sea without finding oneself back in a figural slave ship of exploitation?" (Browning, this volume).

One answer to this question comes from Taylor (2007), who urges us to return to the question of political economy: "'World music' as a category of music . . . is not simply the soundtrack to globalization; it is a symptom of global capitalism." Many of the authors in the volume draw from the critical tradition of cultural Marxism, some indirectly and some employing the basic concepts of Marxist theory in surprisingly fresh ways. Steven Feld's analysis uncovers the way that alienation occurs through participation in wider global markets: "world music—whatever good it does, whatever pleasure it brings—rests on economic structures that turn intangible cultural heritage into detachable labor." Ariana Hernandez-Reguant presents a breathtaking description of global markets for Afro-Cuban cultural products in the era of "world music": "the point was to allow Western audiences to enjoy Cuban music without necessarily having to turn aesthetic enjoyment into an ideological statement." While her analysis differs considerably from

Hayward's discussion of the local music industry in Vanuatu, together the two chapters demonstrate that everywhere markets matter but they are not everywhere the same. A number of contributors show the extent to which the effects of these globalizing market flows are often disastrous not only for local economies but also for individuals (Browning, Noveck). As Daniel Noveck explains regarding the newfound mobility of traditional musician-artisans from Mexico, the problems that arise are markedly quotidian: then as now, Rarámuris on these trips complain that they don't get enough to eat.

In the context of intercultural communication and encounters, the playing field on which actors encounter one another is rarely level, but this need not be an obstacle to the production of meaning and the articulation of sound (Martin, Shain, Hayward, this volume). Instead, it is the erasure of this difference, or the denial of this shared time and space (Fabian's "coevalness" [1983]), that characterizes most exchanges across cultural lines. Similar processes of denial and erasure occur in the production of music for global consumption. As White shows in his chapter about cosmopolitan yearning among fans of world music in the West, promoters and consumers of world music reproduce essentialist discourses and practices that actually hide behind a rhetoric of non-essentialism, in many ways assuaging the anxieties associated with global capitalism: "World music is not a problem per se; it becomes a problem when the listener-consumer makes claims about the world via music without attempting to go beyond the simple projection of a personal listening utopia." In a similar vein, the seemingly innocuous idea of world music as "infectious"—meaning desirable—has deeply troubling implications across national and racial divides, as Barbara Browning shows in her chapter about the symbolic and historic connections between Fela Kuti, Gilberto Gil, and the HIV-AIDS pandemic.

Writing about slavery and cultural creation in the context of the transatlantic slave trade, Denis-Constant Martin explains that "understanding the processes of cross-fertilization and creation that led to the invention of original genres in the slave societies and their successor societies should help us analyze the mechanisms of current globalization," reminding us that there is no globalization outside of history. Barbara Browning's analysis of the lyrical yearnings of the Brazilian superstar Gilberto Gil suggests that historical narrative is linked to social memory: the metaphor of the transatlantic vessel is a melancholy memory of slavery but also a lifeboat that provides access to the future via "the infosea." Similarly Steven Feld's discussion of musical appropriation in Western avant-garde pop music explains how the conflicting narratives of world music "embed a fraught cultural politics of nostalgia, that is, each is deeply linked to the management of loss and renewal in the modern world." Thus, in some sense, memories of encounters (some deeply traumatic) are activated through the encounter with other subjects, recursively permitting new kinds of collective memory and new versions of historically specific individual memory.

The Organization of This Volume

The contributors to this volume have a deep understanding and appreciation of musical practice, but they struggle to understand how music itself creates the conditions of globalization. How they render the complex relationship between musicians and cultural brokers, the expressive forms they are driven to produce and promote, and the political and economic forces through which they must navigate varies from one author to the next. Uniting them all, however, is their desire to use fine-tuned historical and ethnographic data as a way to understand music both as product and process. Through the notion of the encounter (metaphorical or otherwise), they explore the modalities of different cross-cultural encounters as the channels through which the worlds of music and globalization are constantly rearticulated. Whether in person or completely virtual, the encounters in this collection demonstrate how power actually operates in the context of cross-cultural contact, as well as how various types of "selves" and "Others" are constituted, misconstrued, and misunderstood through uneven forms of exchange and mutual self-interest.

Part 1 includes four case studies that reveal how history is inscribed in today's global encounters. Each chapter in this section addresses one aspect of the larger political economy (for example, slavery, colonialism, or capitalism) that in some way structures the terms and outcomes of particular encounters. Denis-Constant Martin's detailed analysis of various processes of musical creolization under conditions of slavery (involving instruments, sounds, and structures) enables us to grasp the underlying dynamic of cultural production under globalization, specifically that "domination never extinguishes creation; that, behind the musically empty and commercially profitable label of 'world music,' strategies of invention may be deployed that continue and extend the creolization initially begun in the brutality of servitude."

Steven Feld's analysis of the groundbreaking experimental rock album *My Life in the Bush of Ghosts* examines how Brian Eno and David Byrne's use of exotic voices, beats, and sounds tapped into Western liberal critiques of organized religion at the same time that it drew in Western listeners in search of a new spiritualism. Feld explains how the production of world music depends on the mechanism of schizophonia, "the splitting of sounds from sources." He also reminds us that this dynamic must be understood in a logic of late industrial capitalism, since world music, "whatever good it does, whatever pleasure it brings—rests on economic structures that turn intangible cultural heritage into detachable labor."

Philip Hayward's discussion of the local music industry in postwar Vanuatu demonstrates the impact that numerous waves of foreign intervention have had on cultural performance and identity in the region. In Hayward's analysis, globalization is more of a resource than a restriction, since locally orchestrated manifestations of *kastom* culture are a source of pride as a cultural heritage and also provide jobs. The emergence of new forms of local popular music has led to what appears to be a form of cultural self-sufficiency, which enables local artists to reap the benefits of being recognized as local and regional players.

In what he refers to as an anthropology of the encounter between British pop superstar Sting and Amazonian indigenous leader Raoni, Rafael José de Menezes Bastos describes how the stars of the global environmental movement seemed to be temporarily aligned with those of the indigenous rights movement in Brazil and how the political semantics of this encounter were marked by the musical universes in which these two men were seen as having cultural legitimacy. But Bastos warns against reading this meeting either as an intersection of the logics coming into contact with each other or as a third logic born from their sum, arguing that instead it must be interpreted as a form of inter-societal contact that is inseparable from the colonial encounter.

The structuring effect of institutions such as slavery, colonialism, and capitalism creates certain possibilities and rules out others. Having established this groundwork in part 1, part 2 considers what individual actors (artists, promoters, and producers) do to position themselves as artistic or commercial agents within these structures. Much of what is described in these chapters has to do with the Janus-faced nature of any process of mediation, in this case a constant interplay between perceptions of consumers' desire and artists' authenticity.

In a provocative essay about the globalization of an indigenous community from Northwest Mexico (the Rarámuri) and a not so indigenous musical instrument (the violin), Daniel Noveck poses a question that is central for much of this book: How might we understand music as mediation, not simply expressing culture but actively producing forms of difference, locality, and value in its moments of performance and circulation? He examines two moments in the trajectory of this community of musicians—a folkloric dance performance in Texas and a trip to an Italian violin maker—to show exactly how different types of cultural brokers bring their knowledge and power to bear on the outcomes of particular encounters.

Ariana Hernandez-Reguant's analysis of the Cuban world music "frontier" examines how foreign-born independent music producers, despite a great deal of financial risk and uncertainty, "came to be seen as the faces of the global economy." She describes how, in a fascinating turn of events, the reintroduction of Afro-Cuban music into global markets for Western music was actually precipitated through its historical and aesthetic links to African popular music, which, according to most accounts, constituted the vanguard of the world music wave of the 1980s.

It is not coincidental that Richard Shain's chapter immediately follows Hernandez-Reguant's, as the two complement each other. Shain presents a harrowing tale of cultural and musical mediation in his detailed analysis of the career of Senegalese musician Laba Sosseh, who is fascinating not only because of his attachment to the idea of faithfully reproducing the canon of Afro-Cuban music in an African setting but also because of the extraordinary effort he made to "Africanize" Afro-Cuban music in various parts of the New World, including Cuba itself. Shain's analysis is steeped in historical detail, enabling the reader to see not only the dynamics and mechanisms of cross-cultural collaboration between artists but also what is at stake politically when cultural brokers such as Sosseh bypass the traditional north-south circuitry of the music industry to focus his energies on the "global south."

Part 3 examines manifestations of globalization and music that do not involve personal encounters through music, as is the case in most of the chapters in parts 1 and 2. Thus the encounters presented in this final section can be seen as imagined in the sense that the self experiments with ideas about the Other rather than with the Other's ideas themselves. This does not mean, however, that the work of imagination is inconsequential. On the contrary, the chapters in part 3 show exactly how much can be done without the Other and the extent to which the idea of the Other enables the self to rework or confirm its place in the world.

Barbara Browning builds from her previous research on the metaphor of contagion to weave an intricate narrative about the connections between the complex political and musical legacy of Nigeria's Fela Kuti and the transatlantic wanderings of Brazilian superstar Gilberto Gil. Acting as a spokesperson for the diversity of experience of black people, Gil uses the imagery of the slave ship to call attention to the commodification of African bodies, "but," as Browning tells us, "he simultaneously envisions the possible liberatory potential of new technologies, which might allow black artists, in particular, to critique, and contaminate, the circulation of their political and artistic productions."

Timothy Taylor's chapter on the recording and compositional practices of culture industry specialists in the United States argues that, as a genre, world music has had more influence in terms of its sounds than its genres or artists. His ethnography of music intended for advertising shows how marketing experts have come to depend on bits of sound (melodies, timbres, and instruments) to mark particular products as "Other" for Western cosmopolitan audiences. In this sense, Taylor suggests that world music has become integral to how the West imagines itself, as it "has seeped into the broader musical soundscape of the contemporary West."

White, in the concluding chapter, is also concerned with how the West imagines non-Western musical Others, although his analysis focuses on the practices of consumers. His discussion of how to reform listening practices is intended not so much as a critique as a call to action for critically minded consumers, a pedagogical formula that provides everyday consumers (including professors and their students) with the tools to undermine their assumptions about cultural difference and invest real energy into the work of understanding cultural complexity outside the West. Music, White tells us, "can be a window into this complexity, but it can also be a brick wall."

The inspiration for this volume comes from Critical World. Although initially conceived as a website to provide information and resources for the critical study of world music, Critical World gradually took on a life of its own, becoming a kind of virtual laboratory for teaching and research on music and globalization, with a strong emphasis on critical approaches to ethnography.[5] Critical World consists of various projects, each making use of at least four different media types (images, videos, sound, and text). This feature, together with the fact that the media content of each project is generated based on the principal of free association, make it possible for users to consult different media in personal and novel ways. One objective of the Critical World laboratory is to experiment with the meaning-spaces between different types of media—a phenomenon known as "intermediality"— and the publication of this book is an important step in that direction, as most audiovisual material that accompanies the written word is limited by its status as an illustration of something being described in the text. Each chapter in this volume has a corresponding multimedia module online that refers to the content of the chapter but also gestures beyond the written word.[6] Thus, while one may discover the online multimedia project by exploring the chapters of this book, the reverse is also true. This method of presentation is intended to encourage critical thought regarding the representation of culture and the production of knowledge, whether expert or otherwise. As the multimedia modules on Critical World contain a comments window, the contributors to this volume hope that readers will take the time to consult the book and the virtual laboratory simultaneously and look forward to feedback on their work.

Notes

1. See http://www.frootsmag.com.

2. See, for example, Feld's (2001) discussion of "anxiety" and "celebration" or Meyer and Geschiere's (2003) use of the terms "flux" and "fix."

3. One could probably argue the same for Gidden's discussion of "distanciation" or "disembedding," in which an increasing number of people's lives are "shaped by events occurring many miles away" (1990, 64). For further analysis of this question, see Inda and Rosaldo 2008 and Tomlinson 1999.

4. Here I am using the term in the same sense as did Hans-Georg Gadamer to mean a series of dispositions or prejudices that are transmitted from one generation to the next but that are not necessarily limited to the realm of culture in the anthropological meaning of the term. For a more detailed discussion, see White, forthcoming.

5. Visit Critical World at http://www.criticalworld.net.

6. To consult the module for a particular chapter, visit http://www.criticalworld.net.

References

Asad, Talal, ed. 1973. *Anthropology and the Colonial Encounter*. London: Ithaca.

Askew, Kelly. 2002. *Performing the Nation: Swahili Music and Cultural Politics in Tanzania*. Chicago: University of Chicago Press.

Averill, Gage. 1997. *A Day for the Hunter, a Day for the Prey: Popular Music and Power in Haiti*. Chicago: University of Chicago Press.

Bauman, Zygmunt. 1998. *Globalization: The Human Consequences.* New York: Columbia University Press.

Brennan, Timothy. 2001. "World Music Does Not Exist." *Discourse* 23.1 (winter): 44–62.

Byrne, David. 1999. "I Hate World Music." *New York Times,* October 3.

Denselow, Robin. 2004. "We Created World Music." *The Guardian,* June 29. Retrieved from http://www.guardian.co.uk/music/2004/jun/29/popandrock1.

Erlmann, Veit. 1996. "The Esthetics of the Global Imagination: Reflections on World Music in the 1990s." *Public Culture* 8:467–487.

Fabian, Johannes. 1983. *Time and the Other: How Anthropology Makes Its Object.* New York: Columbia University Press.

Feld, Steven. 2001. "A Sweet Lullaby for World Music." In *Globalization,* ed. Arjun Appadurai, 189–216 Durham, NC: Duke University Press.

Gadamer, Hans-Georg. 1989. *Truth and Method.* 2nd rev. ed. Translated by J. Weinsheimer and D. G. Marshall. New York: Crossroad.

Goodwin, Andrew, and Joe Gore. 1990. "World Beat and the Cultural Imperialism Debate." *Socialist Review* 20:63–80.

Gronow, Pekka, and Ilpo Saunio. 1998. An International History of the Recording Industry. Translated by Christopher Moseley. London: Cassel.

Guilbault, Jocelyne. 1993. *Zouk: World Music in the West Indies.* Chicago: University of Chicago Press.

Hannerz, Ulf. 1996. *Transnational Connections: Culture, People, Places.* New York: Routledge.

Hayward, Philip. 1999. *Widening the Horizon: Exoticism in Post-War Popular Music.* Sydney: John Libbey.

Hymes, Dell, ed. 1969. *Reinventing Anthropology.* New York: Random House.

Inda, Jonathan Xavier, and Renato Rosaldo, eds. 2008. *The Anthropology of Globalization: A Reader.* Malden, MA: Blackwell.

Jones, Andrew F. 2001. *Yellow Music: Media, Culture, and Colonial Modernity in the Chinese Jazz Age.* Durham, NC: Duke University Press.

Keightley, Keir. 2004. "Adventures in Sound: Audio Technology and the Virtual Global." Conference presentation, "Critical Worlds I," University of Montreal, November 13.

Konaté, Yacouba. 1987. *Alpha Blondy.* Paris: Ceda.

MacCannell, Dean. 1976. *The Tourist: A New Theory of the Leisure Class.* New York: Schocken.

Mallet, Julien. 2002. "World Music": Une question d'ethnomusicologie? *Cahiers d'études africaines.* 42 (4), 168: 831–852.

Mazzarella, William. 2004. Culture, Globalization, Mediation. *Annual Review of Anthropology.* 33:345–67.

Meintjes, Louise. 1990. "Paul Simon's *Graceland,* South Africa, and the Mediation of Musical Meaning," *Ethnomusicology* (winter): 37–73.

———. 2003. *Sound of Africa: Making Music Zulu in a South African Studio.* Durham, NC: Duke University Press.

Meyer, Birgit, and Peter Geschiere. 2003. *Globalization and Identity: Dialectics of Flow and Closure.* Malden, MA: Blackwell.

Moore, Robin D. 1997. *Nationalizing Blackness: Afrocubanismo and Artistic Revolution in Havana, 1920–1940.* Pittsburgh, PA: University of Pittsburgh Press.

Rice, Timothy. 2003. "Time, Place, and Metaphor in Musical Experience and Ethnography." *Ethnomusicology* 47 (2): 151–179.

Shain, Richard. 2002. "Roots in Reverse: Cubanismo in Twentieth-Century Senegalese Music." *International Journal of African Historical Studies* 35 (1): 83–101.

Sterne, Jonathan. 2003. *The Audible Past: Cultural Origins of Sound Reproduction.* Durham, NC: Duke University Press.

Taylor, Julie. 1998. *Paper Tangos.* Durham, NC: Duke University Press.

Taylor, Timothy D. 2007. "The Commodification of Music at the Dawn of the Era of 'Mechanical Music.'" *Ethnomusicology* 51 (2): 281–305.

———. n.d. "Global Capitalism and the Commodification of Taste."

Tomlinson, John. 1999. *Globalization and Culture.* Chicago: University of Chicago Press.

Trouillot, Michel-Rolph. 2003. *Global Transformations: Anthropology and the Modern World.* New York: Palgrave.

Tsing, Anna. 2000. "The Global Situation." *Cultural Anthropology* 15 (3): 327–360.

Vianna, Hermano. 1999 *The Mystery of Samba: Popular Music and National Identity in Brazil.* Translated by John Charles Chasteen. Chapel Hill: University of North Carolina Press.

Wade, Peter. 2000. *Music, Race, and Nation: Musica Tropical in Colombia.* Chicago: University of Chicago Press.

White, Bob W. 2002. "Congolese Rumba and Other Cosmopolitanisms." *Cahiers d'études africaines* 42 (4), 168: 663–686.

———. 2008. *Rumba Rules: The Politics of Dance Music in Mobutu's Zaire.* Durham, NC: Duke University Press.

———. 2011. "The Power of Collaboration." In *Affirming Collaboration: Community and Humanist Activist Art in Québec and Beyond,* edited by Louise Lachapelle and Devora Neumark. Montreal: Levier/Engrenage Noir.

Part 1.

Structured Encounters

1

The Musical Heritage of Slavery: From Creolization to "World Music"

Denis-Constant Martin

Most forms of music described today as "popular" or "mass" music (Martin 2006) are derived, in one way or another, from practices that appeared within societies organized around slavery in territories conquered by Europeans: from the French odes of Georges Brassens to the Chinese rock of Cui Jan, from Japanese reggae to the Spanish ska of Ska-P, from the vagabond rovings of Emir Kusturica to the inventions of Yothu Yindi, from the songs of Björk to the modernized rebetiko of Manolis Hiotis, beginning with the countless genres invented in North and South America and the Caribbean. These musics are the product of cultural contacts (Turgeon 1996) that occurred in peculiar conditions of inequality and absolute violence, all based on the denial of the humanity of people removed from their homelands.

The first forms of musical expression by slaves, of which all these contemporary forms to a greater or lesser degree bear the stamp, were harbingers of what is now called globalization. Understanding the processes of cross-fertilization and creation that led to the invention of original genres in the slave societies and their successor societies should help us analyze the mechanisms of current globalization. This history of cross-fertilization and innovation, of creolization in Édouard Glissant's sense (Glissant 1990, 1997), indicates at the very least that the spread of certain phenomena, including musical phenomena, throughout the planet is linked to systems of oppression and the inextricable strategies of resistance, accommodation, and power they have brought into being and continue to produce. The study of the modalities of the emergence of new musics in slave societies—or at least the attempt to reconstruct them from fragmentary data—should enable us to understand the functions of musical creation in the face of slavery, and hence to reevaluate the meaning of "world music" in today's world. Given that it is impossible, in the limited scope of this chapter, to cover all the musical forms that emerged from slavery, I simply base my argument on two examples: the musics of North America and of South Africa.[1]

Cross-Fertilization and Innovation

A great number of the musics widely listened to today are the product of the blending and innovation that has occurred in North America. Two strands have been particularly fertile: a secular strand leading from blackface minstrels to an infinite range of light musical forms but also to the blues, country and western, jazz, rock, and all their offshoots; and a second, initially sacred strand beginning with spirituals and leading, after many twists and turns, to soul, reggae and rap.

THINKING CROSS-FERTILIZATION

Despite the inequality and violence that characterized them, slave societies were also universes of contact, exchange, and blending. Slavery was also a cause of cultural cross-fertilization in which all took part, masters and slaves alike. It is difficult, however, for Western social sciences to think in terms of cross-fertilization in view of the long habit within that discipline to classify events and seek out a supposed purity or "authenticity" (Amselle 1990). To achieve this, we must abandon the idea that blending and cross-fertilization necessarily produce mongrelization and impoverishment, and recognize instead that they are sources of "fundamental dynamics" (Gruzinski 1999, 54) that unfold in "strange zones" and bring into play previously unknown procedures (ibid., 241) capable of engendering creative activity.

In the beginning comes the encounter: people move of their own free will or are moved by some force and come up against others: they are all human beings (even if some argue otherwise), and therefore they are similar, yet different. What differentiates them frightens them at times but, inevitably, also fascinates them. This ambivalence underlies the contact they establish and frames the exchanges that ensue. Those exchanges may be, and often have been, violent, by dint of the fears that seize human beings or by their will to dominate or their ambitions of conquest. But brutality never prevents objects from circulating (Turgeon 2003), bodies from rubbing up against one another, words from mingling (Alleyne 1980; Valkhoff 1972), or musical forms from becoming entangled with one another (Dubois 1997; Pacquier 1996). Meetings between human groups are thus almost always opportunities to establish a relationship, though, admittedly, one of domination. For example, when the meeting occurs at the end of a voyage on land which some people wish to settle and control, and when people are brought from other continents to exploit those lands, the exchanges between natives, conquering settlers, and slaves or indentured servants shape a new world. Though asymmetrical, those exchanges are based on a degree of reciprocity (Turgeon 1996, 16). All are transformed by them. Against a background of incomprehension, cruelty, collusion, and solidarity, and through misunderstandings and approximations (Gruzinski 1996, 144), all parties forge markers for themselves in which the Other necessarily plays a part, and these markers—on both sides—together delimit the mixed universe they now share.[2]

Contacts between settlers, slaves, and natives give rise to cultural transfers (Turgeon 1996) that produce the cross-fertilization from which creative activity emerges. At stake for all parties to the mix is nothing less than the invention of a society in which all must live—by choice, chance, or force. That society not only has to be built but also has to be given meanings, which will vary according to the groups devising them but cannot be impermeably isolated from one another. The cross-fertilization that is the launching pad for creolization must be understood then, first, as a creative activity with the goal of mastering the environment and understanding—and then often changing—the respective positions occupied by its various inhabitants. In the Americas, languages and religions have provided many confirmations of this. It is no different for musics.

CONQUEST AND SLAVERY: A NEW WORLD

In North America, in the areas where the United States was to form, there were, of course, indigenous peoples, but Europeans from various countries settled there and gradually took control of the lands stretching between the Atlantic and the Pacific. The colonialists of the Eastern seaboard, and then of the Southeast, imported African slaves. From 1619 to 1865 between four hundred thousand and six hundred thousand persons, depending on the estimates one accepts, were removed from their homelands in this way. American Indian populations were varied, whereas the European invaders were not as diverse and, in the early years, usually came from England, Scotland, and Ireland. Meanwhile, Africans belonged to a great many societies established between present-day Senegal and Angola, and sometimes in the interior quite far from the coasts, if not indeed in Mozambique or Madagascar (Curtin 1969; Davidson 1980). The social systems, religions, languages, food customs, and music of their areas of origin were therefore extremely diverse. Moreover, slaves were systematically dispersed on arrival so that those from the same original locality could not reestablish their group (Genovese 1974). They lived, particularly in the seventeenth and eighteenth centuries, in intimate contact with the settlers, most often on small farms where a small number of slaves lived alongside a European family. Until the late nineteenth century, the poor found themselves mingled together in the northern cities with no distinctions of origin. From these contacts came new musics.

The natives certainly contributed to the new musical mixes, although their decimation probably restricted their influence. In any case, the Amerindian contribution to the creole musics of North America has received little scholarly attention (Conway 1995, 315; Nash 1974). Though I postulate its existence, I am unable to take account of it here. Historians generally recognize the existence of an Anglo-Celtic core among the Europeans around which new musical practices aggregated (Cockrell 1997; Conway 1995). As far as the Africans were concerned, having been dispersed and with no great way to communicate among themselves, they had to invent the means by which they could collectively make sense of their condition and their physical and social environment They therefore had to overcome their differences in order to reconstitute tools for thinking, communicating, and acting in concert. Language, religion, and music were some of the main areas in which they exerted their will to create in order to survive.

The most realistic hypothesis is that, having been cast into a state of social death (Patterson 1982) and denied their humanity, they reacted by striving to restore their sense of humanity, the better to proclaim it against those who refused to accept it. In pursuing this aim, the captives employed two strategies for creating shared musics, proclaiming their humanity while providing bonds indispensable to social life. The first was to use whatever similar or compatible elements might exist within the musical systems of the areas from which the slaves originated, to elaborate, so to speak, a "pan-Africanism of exile" (Martin 1991). The second was to appropriate elements of the musical practices of the masters—but, again, especially practices that were compatible with "pan-African" forms (Nettl 1978; Storm Roberts 1972)—and reinterpret and transform those elements. These two strategies were probably governed by the need to give meaning to the absurdity of life as a slave and to regain hope (Depestre 1980).

Minstrels and Saints

The dearth of sources on the musical practices of slaves in the seventeenth and eighteenth centuries prevents us from precisely reconstructing the emergence of North American creole musics. The writings or reproductions studied by Dena Epstein (1977) and reassessed by Ronald Radano (2003) point to some general features. In settlers' memoirs and travelers' accounts, the slaves' liking for music is stressed. Such writings show them playing instruments of African origin, including drums, musical bows, flutes, and xylophones, all of which will almost disappear by the nineteenth century, as well as the fiddle, which they particularly liked, and various lutes that prefigured the banjo. As the general evangelization of the slaves began only with the religious "Awakenings" in 1734 and, more emphatically, in 1801, this first generation of creole music was almost certainly secular. The slaves played this music at work but also played for their own pleasure, dancing to its sounds, although we cannot know what those sounds were. Domestic slaves were organized into musical bands which performed the then fashionable European dances for the entertainment of their masters.

FROM BLACKFACE MINSTRELS TO MUSICAL REVUE

Even before Northern scholars began collecting religious songs during the Civil War (Allen, Ware, and Garrison 1951), white entertainers were struck by what the black slaves of the South and the free African American proletarians of the North played, sang, and danced to. From the eighteenth century on, the English theater had staged "Negro songs" during intervals, and blackened faces were common in certain carnavalesque or charivari rituals. These practices were transposed to North America (Cockrell 1997, 32–33), where the presence of a large number of black people could not fail to change the nature of these first blackface comedians.

The surviving sheet music from the period enables us to discern that a form of musical Americanization asserted itself onstage as early as 1827, with "Long Tail Blue," a song describing a smart, clever black dandy—a character which was, overall, rather positive (Lewis 1996). *Jim Crow*, produced by Thomas D. Rice at the Bowery Theater in New York in 1832, changes this character's style: the Negro played by a white man becomes a parody of the aspirational (black) American portrayed in "Long Tail Blue," yet he remains highly ambiguous.[3] Jim Crow is a black man who is animalized and dressed in rags, but he is a skillful dancer and the exploits related in the lyrics of his song incline at times toward abolitionism (Cockrell 1997). The year 1834 sees the birth of *Zip Coon,* where the animalization continues with the term "coon" (derived from racoon), a term which, as a description of African Americans, remains extremely insulting. This time the black man is ridiculed and his claim to be well educated and cultivated harshly mocked. Yet the man who actually played Zip Coon, George Washington Dixon, a singer, journalist, moral campaigner, and frequent visitor to the courtroom who was suspected of being a mulatto, no doubt gave the character a more complex image, underscoring by its grotesque nature the injustices done to the common people in the days when Andrew Jackson was president of the United States (Cockrell 1997).

Until the late 1830s blackface minstrels performed individual numbers in shows not exclusively devoted to them. Some of these famous solo performers were, in fact, black, such as the most famous of the dancers, William Henry Lane, known as "Juba" (ca. 1825–1852), whose virtuosity was acclaimed by Charles Dickens (1997, 100). An important change occurred at the beginning of the 1840s with the appearance of minstrel troupes, initially a quartet combining violin, banjo, tambourine, and bones (pieces of bone, metal, or wood that were struck together), whose members sang, danced, and told jokes. The model of the genre, Dan Emmett's Virginia Minstrels, appeared in New York and Boston in 1843 and were to have many emulators (Nathan 1977). From this point on, the minstrels presented the black man as grotesque; the blackface minstrel, born of cross-fertilization with the aspirations of a motley youth ill used by the beginnings of American industrialization (Bean, Hatch, and McNamara 1996; Cockrell 1997; Lhamon 1998), was turned into a racist caricature. The music, on which lyrics, supposedly funny stories, and brief scenes were superimposed, does, however, retain its characteristics as a cross-bred production, evincing—particularly after songs such as "Jim Crow" and "Zip Coon"—a rhythmic sense that is distinct from that of European song and dance tunes (Winans 1998 [1985]).

In these conditions, it was to African American artists that the ambivalence and paradoxicality were to devolve. William Henry Lee was a lone star who in 1848 chose to move overseas to Great Britain. After 1865 troupes of blackface minstrels increased in number. The conventions of the genre remained: the performers were dark-skinned, but still they blackened their faces. Their repertoire was expanded, however, to include, among other things, spirituals and operatic arias, and though we lack precise data in this area, it seems reasonable to believe that their interpretation of the "plantation songs" necessarily stood out from that of the white performers. Moreover, these troupes afforded black composers an opportunity to showcase their talents. Even when, like Will Marion Cook (1869–1944), they had a solid, Western-style training, gleaned from American schools and European conservatories, being black was an obstacle to any "legitimate" musical career, and the only outlet for creative ambition was the entertainment scene that came out of blackface minstrelsy.[4] Thus we can only cursorily follow the development of African American performing arts, beginning with the Georgia Colored Minstrels, created as early as 1865 at Indianapolis, to dancers Bert Williams (1874–1922) and George Walker (1873–1911), inventors of the musical revue (Riis 1989; Winter 1996), to the composers and band leaders Ford Dabney (1883–1958) and James Reese Europe (1881–1919), who played a notable role in the development of jazz. Revues and musical comedies were to take the place of the minstrel shows, but it was a blackened face, belonging to a white man, Al Jolson, that would sing "Dirty Hands, Dirty Face" in the first "talkie" in the history of cinema, Alan Crossland's *The Jazz Singer* (1927). In the fields of secular music, song, dance, and performance in general, the minstrels exemplify all the contradictions and cruelties that marked the invention of a profoundly creole form of entertainment in North America. The originality of this kind of show was the root of its success, both in the United States and throughout the world, as it was exported to Europe, Asia, the West Indies, and to West and South Africa.

FROM SPIRITUALS TO SOUL MUSIC

The forms of music and dance that fascinated young white people in the first half of the nineteenth century, to the point where they sought to adopt them and were spurred to become performers themselves, had doubtless taken shape during the eighteenth century. The banjo existed at that time and was sometimes accompanied by drums; it was principally a dance instrument, at times also for white people (Conway 1995). Clearly slaves also practiced secular singing. During the same period we find traces of blacks participating in the foundation of the American Christian churches: the religious "Awakenings" of 1734 and 1801 combined a style of emotional, fiery preaching with communal singing, and blacks and whites mingled in the "Camp Meetings."[5] In the first phases of African Americans entering the Christian churches, the range of songs mainly included European hymns, which were most often modal and without regular accents. They were melodically close to Anglo-Irish songs, but were subject to individual embellishment, which meant that group singing was not done in strict unison. The practice of "lining-out" was also developed in America, a technique where the leader speaks a line that is then taken up by the congregation, lending a responsorial quality to the interpretation but also leaving room for the two to overlap. The classic hymns, taken from the *Bay Psalm Book* of 1640 and from *Hymns and Spiritual Songs* published by Isaac Watts in 1707, would never be abandoned, but songs of an entirely new type appeared, particularly in the maelstrom of the Camp Meetings, where they received the generic title "spiritual songs." This repertoire was partly shared by blacks and whites, but each also created songs they regarded as their own. Where African Americans were concerned, these were the songs collected during the Civil War by Northern men and women and compiled into *Slave Songs of the United States*.

After abolition, schools and colleges were created for former slaves, where they were taught to sing as part of a choir, performing Negro spirituals and molding them into European forms, particularly four-part harmony. From these ensembles, which were often called "Jubilee Singers," such as the Fisk Jubilee Singers of Nashville, Tennessee (Ward 2000), would come the quartets that became the foremost purveyors of modernized African American religious singing: the "gospel songs," widely distributed and marketed from the late 1920s on. These songs emerged when elements borrowed from secular genres, such as blues and jazz (Martin 1998), were included in hymnal music, an example of the interaction between black sacred and secular music. In later years, this interaction would spur the development of religious musical forms and fuel the creation of new secular styles, specifically "soul music" in the 1960s and then "rap," which was inspired by all forms of African American speech, particularly as preached and sung in the Protestant churches. Gospel singing and soul music would also travel, as spirituals had in the late nineteenth century, and reggae would doubtless never have been devised if young Jamaicans had not been raised on these musical forms (Constant 1982).

The Cape Colony, a Hub of Cross-Fertilization

Spirituals and gospel songs had such an effect on South Africa that African hymnody became deeply imbued with them. Jazz, rap, and reggae were adopted and reformulated in the Cape Colony (Coplan 1985, 44–46; Martin 1992). Before that, in the second half of the nineteenth century, the blackface minstrels had made an impact there, with a force that is difficult for us to imagine today—not only among the whites but even more so among the Africans (Erlmann 1991) and those termed "coloureds." The way these essential elements of American minstrelsy were taken up in South Africa is significant because it further illustrates the cross-fertilization arising out of slavery (Martin 1999).

SLAVES AND THE NEW YEAR

The experience of the South African "coloureds" has a number of points in common with the experience of African Americans. The first of these is slavery, which, in the Cape Colony, lasted from 1652 to 1834. Some 26.4 percent of slaves came from Africa (especially Mozambique and West Africa), 25.9 percent from India (Bengal, Malabar, and Coromandel) and Ceylon, 25.1 percent from Madagascar, and 22.7 percent from present-day Indonesia and Malaysia (Shell 1994). As in North America, it was impossible for them to re-form their original communities, and, in order to survive, they had to reinvent an original culture that blended contributions from their homelands with elements borrowed from their masters, who were mainly Dutch. When a systematic policy of racial segregation was established at the end of the nineteenth century, the authorities saw the coloureds as people who were neither visibly European nor African. Thus, included among the coloureds were the descendants of slaves; the products of unions between European settlers and khoikhoi natives ("Hottentots," in colonial parlance); the descendants of "free blacks," who were mainly Muslims from the East Indies; and all "people of colour" from elsewhere—among others, black Americans and West Indians who had opted to settle in the Cape.

In the nineteenth century, during the time of slavery, one of the most important events in the social life of the Cape was the New Year, which was celebrated with street parades, singing, and dancing, inspired no doubt both by Christmas and Epiphany festivities in the Netherlands and by the British end-of-year charivaris. Slaves and, after abolition in 1834, their descendants took part in these celebrations; as in the United States, their enjoyment of music and talent for it were evident, and on this occasion they could give free rein to both. We also know of slave bands in South Africa that played the dances and music then fashionable in Europe, and after emancipation "coloureds," alongside the military, were the Cape's most active musicians. When troupes of blackface minstrels—first white groups in 1862 and then the African American Virginia Jubilee Singers of Orpheus McAdoo in 1890 (Erlmann 1991, 21–53)—visited South Africa, they provoked such fascination among their audiences that many coloured musicians in the Cape copied them. As a result, "Coons"[6] would regularly be featured in the carnival troupes of the early twentieth century, and their costume would become almost exclusively the costume of the Coon Carnival in the late 1930s.

CREOLE AND IMPORTED REPERTOIRES

These festivals and their music were, moreover, greatly influenced by eastern Islam, which was practised discreetly from the late seventeenth century on by religious and political personalities deported to South Africa from the Dutch East Indies. In the early nineteenth century many people converted to Islam, particularly slaves and former slaves but also Europeans. The Islam that developed in the Cape Colony was Sufi, and music had a prominent role in its rituals. The social life of Muslims was also alive with various styles of music, whether it was singing at weddings, dancing at picnics, or New Year's Eve celebrations. In the late nineteenth and early twentieth centuries mixed repertoires emerged that became the prerogative of the "coloureds" and were performed at family, religious, or social gatherings but also at various times in the New Year celebrations: street parades on the night of New Year's Eve; the Coon Carnival on January 1 and 2, and then on a number of Saturdays in January; and the Malay Choirs[7] competitions, which generally began in January. These repertoires were essentially vocal and can be classified mainly as either w-4 creole or imported repertoires (The Tulips 2002).

Today, imported repertoires include the appropriation and adaptation, without radical transformation, of musical forms that were popular elsewhere, particularly in the United States: American songs, jazz "standards," "variety" tunes, soul music, rap, techno, and sometimes even operatic arias are all performed during the Coon Carnival. Creole repertoires resulted from the particular cross-fertilization that took place in the Cape and provided one of the foundations on which contemporary South African cultures are built. On one side are the *Moppies,* comic songs performed by carnival troupes and Malay Choirs in competitions. Their melodies are often taken from the international fund of popular songs and strung into a medley, but their style of performance is specific: accompanied by the simple rhythm of the *ghoema* drum[8] at a brisk tempo, a soloist sings an amusing lyric, underscoring it with arm and hand movements (partly inspired by the blackface minstrels), and a choir sings back to him while performing a kind of dancing march in place. On the other side were the *nederlandsliedjies.*[9] In this repertoire, following an introduction in which vocalists are accompanied by a small string ensemble (guitar, banjo, mandolin, cello, and sometimes violin), positioned in front of a choir singing chords from the stock of European tonal harmony, a soloist ornaments the whole with an oriental flavor redolent of *kroncong.* The latter is a genre that itself arose out of the appropriation of Portuguese instruments and songs by Indonesians, and was developed largely by people of mixed Portuguese and Indonesian ancestry from the sixteenth century on (Becker 1975; Heins 1975; Kornhauser 1978). An early form of *kroncong,* brought over by Indonesian slaves, was probably one of the initial components of the Muslim wedding songs from which the *nederlandsliedjies* issued and likely shaped the style of the plucked-string music that precedes and accompanies them.

The New Year celebrations provide the chief opportunity to display these musical mixes that relate the history of the Cape. On the night of December 31 the Malay Choirs sing *moppies*—and sometimes *nederlandsliedjies*—to a *ghoema* and string accompaniment, and on January 1 the song, band, and dance competitions are held between the Coon troupes. Their "uniform" is a distant descendant of the costume worn in the American minstrels that visited South Africa. Some performers still blacken their faces, tracing their mouths and eyes in white, and most now sport colorful costumes studded with brilliant sequins. The musical program includes *moppies* and all kinds of imported songs. Somewhat later in January, if Ramadan does not coincide, the Malay Choirs competition begins, with singers performing four repertoires, including *moppies* and *nederlandsliedjies* along with the less original "combined choruses" and "solos." Taken together, these festivities[10] clearly constitute an event that is as important socially as it is musically.

The Cape affords an insight into how crossbred forms interlock and reproduce themselves. Encounter leads to exchange, which produces the cross-fertilization from which creation emerges; this creation, in turn, inevitably circulates to play a part in new encounters and enter into new mixes, leading to yet other creations. In South Africa, colonization and slavery gave rise to cultural contacts in a situation of violence and inequality; the resulting creations circulated within South Africa and inspired the invention of new South African musical forms (Coplan 1985). The creole inventions that appeared in the Cape, and the innovations they prompted within the other territories forming the Union of South Africa, were in turn enriched by musical forms from elsewhere, themselves formed under conditions of slavery. In South Africa, then, two itineraries of musical production that arose out of slavery are conjoined. The history of mass-market musical forms in the twentieth century extends and multiplies these musical journeys, these "cross-fertilizations," which have now spread throughout the world and which, at every point on the globe—because each encounter is unique—generate something original. In some cases there may be total fusion, to the point where it becomes difficult to distinguish the initial components: this is generally the case with African American music of North America, a style that became fixed in the late nineteenth and early twentieth centuries. Elsewhere, in Guadeloupe, for example, creole repertoires of varying degrees may remain alongside one another (Lafontaine 1983, 1985). Creole repertoires in the Cape still bear the tangible stamp of the original influences. They coexist with imported repertoires, but it is the performances during the New Year celebrations that give them their full meaning (Martin 1995, 2002a).

Engines of Cross-Fertilization

In North America and South Africa two lines of cross-fertilization developed that ended up entwined (Erlmann 1999). North American mixes played their part in the elaboration of the creole musical practices of South Africa, just as they served as a leaven for the development of most contemporary mass-musical forms. Attempting to reconstruct the processes that took place in the United States and in South Africa will perhaps enable us to derive some general lessons from the dynamics of musical cross-fertilization and the meaning of those dynamics.

The Banjo and Minstrel Songs

In the beginning the only certainty is that the slaves of North America made music, and the first indication of the creole nature of their production is undoubtedly the banjo. Mentioned as early as 1754—when it was described as the *bandore* or *banjor*—it is not, as Cecelia Conway (1995) would have it, a transplanted African instrument; rather, it is a cordophone of a new type, a cobbled-together form of guitar—perhaps also of the Iberian *bandurria*—with the flat fingerboard and the bridge of those instruments and of various types of the African lute from which it derives its sounding box, made originally from a gourd covered with stretched skin. The techniques for playing the banjo could have been inherited from Europe or Africa and did, in fact, probably come from both. It is difficult to describe precisely the music initially played on it except to note that a late-eighteenth-century observer spoke of it as improvised (Conway 1995, 304–305). The instrument was appreciably reshaped by the white musicians of the nineteenth century. It acquired frets and a fifth string pegged halfway along the neck and, before assuming its place in the first jazz bands and in the white groups playing country and western music, it became the emblem of the minstrels. As a cross-bred instrument devised by the earliest African Americans, it became a symbol of American musical identity (Bardinet 2003).

The blackface minstrels provide a more complex example of the exchanges that led to cross-fertilization. In the beginning white performers took over creole forms that had been created by blacks, though some blacks managed to win recognition for their talent as "blackfaces" to the point of tangibly modifying the genre after the Civil War. Attempts to reconstruct the music of the minstrel shows bring out the following characteristics, which might have been typical of the Virginia Minstrels (Winans 1996, 1998 [1985]): a predominant melodic function—the banjo playing the melody note by note and not in chords—based on very short, repeated motifs, most often using conjoint intervals; the music was generally in a major key, in the tradition of the British Isles, with modal or pentatonic episodes, but around 1844 it began to incorporate elements of the blues (Nathan 1977). These elements include four beats in a bar, regularly accented but becoming irregular at times, which, combined with syncopation, tends to place the accents on the European off-beat. Instrumental solos were frequent, allowing the banjo and fiddle to embellish the melody. The four voices of the first Virginia Minstrels sang in unison, but the minstrels soon adopted a four-part polyphony, an intimation of which we can no doubt still glean today from barbershop singing (Averill 1999, 2003). An examination of the published sheet music of some famous songs—"Jim Crow" (Cockrell 1997, 77), "Zip Coon," which will survive for many years as "Turkey in the Straw" (ibid., 95), and "Old Dan Tucker" (ibid., 158–159)—enables us to specify other features: the construction of melodies on four-bar segments, which give the theme a standard sixteen-bar structure; the frequent presence of an underlying anhemitonic pentatonism, whatever the key signature indicated, built on a succession counted in semitones 2 2 3 2 3 (Arom 1997), and the recurrent use of a dotted quaver/semiquaver rhythmic figure. The latter, which is the true signature of "Jim Crow," as it appears systematically in the bars where the character dances, introduces a particular rhythmic dynamic that will continue to develop in subsequent years. One begins to see how creole elements were grafted onto a European trunk, solidly rooted in Anglo-Irish-Scottish soil, particularly concerning harmony and rhythm.

BLUE NOTES AND SACRED SONGS

The descriptions we have of religious singing before and after the abolition of slavery enable us to refine this reconstruction of the American process of musical cross-fertilization. Anthologies of spirituals, first committed to paper by whites, and then collected by former slaves, confirm the melodic and harmonic characteristics we glimpsed in the minstrel songs; they bring out the systematic use of progressions based on the tonic-subdominant-dominant succession (I–IV–V), which will remain present, in several variants, in most American twentieth-century music beginning with the blues. White listeners to black religious services stress, however, that they have difficulty discerning whether the mode employed is major or minor, as it seemed to them at times that the singers shifted from one to the other. This impression, heightened by the mention of melismatic ornamentation, glissandos, and improvised trills, suggests that, in the practice of singing, frequent alterations could sweep away the European major/minor distinction. These alterations probably heralded what later came to be called "blue notes," as they were impossible to fix rigidly on a stave—all the more so given the richness of the vocal timbres, which tended to make an exact perception of pitch difficult, and given the complex polyphonies.[11] Here again descriptions falter. Although responsorial structures no doubt exist, they do not exclude overlap between soloist and choir, and the ensemble sections were sung in unison, in false unison, or as polyphonies without parts or with several parts. Undoubtedly, too, a great variety of ways were found for singing together during the services. In African American Methodist chapels of the North, the singing resembled that in European Methodist chapels. In the Southern gatherings, however, the singing was quite different, with additional differences apparent in the various regions. The most pertinent analysis of this collective singing may be found in the introduction provided by the collectors of *Slave Songs of the United States* (Allen, Ware, Garrison 1951):

> There is no singing in parts, as we understand it, and yet no two appear to be singing the same thing—the leading singer starts the words of each verse, often improvising, and the others, who base him, as it is called, strike in with the refrain, or even join in the solo, when the words are familiar. When the "base" begins, the leader often stops, leaving the rest of his words

to be guessed at, or it may be they are taken up by one of the other singers. And the "basers" themselves seem to follow their own whims, beginning when they please and leaving off when they please, striking an octave above or below (in case they have pitched the tune too low or too high), or hitting some other note that chords, so as to produce the effect of a marvelous complication and variety, and yet with the most perfect time, and rarely with any discord.

One finds these forms of polyphony today in the recordings of congregational singing (Wade in the Water 1994) or the female vocal group Sweet Honey in the Rock (1995).

Some songs, or phases of the performance of songs, seem to have been constructed not in measured fashion but on a surge or wave rather than a regular beat. This practice is still maintained today. When the music is clearly measured, it is described as syncopated, with the accents placed, seemingly deliberately, on the offbeat and systematically away from the downbeats of European music. Moreover, the vocal accents, the hand clapping, foot stamping, and, when dance is involved, the body movements do not coincide and hence an intricate polyrhythmy is produced.

From this brief overview of the American musical forms that emerged between the seventeenth and nineteenth centuries, it seems that, despite the gaps that remain in our historical knowledge, we may assume that it took the following course. In an initial period, following cultural contacts brought about by slavery, some early mixing took place, with musical results that remain virtually unknown to us: on the one hand, there was a blending of different African musical forms, and, on the other, mixtures occurred between those musical forms, the products of the "pan-Africanism of exile" to which they gave rise, and various European musical forms that probably were centered on practices specific to the British isles. The most convincing evidence of this first stage of creolization that has come down to us is the banjo, adopted by the blackface minstrels. These minstrels, heirs to the theatrical tradition of Negro songs and songsters familiar with the British repertoire, took over (probably not without fidelity before 1840) the creole practices they found among the blacks. In their work we see the first signs of the features that would typify American twentieth-century music, particularly embellishment, which would develop into improvisation; the reshaping of academic tonal harmony which, when combined with the anhemitonic pentatonisms of both African and Anglo-Celtic music, would come to promote the use of inflections on blue notes; and the tendency of modern American music, still mild back then, to shift the accent to the offbeat. Religious songs followed a parallel path, undoubtedly with many crossovers. In them we see a greater preference for ornamentation, and we can also decipher polyphonies that do not correspond to any European or African formula. Also present is a persistent inclination toward polyrhythmy. In the late nineteenth century the elements that would eventually define jazz began to form: these were the African American minstrel shows that included "spirituals" sung by the Jubilee Choirs and the early revues that replaced the minstrel shows and had orchestra scores sensitive to the innovations of ragtime composers. The music played by the first banjos also continued to develop in rural areas, alongside the singing of British ballads and epic songs. Condensing this history, one might conclude that this, together with the vocal techniques associated with the "field hollers," was the source of the blues, which was given a fixed form[12] by collector-composers such as William Christopher Handy[13] and formatted by the recording industry that would assign the blues exclusively to black musicians and, in so doing, induce these musicians to abandon other types of songs in their repertoires, for example, ballads, coon songs, and ragtime songs (Oliver 1984). Religious songs, jazz, and blues were nothing less than the origin of most contemporary mass-market music.

The Cross-Fertilization of Cross-Fertilizations at the Cape

The example of the coloured musicians of the Cape Colony of South Africa underscores two important facts: that American cross-fertilization spread to the four corners of the earth as early as the nineteenth century, before the age of recording, and that crossbred forms combine easily, as the history of the United States already suggested. In the Cape Colony, as in North America, the mix of musical practices from the slaves' original homelands was an essential element in this cross-fertilization. The mix included previously crossbred elements from *kroncong*, combined with European forms of choral singing. It probably also absorbed elements from East Africa, the Arabian peninsula, and Turkey, as the Cape Muslims were in contact with their co-religionists from those regions. Added to this creole substrate was the influence of the American blackface minstrels. Thus we can distinguish three types of cross-fertilization at the Cape: in a crucible containing every possible mix, a peculiar creolism was melded, and into this particular mix, alongside European, African, and Asian components, were Portuguese-Asian and American crossbred forms.[14]

From the Musics of Slavery to World Music

American crossbred products, which have served almost everywhere as ingredients in other mixes, may be described as a variety of melodic types that still exist. Among the minstrels, melody still seems closely linked to the British model, although one can discern arrangements of short repeated motifs also found in spirituals where the melody is more discontinuous in style. These productions evince a great melodic plasticity, all the more so as the minstrels and religious singers did not deem it important to render a fixed composition precisely but preferred to add ornamentation or variations. On this point European popular practices and African practices converged.

LIMITLESS MIXES

The harmonic foundations are clearly borrowed from Europe: the I–IV–V progression, which is very widespread in nineteenth-century hymns, particularly methodist hymns, provides the elementary structure. Within this framework, however, the influence of anhemitonic pentatonisms—known in British music, seen in Methodist bible songs, and common in Africa—still retains a presence. These pentatonisms are of various types, particularly in the spirituals; one of the most common is the first (2 2 3 2 3) (Maultsby 1974). They afford scope for ornamentations that, when sung or played on an initially fretless banjo or fiddle, makes generous use of inflections and glissandos. The latter incorporate pitches that blur the major/minor opposition and that will be fixed as blue notes, particularly when played on the keyboard or written down. This reformulation of European harmony, one of the crucial innovations of American crossbred forms, probably began amid embellishments within original polyphonies that owed much to Africa and were embedded within a cyclical conception of time concretized in twelve-, sixteen-, or thirty-two-bar forms, thus setting the framework for improvisation.

The other innovation is rhythmic in nature. In the minstrel songs, as in the spirituals, one senses the beginnings of a displacement of accents from the European downbeats to the offbeats. We may wonder whether, in the amalgam of European musics that regularly alternate between downbeats and offbeats and of African and European musics (psalms) that use no such alternation, the pan-African propensity for countermetricality[15] did not give rise to this slippage. Polyrhythmia, which religious singing would never abandon and which jazz was to incorporate and redevelop, certainly encouraged this tendency which was to become one of the rhythmic features of blues and jazz.

Lastly, American processes of cross-fertilization would produce the banjo, a cross between European and African plucked string instruments, which the white Americans would eventually preserve more enthusiastically than the black. These cross-fertilizations would also bring into common usage a noncanonical approach to vocal and instrumental tone; with priority given to expressiveness and the conveying of emotion, all sounds could be used to that effect. Extending European and African popular practices, religious singers demonstrated the range of possibilities offered by this flexibility, as did instrumentalists in jazz, blues, "rhythm and blues," and today's rap DJ "scratch masters."

Most striking, ultimately, is the point that Margaret Kartomi (1981, 240) already emphasized: all musical forms are, to a certain degree, similar or compatible, and hence capable of becoming part of cross-fertilization processes. We should point out, however, that the musical forms or characteristics that trigger dynamics of innovation are most often those that overlap, that are closest to each other—most compatible, so to speak. From this point of view, America reminds us that there were convergences between the many African musical forms and European popular music, particularly the music of the British Isles (Martin 1991). In the process of musical innovation and exchange, certain groups may, by dint of their social position or the unifying character of their music, have an important influence that is not necessarily related to their demographic impact. This is true among the powerful, the conquerors, as indicated by the British of North America, and also among the downtrodden, as exemplified by the Muslims of Indonesian origin in the Cape Colony.

CREOLIZATION AND "RELATIONSHIP"

When musics arise out of slavery, one cannot merely content oneself with a technical analysis of the processes of blending or fusion that are triggered by cultural transfers: neither the processes nor their products can be dissociated from the conditions in which they are produced. Here lessons about musical production may be drawn from the theory of creolization proposed by Édouard Glissant.[16] He hypothesizes a dynamic of encounter/cross-fertilization/novel dimension, which implies that cross-fertilization is limitless, that it leads necessarily to innovation, and that we cannot, as a consequence, limit its *élan* to syncretism or hybridity.[17] Creolization begins in the exploitation of slavery, a space of closure and constraint in which the aspiration to Relationship is born, a site of oppression and dehumanization, where the will to humanity rises up.[18] Creolization—like the Relationship that ensues from it—is engendered by violence and domination; therefore it cannot be conceived simply as the harmonious, peaceful mix of cultural features of different origins. With a distinctly different vocabulary, Glissant echoes Rex Nettleford, when the latter asserts: "[creolization] refers to the agonizing process of renewal and growth that marks the new order of men and women who came originally from different Old World cultures (whether European, African, Levantine or Oriental) and met in conflict or otherwise on foreign soil. The operative word here is 'conflict'" (1978, 2).

Yet, the violence and social death inflicted on the slaves engendered creation, that "new, totally unforeseeable fact," and this cleared the path to the rehumanization of the oppressed. Creation, fueled by blending, contaminates the masters along with the slaves. Often they invent together, sometimes separately, but out of the same elements they share by virtue of their coexistence. Generally, however, the slaves and their descendants have cultural ownership of creole inventions, whereas the masters and the dominant take refuge behind a fixation on the supposed nobility of their origins, their fictive purity, to deny their own creoleness and reject everything springing from it as mongrel and degenerate. As a result, they offer a gift of creoleness to the oppressed,[19] who, in the examples presented above, are African Americans or "coloureds." Creole musics thus become badges of identity for these groups all the more easily because their characteristics have meaning within racially organized societies in which the body is stigmatized as a sign of inferiority. If African rhythmic elements pervaded North American creole musics, this was not the result of some sort of atavism but because there were common elements in many African musical cultures, and the link between rhythm, dance, and the body was of prime important to people whose slave status and dehumanization were denoted by their bodies. The implicit rehabilitation of the body, thanks to the use of shared rhythmic principles, provided a means to regain self-esteem, a communal cement, at the same time as it was an instrument of musical creation.

Creolization is a process, not a fixed condition, and it has no end. It introduces Relationship but does not universalize (Glissant 1990, 103), for, in the contemporary world, the "Whole-World," the "Chaos-World" (Glissant 1997), Relationship can only be contradictory. The "Poetics of Relationship," in which poetics, restored to its Greek etymological base in *poiein* (to make), designates an act of thought and an act of production, indicates that Relationship possesses a potential for transcending violence and recovering together the humanity of being by constructing the subject in circumstances that are unique and yet, in no sense, isolated from each other. But it also indicates that Relationship can be manipulated either by un-binding it or by playing artificially on the seduction of its fusion. The "gift" of creole musics to the oppressed is an example of this former phenomenon: negation, the rejection of bonds. The combinations of world music illustrate the latter, as they are responses to a demand for exoticism by selling encounter and harmony, by trading in untroubled dreams and selling an "Other" that is to be consumed rather than frequented (Aubert 2001; White this volume).

Reconstructing this historic bridge between the musics of slavery and the world music that has now been on sale for two decades involves, in the first instance, reweaving the continuity of creative dynamics that have never ceased to mingle, without, for all that, producing any kind of uniformity. Circulation, appropriation, blending, creation, and new circulation engender one another in a ceaseless round. The universalizing pretension of the label "world music" conflicts with concrete creative practices that draw on diverse, heterogeneous elements to produce original versions locally. My intention in this chapter is also to provide a reminder that, as a source of immense auditory, physical, and social pleasures, the mass-market music we enjoy today, including "world music," emerged in and from violence and domination, and that the mechanisms of musical "production" (in all senses of the term) and marketing that prevail in a world dominated by financial interests are always mechanisms of domination engendering inequality. Yet, the heritage of slavery also tells us that domination never extinguishes creation; that behind the musically empty and commercially profitable label of "world music," strategies of invention may be deployed that continue and extend the creolization initially begun in the brutality of servitude (Arom and Martin 2006; Martin 2002b).

Notes

1. This essay, translated by Chris Turner, is an enlarged and revised version of an earlier paper published in French as "Le métissage en musique, un mouvement perpétuel, création et identité, Amérique du Nord et Afrique du Sud," which appeared in *Cahiers de musiques traditionnelles* 13 (2000): 3–22.

2. Serge Gruzinski (1996, 147) sums up clearly the consequences of conquest: "The exchange of objects, women and food [to which we must, of course, add music—D.-C. M.], is quite clearly a form of communication. In this sense, it permits of a more or less extensive exchange of information. But it cannot be reduced to that dimension, to the deployment of a material language the Other would, with greater or lesser ease, manage to decipher. Because it unfolds in contexts that did not exist before—the interface of invaded and invaders—it is also creative of something original."

3. Subsequently all ambiguity would disappear from the references to this song, and its title was to become synonymous with racism; the segregationist laws adopted after the emancipation of the slaves and Reconstruction would be termed the "Jim Crow" laws.

4. For example, the African-American singer Matilda Sisieretta Jones (1869–1933)—nicknamed the "Black Patti" because her qualities so reminded audiences of Adelina Patti, the most popular diva of the day—had to create her troupe of minstrels, because she could not appear on the "classical" stage. Composers such as Harry T. Burleigh (1866–1949), a pupil of Antonin Dvorak, who had a career in publishing, or R. Nathaniel Dett (1882–1943), who made a living as a teacher, are exceptions to this rule.

5. "Camp Meetings" were religious gatherings, attracting large crowds—freemen and slaves, whites and blacks—held in the open air or in tents and usually lasting several days. Preaching and singing were the high points of these meetings.

6. The term "coon" arrived in South Africa with the blackface minstrels and the titles of their songs. Those who still currently use it in the Cape, carnival celebrants and "troupe captains," are unaware of the racist meaning it has assumed, which it still retains in the United States today. In their usage it refers to the main figure in the New Year Carnival (dressed in a costume derived from that of the nineteenth-century minstrels, which in the past consisted of a tailcoat, top hat, and large bowtie but today is reduced to trousers and a jacket in troupe colors, and a T-shirt, small hat, parasol, and face makeup) and symbolizes the celebrations in which they could then participate. This is one of the rare moments of the year when, in the twentieth century, they managed to forget the humiliations they suffered and the economic difficulties they faced.

7. These are male choirs comprised largely of Muslims. Some singers and musical directors from the Malay Choirs are also members of the Coon troupes' vocal ensembles.

8. The *ghoema* drum is specific to the Cape, though it is modeled after a small cask-shaped instrument found elsewhere, with skin covering one of the ends of the cask. Accompanying the four-beat *moppies,* the *ghoema* drum most often beats out a rhythm based on the dotted quaver-semiquaver-crotchet formula, known as the *ghoema* beat.

9. Their name, which means "Dutch songs" in Afrikaans (the creole produced by the interaction of the Dutch masters and the slaves that is the mother tongue of most "coloureds"), suggests that some tunes came from the Netherlands in different periods. These songs are, nevertheless, an original creation by the coloured musicians of the Cape; they are sung exclusively by the Malay Choirs on New Year's Eve and in competitions.

10. The festivities also include the Christmas Choirs competition, in which Christian brass bands play hymns in the fashion of Salvation Army bands.

11. Blue notes are notes that are lowered by a semi-tone of the third, seventh, and fifth of a major diatonic scale, a technique used systematically in blues and jazz, and their derivatives.

12. This "fixed form" was a twelve-bar song with an A–A–B structure on a I–IV–V progression.

13. W. C. Handy (1873–1958) began his career singing in a choir and then taught himself the cornet, joined a minstrel troupe, formed his own brass band, and ultimately acquired a solid reputation as band leader, arranger, and composer. He toured a great deal in the South, where he heard rural singers, committed their tunes to paper, and used them in compositions with the word "blues" in the title, most notably "Memphis Blues" and "Saint Louis Blues."

14. The *ramkie* perhaps provides evidence of this. This lute, adopted by the Khoikhoi aboriginal people in the eighteenth century, was no doubt an adaptation—based on a native model—of a Portuguese instrument (the *rabequinha*) brought to South Africa by slaves from the Dutch Indies. From the Khoikhoi it was to pass to the Cape coloureds and Bantu-speaking Africans. Often used for playing chords, it would be supplanted by the banjo, which took over its function but not without intermediate forms appearing, including, in particular, a high-pitched string pegged halfway along the neck, as on the minstrels' instrument (Kirby 1939; Rycroft 1984).

15. "The symmetry of metric organization is systematically counteracted by rhythmic configurations producing a permanent conflictual relationship between the isochrony of the period and the rhythmic events that take place within it" (Arom 1998, 183; see also Arom 1988).

16. "Creolization is the bringing into contact, in some place in the world, of two or more cultures or, at least, of two or more elements of distinct cultures, in such a way that a new state of affairs ensues that is totally unpredictable when compared with the mere synthesis or sum of these elements" (Glissant 1997, 37; see also Glissant 1990, 46).

17. The term "hybridity," freely used by Anglo-Saxon postmodernists, raises many questions that we cannot examine in depth here or be more specific. In short, it connotes the static rather than the dynamic, and retains the stamp of an original meaning that implied the incapacity of such entities to reproduce themselves (See article: "hybrid," *Webster's Interactive Encyclopaedia,* CD ROM 1998; article: "hybride," *Dictionnaire Le Littré,* CD ROM version 2.0). It therefore seems particularly ill-suited to the analysis of creative dynamics.

18. "The Plantation was one of the focal sites where some of the current modes of Relationship were elaborated. In that universe of domination and oppression, of veiled or overt de-humanization, humanities persisted powerfully. In that outmoded place, cut off from any sort of dynamic, the trends of our modernity began to take shape" (Glissant 1990, 79).

19. "The reality of that 'music' [of what is described as "Negro music"], while recognized as such and while growing out of the interracial participation of whites, could never be acknowledged as a fruitful interracial offspring. As a result, its value, power and invention lay completely with African-America. This odd turn of events would give to blacks a remarkable gift, inadvertent as it was, and one they proceeded to employ in casting a viable place in America" (Radano 2003, 115).

References

Allen, William Francis, Charles Pickard Ware, and Lucy McKim Garrison, eds. 1951 [1867]. *Slave Songs of the United States*. New York: Peter Smith.

Alleyne, Mervyn C. 1980. *Comparative Afro-American, An Historical-Comparative Study of English-Based Afro-American Dialects of the New World*. Ann Arbor, MI: Karoma.

Amselle, Jean-Loup. 1990. *Logiques métisses, anthropologie de l'identité en Afrique et ailleurs*. Paris: Payot.

Arom, Simha. 1988. "Du pied à la main: les foncements métriques des musiques traditionnelles d'Afrique centrale." *Analyse musicale* 1:16–22.

———. 1997. "Le syndrome du pentatonisme africain." *Musicae Scientiae* 1 (2): 139–163.

———. 1998. "'L'arbre qui cachait la forêt', principes métriques et rythmiques en Centrafrique." *Revue belge de musicologie* 52:179–195.

Arom, Simha, and Martin Denis-Constant. 2006. "Combiner les sons pour réinventer le monde, la world music, sociologie et analyse musicale." *L'Homme* 177–178 (January–June): 155–178.

Aubert, Laurent. 2001. *La musique de l'autre, les nouveaux défis de l'ethnomusicologie*. Geneva: Georg/Ateliers d'ethnomusicologie.

Averill, Gage 1999. "Bell Tones and Ringing Chords: Sense and Sensation in Barbershop Harmony," *World of Music* 41 (1): 37–51.

———. 2003. *Four Parts, No Waiting: A Social History of American Barbershop Harmony*. New York: Oxford University Press.

Bardinet, Nicolas. 2003. *Une histoire du banjo*. Paris: Outre Mesure.

Bean, Annemarie, James V. Hatch, and Brooks McNamara, eds. 1996. *Inside the Minstrel Mask: Readings in Nineteenth-Century Blackface Minstrelsy*. Hanover, CT: Wesleyan University Press.

Becker J. 1975. "Kroncong, Indonesian Popular Music," *Asian Music* 7 (1): 14–19.

Cockrell, Dale. 1997. *Demons of Disorder: Early Blackface Minstrels and Their World*. Cambridge: Cambridge University Press.

Constant, Denis. 1982. *Aux sources du reggae, musique, société et politique en Jamaïque*. Marseille: Parenthèses.

Conway, Cecelia. 1995. *African Banjo Echoes in Appalachia: A Study of Folk Traditions*. Knoxville: University of Tennessee Press.

Coplan, David B. 1985. *In Township Tonight! South Africa's Black City Music and Theatre*. London: Longman.

Curtin, Philip D. 1969. *The Atlantic Slave Trade, a Census*. Madison: University of Wisconsin Press.

Davidson, Basil. 1980. *Black Mother: Africa and the Atlantic Slave Trade*. Harmondsworth, UK: Penguin.

Depestre, René. 1980. *Bonjour et adieu à la négritude*. Paris: Robert Laffont.

Dickens, Charles. 1997 [1907]. *American Notes and Pictures from Italy*. London: Everyman.

Dubois, Paul-André. 1997. *De l'oreille au coeur, naissance du chant religieux en langues amérindiennes dans les missions de la Nouvelle-France, 1600–1650*. Sillery, Québec: Septentrion.

Epstein, Dena J. 1977. *Sinful Tunes and Spirituals: Black Folk Music to the Civil War*. Urbana: University of Illinois Press.

Erlmann, Veit. 1991. *African Stars: Studies in Black South African Performance.* Chicago: University of Chicago Press.

———. 1999. *Music, Modernity, and the Global Imagination: South Africa and the West.* New York: Oxford University Press.

Genovese, Eugene D. 1974. *Roll, Jordan, Roll: The World the Slaves Made.* New York: Pantheon.

Glissant, Édouard. 1990. *Poétique de la Relation, Poétique III.* Paris, Gallimard.

———. 1997. *Traité du Tout-Monde, Poétique IV.* Paris, Gallimard.

Gruzinski, Serge. 1996. "Découverte, conquête et communication dans l'Amérique ibérique: avant les mots, au delà des mots." In Patrimoines métissés, contextes coloniaux et postcoloniaux, ed. Laurier Turgeon, Denys Delâge, and Real Ouellet, 141–154. Paris: Éditions de la Maison des sciences de l'homme; Québec: Presses de l'Université Laval.

———. 1999. *La pensée métisse.* Paris: Fayard.

Heins, E. 1975. "Kroncong and Tanjidor—Two Cases of Urban Folk Music in Jakarta," *Asian Music* 7 (1): 20–32.

Kartomi, Margaret. 1981. "The Processes and Results of Musical Culture Contact: A Discussion of Terminology and Concepts." *Ethnomusicology* (May): 227–249.

Kirby, Percival R. 1939. "Musical Instruments of the Cape Malays," *South African Journal of Science* 36 (December): 477–488.

Kornhauser, B. 1978. "In Defence of Kroncong." In *Studies in Indonesian Music,* ed. M. J. Kartomi, 104–183. Victoria: Monash University, Centre of Southeast Asian Studies.

Lafontaine, Marie-Céline. 1983. "Le carnaval de l'"autre': A propos d'"authenticité' en matière de musique guadeloupéenne, théories et réalités." *Les Temps modernes* (May): 2126–2173.

———. 1985. "Terminologie musicale en Guadeloupe, ce que le créole nous dit de la musique." *Langage et société* 32: 7–24.

Lewis, Barbara. 1996. "Daddy Blues : The Evolution of the Dark Dandy." In *Inside the Minstrel Mask: Readings in Nineteenth-Century Blackface Minstrelsy,* ed. Annemarie Bean, James V. Hatch, and Brooks McNamara, 257–272. Hanover, CT: Wesleyan University Press.

Lhamon, W. T., Jr. 1998. *Raising Cain: Blackface Performance from Jim Crow to Hip Hop.* Cambridge, MA: Harvard University Press.

Martin, Denis-Constant. 1991. "Filiation or Innovation? Some Hypotheses to Overcome the Dilemma of Afro-American Music's Origins." *Black Music Research Journal* 11 (1): 19–38.

———. 1992. "Music beyond Apartheid?" In *Rockin' the Boat: Mass Music and Mass Movements,* ed. Reebee Garofalo, 195–207. Boston: South End.

———. 1995. *Les ménestrels du Cap.* Meudon: CNRS Audiovisuel (documentaire vidéo VHS, 28', couleur).

———. 1998. *Le gospel afro-américain, des spirituals au rap religieux.* Paris: Cité de la musique/Actes Sud.

———. 1999. *Coon Carnival: New Year in Cape Town, Past and Present.* Cape Town: David Philip.

———. 2002a. "Le Cap ou les partages inégaux de la créolité sud-africaine." *Cahiers d'études africaines* 52 (4): 687–710.

———. 2002b. "Les 'musiques du monde,' imaginaires contradictoires de la globalization."

In *Sur la piste des OPNI (Objets politiques non identifiés)*, dir. Martin, Denis-Constant, 397–430. Paris: Karthala.

——. 2006. "Le myositis, et puis la rose . . . , pour une sociologie des 'musiques de masse.' *L'Homme* 177–178 (January–June): 131–154.

Maultsby, Portia K. 1974. "Afro-American Religious Music, 1619–1861." Ph.D. diss., University of Wisconsin, Madison.

Merriam, Allan. 1955. "The Use of Music in the Study of a Problem of Acculturation," *American Anthropologist* 57:28–34.

Nash, Gary. 1974. *Red, White, and Black: The Peoples of Early America*. Englewood Cliffs, NJ: Prentice Hall.

Nathan, Hans. 1977. *Dan Emmett and the Rise of Early Negro Minstrelsy*. Norman: University of Oklahoma Press.

Nettl, Bruno. 1978. "Some Aspects of the History of World Music in the Twentieth Century: Questions, Problems, and Concepts," *Ethnomusicology* 22 (1): 123–136.

Nettleford, Rex M. 1978. *Caribbean Cultural Identity: The Case of Jamaica, An Essay in Cultural Dynamics*. Kingston: Institute of Jamaica.

Olivier, Paul. 1984. *Songsters and Saints: Vocal Traditions on Race Records*. Cambridge: Cambridge University Press.

Pacquier, Alain. 1996. *Les chemins du baroque dans le Nouveau Monde, de la Terre de Feu à l'embouchure du Saint-Laurent*. Paris: Fayard.

Patterson, Orlando. 1982. *Slavery and Social Death: A Comparative Study*. Cambridge, MA: Harvard University Press.

Radano, Ronald. 2003. *Lying up a Nation: Race and Black Music*. Chicago: University of Chicago Press.

Riis, Thomas L. 1989. *Just before Jazz: Black Musical Theater in New York, 1890 to 1915*. Washington, DC: Smithsonian Institution Press.

Rycroft, David K. 1984. "Ramkie." In *The New Grove Dictionary of Musical Instruments*, ed. Stanley Sadie, 3:190–191. London: McMillan.

Shell, Robert C. 1994. *Children of Bondage: A Social History of the Slave Society at the Cape of Good Hope, 1652–1838*. Johannesburg: Witwatersrand University Press.

Storm Roberts, John. 1972. *Black Music of Two Worlds*. New York: Morrow.

Turgeon, Laurier. 1996. "De l'acculturation aux transferts culturels" in *Patrimoines métissés, contextes coloniaux et postcoloniaux*. ed. Laurier Turgeon, Denys Delâge, and Real Ouellet, 11–32. Paris : Éditions de la Maison des sciences de l'homme.

Turgeon, Laurier, Delâge Denis, and Ouellet Réal, ed. 1996. *Transferts culturels et métissages Amérique/Europe, XVIe–XXe siècle*. Québec: Presses de l'Université Laval.

Valkhoff, M. F. 1972. *New Light on Afrikaans and "Malayo-Portuguese."* Louvain: Peeters.

Ward, Andrew. 2001. *Dark Midnight When I Rise: The Story of the Fisk Jubilee Singers*. New York: Amistad.

Winans, Robert. 1996. "Early Minstrel Show Music, 1843–1852." In *Inside the Minstrel Mask: Readings in Nineteenth-Century Blackface Minstrelsy*, ed. Annemarie Bean, James V. Hatch, and Brooks McNamara, 141–162. Hanover, CT: Wesleyan University Press.

Winter, Marian Hannah. 1996. "Juba and American Minstrelsy." In Inside the Minstrel Mask: Readings in Nineteenth-Century Blackface Minstrelsy, ed. Annemarie Bean, James V. Hatch, and Brooks McNamara, 223–241. Hanover, CT: Wesleyan University Press.

Discography

Sweet Honey in the Rock. 1995. *Sacred Ground*. Redway, CA: Earthbeat (CD 9 42580-2).

The Tulips. 2002. *Les ménestrels du Cap, chants des troupes de carnaval et des chœurs "malais."* Paris : Buda Music (CD 1986102).

Wade in the Water. 1994. "Volume 2: African American Congregational Singing." Washington, DC: Smithsonian Institution/Folkways (CD SF 40073).

Winans, Robert. 1998 [1985]. *The Early Minstrel Show*. New York: New World Records (CD 80338-2).

2

My Life in the Bush of Ghosts: "World Music" and the Commodification of Religious Experience

Steven Feld

Schizophonia and Its Discontents

Since the early 1980s I have been tracking "world music," a term I do not use transparently, as a benign generic gloss for human musical diversity. My interest is specifically in "world music" as a label of industrial origin that refers to an amalgamated global marketplace of sounds as ethnic commodities. Once more idiosyncratically and unevenly collected and circulated under labels like "primitive," "folk," "ethnic," "race," "traditional," "exotic," or "international" music, today's world music tells a new story, one about intersections of transnational capital, global economic niche expansion, technological ubiquity, and the contradictions of aesthetic pluralism and product homogenization. It is a story about the shaping power of a global recording industry that sees the marketplace as the actual arbiter and guarantor of musical authenticity. This is to argue that the existence of the category of "world music"—like the category of "fine art" examined by Fred Myers (2001)—derives from and is chiefly dependent on the marketplace, and not from formal genre distinctions, autonomous aesthetic qualities, or geographic categories.

Like other contemporary anthropological projects, mine owes a certain impetus to Michel Foucault's (1977) insistence that the modern world is full of categorizations experienced as normalizing routines that render things invisible but known. I find it useful to examine many invisible but known qualities of world music through the concept of "schizophonia," a term introduced by Canadian composer R. Murray Schafer (1977, 90) to refer to the splitting of sounds from their sources. Unlike Schafer, I do not use the term principally or simply to refer to the technological process of splitting that constitutes sound recording. Rather, I am concerned with the larger arena where sound recordings move into long- and short-term routes of circulation and patterns of consumption. At stake, then, in the splitting of sounds from sources is the possibility of new social life, and this is principally about the recontextualization and resignification of sounds. It is the relationship of these social processes of resignification and their relationship to commoditization that I have been following, specifically how schizophonic things participate in what Arjun Appadurai (1986) has called "regimes of value."

My larger goal is to theorize how the experience of music is now increasingly mediated and tied to recorded commodities, but my specific interest is to explore the role of schizophonia—a decidedly nervous word, of course—in producing a classic form of modernist anxiety. This is the anxiety that world music variously reduces cultural equity or creates deeper cultural cleavages and hierarchies. It is the anxiety that world music—whatever good it does, whatever pleasure it brings— rests on economic structures that turn intangible cultural heritage into detachable labor. It is the anxiety that this detachability marginalizes, exploits, or humiliates indigenous originators and stewards. It is the anxiety that the underlying tale here is about the enrichment of global corporations, the consolidation of music owner- ship in centers of power, and the reproduction of the West touristing the rest for leisure and pleasure.

Alongside the production of these anxious narratives, world music has consis- tently, indeed, dialectically, produced a much more frequent narrative, one of cele- bration. It is this celebratory narrative that sees world music as indigeneity's cham- pion and best friend. This celebratory narrative sees musical hybridity and fusion as cultural signs of unbounded and deterritorialized identities. It sees the produc- tion of both indigenous autonomy and cultural hybridity as unassailable global positives, moves that signify the desire for greater cultural respect, tolerance, and blending. Here is where celebratory discourse virtually proclaims world music as synonymous with anti-essentialism, with borderlessness, with cultural free flow, with a futurist hope or prediction of greater cultural and economic equilibrium.

Anxious narratives tend to focus more sharply on economics and power. They emphasize how the music marketplace is structurally founded on historical ineq- uities in the areas of copyright, royalty structures, ownership regimes, and access to the market. They insist that the industry is currently organized in ways that typically reproduce and amplify these fundamental inequities. Celebratory narra- tives, on the other hand, tend to pay more attention to how pleasure and participa- tion enhance new connections and close old gaps. They emphasize new possibili- ties, new forms of recognition and the potential for respect they bring. In short, embedded in both anxious and celebratory narratives of world music is a fraught cultural politics of nostalgia, that is, each is deeply linked to the management of loss and renewal in the modern world. And they each involve complex suspicions and idealizations about notions like resistance and survival or tradition and heritage. My project is devoted to untangling some of the strands of suspicion and idealization that bind anxious and celebratory narratives. It is in this mutualism and interdependence, this play "from schizophonia to schismogenesis" (see Feld 1994) that I locate the social core of the "world music" story (see Feld 2000).

My Life in the Bush of Ghosts

I now turn to a specific "world music" story to ask what questions schizophonia might open up about the sonic circulation of religious practice. What, in other words, does schizophonia have to say about religion in the "world music" marketplace? What does it have to say about the commodity phase, when material objectification of religious sounds and practices in "world music" recordings achieve particular recognition and value? What role does the incorporation of religious sounds play in world music's larger stories of recontextualization and resignification? I concentrate on the LP/CD *My Life in the Bush of Ghosts* (*MLBG*) and the trend it helped establish, namely, the material incorporation of spirituality and religion—particularly the sounds of religious discourse—into the Western musical avant-garde's well-established primitivist project.

World music was not quite a newly emergent market category when *My Life in the Bush of Ghosts* was released on LP in February 1981. But the LP certainly heralded a great deal of what was to come in the 1980s and 1990s under the banners of "world music" as well as "world beat" and "ethno-techno"—the two subgenre terms that most overtly celebrate exotic alterity as danceable hybridity. The LP is a unique collaboration between British and Scottish art school rockers—trained visual/conceptual/performance artists concentrating on music. Brian Eno's work with Roxy Music, Robert Fripp and solo projects, and his work with U2, David Bowie, and Laurie Anderson clearly established him as an avant-garde electronics and ambient pioneer influenced by Karlheinz Stockhausen and John Cage. David Byrne emerged as well as leader of the hugely popular pop group Talking Heads. *MLBG* was recorded in 1979 and 1980, when Eno was producing two other LPs, *Remain in Light* and *Fear of Music* for Talking Heads. On *MLBG* a whole world of pre-digital ambient atmospherics, electronic effects and multi-track processing, and prominent bass and percussion dance grooves mix with the "found sounds" of radio shows and ethnographic field recordings. The radio segments come from call-in shows featuring indignant hosts, politicians, evangelists, and Christian preachers. The ethnographic recordings come from three LPs, one a compilation about Islamic vocal practice, another of African American spirituals from the Georgia Sea Islands, and the third an anthology of popular Arabic singers. In October

1990 *MLBG* was re-released on CD, the eleven original tracks intact, plus, in the style of many pop LP re-releases, a twelfth bonus track not previously found on the LP. A twenty-five-year anniversary deluxe edition was issued in March 2006.

Now put yourself in the place of a consumer who goes to purchase or preview this recording online at Amazon.com. Like many websites, Amazon's product pages contain consumer reviews. When I visited the site I saw that the first write-in commentary then running on the *MLBG* page was dated July 16, 2004, and was titled "Why is Qu'aran [*sic*] not in this CD ?" The reviewer, from São Paulo, Brazil, writes: "This album is excellent, but a song called Qu'aran [*sic*] (one of my favourite [*sic*]) is not on this CD! Political reasons? I don't know. Fortunately I have a vinyl version. If you don't know this song, try to find [it] in vinyl, the bass line is great!"

The next consumer review, dated March 19, 2004, from Oklahoma City, was titled "A glimpse at the future—but thumbs down to WB/Sire." The reviewer strongly appreciated the CD but withholds a five-star ranking "because, somewhere along the line, one track on the album has been changed. 'Very, Very Hungry' is a nice track, but the original LP contained a track in its place called 'Qu'ran,' which contained a recording of 'Algerian Muslims chanting Qu'ran' (as the original LP notes). I'm assuming the track was removed for political reasons—understandable in these charged times but very disturbing nonetheless. (Since I don't speak Arabic, I don't know what verses from the Qu'ran the Algerians were chanting— something 'inflammatory'?) It practically amounts to censorship, and I'm incensed at the suits at Warner Bros/Sire who (I'm sure) approved the change."

Notice the connected foci in these reviews on autonomous aesthetics (great bass line) and industry suspicion (blaming the corporate lawyers at Warner Bros/ Sire). Notice, too, that the musicians who created and benefit from the CD are not mentioned and thus not imagined to bear any responsibility or authority in its re-edit. The suspicion is that either the copied and contained voices—the Algerian Muslims whose voices are included without their knowledge or permission—or industry management, or both, have made trouble. So what is driving these comments, criticisms, and concerns? Sometime in 1994 all copies of the CD reissue were pulled, and a new edition was put into circulation. On it, the CD's original sixth track, titled "Qu'ran," was deleted, and in its place the original CD bonus track appeared.

The deleted "Qu'ran" piece was a mix of Eno and Byrne's techno dance grooves with excerpts from the first track of an ethnographic LP recording, *The Human Voice in the World of Islam*, published by Tangent Records in the United Kingdom in 1976. It was the first in a six LP anthology on music in the world of Islam (currently available as three CDs) edited by two ethnomusicologists, Jean Jenkins of the Horniman Musical Instrument Museum in London and Poul Rovsing Olsen of the Danish Folklore Archives in Copenhagen. The original LP track was titled "Recitation of Verses," and in the liner notes Jean Jenkins, who made the recording in Algeria in 1970, writes: "Verses of the Qu'ran by members of a religious brother-hood. This is part of the regular Friday religious observance." But on *MLBG* Eno and Byrne credit the track as "Algerian Muslims chanting Qu'ran." This, of course, makes clear that they neither read the liner text *of The Human Voice in the World of Islam* nor grasped the critical point, enunciated there and widely known, that in Islamic practice the Qu'ran is considered a text for recitation, quite inappropri-ate to imagine or render as sung vocal music or music for dance (see, e.g., Nelson Davies 2002).

The Context Changes

Whatever one thinks about Eno and Byrne's grooves, technological prowess with tape loops, hybridophilia, or sloppy liner notes, the global contextualization of their editing work changed radically precisely eight years after the LP's publication. For in February 1989, in what V. S. Naipul famously called "the ultimate extreme in literary criticism," Salman Rushdie was condemned to death by the former Iranian spiritual leader Ayatollah Ruhollah Khomeini. The issue: a character in Rushdie's then new novel, *The Satanic Verses,* was modeled on the Prophet Muhammad, and his transcription of the Qu'ran, quoted in the text, with touches from Rushdie, is portrayed in an unconventional light. The novel was banned in South Africa and India, burned in several locales, and caused riots in others. Forced into hid-ing, Rushdie published, in 1990, an apology in which he reaffirmed his respect for Islam. But Iranian clerics did not repudiate the death threat; indeed, an aide to Khomeini offered a million-dollar reward for Rushdie's death.

In 1993, in an event that generated international publicity, Rushdie's Norwe-gian publisher was attacked and seriously injured outside his home. An overlap-ping incident also generated international publicity. In January 1994 designer Karl Lagerfeld and the House of Chanel officially apologized to Muslims worldwide after it was revealed that three of their dresses, worn in a prime-time tele-spectacle by supermodel Claudia Schiffer, featured texts from the Qu'ran embroidered in gray pearls. Chanel was forced to destroy all the dresses as well as related photo-graphic images and negatives, and urged private makers or holders of photographs and videos to destroy any existing images of the dresses.

The seriousness of these issues was shockingly rekindled more recently by the violent murder of renowned Dutch filmmaker Theo Van Gogh in Amsterdam on November 2, 2004, at the hands of Islamic radicals. Van Gogh was a well-known provocateur, an outspoken opponent of Islamic extremism, and had repeatedly received death threats after the TV transmission, in August 2004, of a short film, *Submission,* which criticized the mistreatment of Muslim women. This film was a collaboration with Ayaan Hirsi Ali, a Somali who fled to Holland in the early 1990s, became a political scientist, and then a member of the Dutch Parliament. She publicly renounced Islam in 2002, after which she also received numerous death threats and had to be protected twenty-four hours a day. In the film Van Gogh reveals passages from the Qu'ran written on the bodies of women; this technique was meant to provoke discussion of whether the texts were hostile to women.

In the light of the Rushdie events of 1989–1993 it is hardly surprising that the "Qu'ran" track was deleted and *MLBG* reissued by 1994. Indeed an earlier wave of protest, from an Islamic organization in the United Kingdom, followed the LP's initial release and led to a prior but more limited withdrawal of the track on some European editions of the LP. But was this unique act of "world music" self-censorship dictated by the record distribution company's legal department, by the conscience of the artists themselves, or both? The answer, until quite recently remained unclear and unobtainable. Neither Eno nor Byrne had ever spoken about the track deletions. Warner Brothers and Sire were silent as well and refused to answer inquiries. The 2006 republication, however, rekindled the question. The package includes a new booklet with extensive liner notes by David Toop, author of *Ocean of Sound* (1995), an authoritative work on ambient music. But Toop's booklet, in keeping with all previous writing, continued the erasure of the story of the "Qu'ran" track. Indeed, his new liner text only added to the confusion by mistaking those who made the original field recordings. It seemed, once again, that the contentious dimension of musical appropriation would be forgotten amid a new flurry of publicity and praise for Eno and Byrne's "pioneering" work in "world music."

But the silence was finally broken, in an interview David Byrne gave to Chris Dahlen of *Pitchfork* magazine, posted online on July 17, 2006. When questioned about the decision to remove "Qu'ran," Byrne indicates that questions posed about blasphemy by an Islamic organization in 1982, shortly after the LP's release, led to the track's removal. Byrne recalls his conversation with Eno in this way: "We're going to get accused of all kinds of things, and so we want to cover our asses as best we can." Lest this be taken for a statement of artistic responsibility, Byrne only contributes to deception by leading readers and listeners to imagine that the track was completely removed from the LP in 1982. In fact, the track remained on many if not most LP issues throughout the 1980s, and then appeared on the initial CD re-release in 1990 and was not completely deleted for several more years.

Before turning to the question of the recording's role in the commodification of the spiritual, a few remarks are in order about its reception history. It is important to note here that the LP was not entirely greeted by celebration in the pop music world. In August 1981 (seven months after publication) *Rolling Stone* published a critical review, written by Jon Pareles, presently chief popular music critic at the *New York Times*.

Pareles writes that, "*My Life in the Bush of Ghosts* is an undeniably awesome feat of tape editing and rhythmic ingenuity. But, like most 'found' art, it raises stubborn questions about context, manipulation and cultural imperialism." Pareles argues that Eno and Byrne's uses of snippets of radio evangelism, preaching, and exorcism constitute "falsified ritual." "Blasphemy is beside the point," he writes, "Byrne and Eno have trivialized the event." And, he goes on, "You'd think if Algerian Muslims had wanted accompaniment while they [*sic*] chanted the Koran ("Qu'ran"), they'd have invented some."

In the end, Pareles quite directly posed the anxious question, the one about power asymmetries: What if, he asks in the review's last sentence, the tables were turned? Indeed, Pareles was perhaps the earliest and is still one of the few critics willing to pose that question. But it is still a major question, namely: How would pop stars and technology gurus like Eno and Byrne (and their record companies) react to being sourced, edited, and remixed by Algerian Muslims, Arabic pop singers, a Lebanese villager (whose name, by the way, they misspelled in the *MLBG* liner and almost everything else written about the project for twenty years), or Georgia Sea Islanders? The question remains poignant. If global sounds can detach from their sources to flow freely into the ears and machines of Western pop stars, could the sounds of pop stars possibly detach, flow freely, and go unnamed or misspelled, unauthorized or unacknowledged into the more local circulatory worlds of Western pop's historical others?

In several interviews published at the time of the LP's appearance, Eno was particularly articulate about *MLBG* as celebratory, indeed, as liberatory hybridity. He rendered the LP unassailable in terms of a politics of unbounded interculture and borderless transculture. "It's almost collage music," he said, "like grafting a piece of one culture onto a piece of another onto a piece of another, and trying to make them work as a coherent musical idea, and also trying to make something you can dance to" (Talking Heads-Net 2000).

But there is a more specific logic to the "grafting" idea, which brings us back to modernist avant-gardism. In a March 1981 interview with Sandy Robertson for *Sounds* magazine, Eno referred to *MLBG* as his "African psychedelic vision." Positioning Africa as "the interface between primitive and futuristic," he says, "rather than the old theory of the modern giving way to the post-modern, linear progression, the interesting ideas are being generated by the primitive, meaning the unchanged aspects of the old world." He adds: "I think we've got to look elsewhere for solutions. Our society has lost a certain strength, partly a strength of tradition, a moral strength." Robertson—the interviewer—then asked Eno about the critical counterview. The "implication is that you're saying the music isn't 'intelligent' enough until you improve upon it, and that therefore what you do is patronising to black culture." Eno responded, calmly, that his work "arrives from a kind of humility rather than a kind of arrogance . . . I regard myself as a student . . . I'm very humble about my understanding of African music, it's a vastly more complicated and rich area than I had dreamed of."

So, is it arrogance or humility? Appropriation or homage? Imperialist poaching or avant-garde boundary transgression? Elitist politics masked by populist dance aesthetics or populist aesthetics triumphing over hybridophobia? Those are the binaries, the anxious vs. celebratory rhetoric that was so clearly established by this and many other projects in the early 1980s. And they have been reproduced and recycled throughout the discursive history of "world music."

Fast forward again. Twenty-five years on from this project, Brian Eno, veteran of numerous technological frontiers, has now assumed the role of techno-futurist pundit and elder statesman, a fixture of the *Wire* magazine set. And David Byrne, producer of the extremely successful Luaka Bop recordings, has assumed a role as a senior entrepreneur, producer, and curator of world music artists and CDs. Notably both are now also active part-time as émigré moralists, lecturing the American masses on the proprieties of citizenship, musical and otherwise.

Time magazine of January 20, 2003, contains an Eno editorial article titled "The US Needs to Open Up to the World," which proclaims how America is "trapped in a fortress of arrogance and ignorance." Eno rails against an "introverted America" and a mass media "thriving on increasingly simple stories and trivializing news into something indistinguishable from entertainment." He rails against the left, too, which he says has retreated into introspection. "It seems content to do yoga and gender studies, leaving the fundamentalist Christian right and the multinationals to do the politics."

Eno's preaching is paralleled by Byrne, who contributed an October 1999 piece to the *New York Times* titled "I Hate World Music." Byrne here rails against "world music" as "a pseudomusical term," lecturing listeners that "it's a none too subtle way of reasserting the hegemony of Western pop culture. It ghettoizes most of the world's music. A bold and audacious move, White Man!"

Isn't it fascinating—or just bizarre—how completely disconnected these rants are from the history of aesthetic choice and representation in the artistic legacies of these two musicians? Eno and Byrne have always carefully excluded themselves from the ranks of the spoilers, those whose acts might in any way be imagined to cheapen or trivialize musical difference, those whose engagements beyond pop might be positioned as appropriation or pillage by anxious discourses. Reviewing all their interviews and projects since *MLBG,* they clearly have never looked back to examine how the history of their projects might contradict their newfound politics. So here, in the role of a lamenting chorus, we have the voices of those who, ironically enough, lack the reflexive capacity to grasp how they are quite centrally implicated in creating some of the very conditions or attitudes they now find so appalling. Put in the anxious language: the bass line is "après moi, le déluge" and the back beat, a "world music" re-spin of the postcolonial dynamic Renato Rosaldo (1989) so poetically dubbed "imperialist nostalgia."

"Unrelated Wanderings": *My Life in the Bush of Ghosts* and Its Phantom Double

These tales qua religious experience may be framed initially through the Amos Tutuola connection. Born in the Nigerian city of Abeokuta, in 1920, Tutuola published his novel *My Life in the Bush of Ghosts* in 1954, after a previously successful novel, *The Palm Wine Drinkard*. Both books are written not in a literary register but in everyday spoken Nigerian English, a stylistic matter that aroused much literary critical commentary (Di Maio 2000). Both, too, are quest narratives, with *My Life in the Bush of Ghosts* more of an underworld odyssey, the story of an eight-year-old boy who becomes lost in the "Bush of Ghosts," a parallel world of spirits and magic.

In the same March 1981 interview with Sandy Robertson for *Sounds* magazine, Eno was asked about the title of the record and how it might be connected to the book. He begins by acknowledging a parallel between the two but then does an about-face:

> It's a bit like the record in a way. The writer portrays himself as a young boy growing up in an African village, and at some point there's an emergency of some kind and he decides to hide in the bush. He dives through this little hole in a hedge and he suddenly finds he's entered this unmapped world of strange spirits. All of the ghosts, I gather, have a certain spiritual place, they're allegories for certain conditions of life. We started making the record before we'd ever read the book, so the record isn't in any way an illustration, or in fact it doesn't really have anything to do with it, except that in a sense it's a series of "unrelated wanderings."

Let us explore that trope for a moment to consider the different quests that the book and LP are after. Of course, by "unrelated wanderings" Eno means the aesthetic autonomy of the LP's music from the book. He wants to share in the power of Tutuola's title and the aura of the book's artistic achievement, but at the same time he insists that he and Byrne owe nothing to Tutuola, either in terms of inspiration or content. The apex of the exchange is the statement that the LP began before they had even read the book, positioning its content as a coincidental afterthought. Even the elisions, what Eno refers to as "an emergency of some kind," is a notable piece of forgetting in the context of calling *My Life in the Bush of Ghosts* his "psychedelic African vision." In fact, that emergency is a harrowing part of the book, where Tutuola's young narrator is abandoned during a slave raid.

Like Tutuola's previous work, Yoruba myth and folklore are clearly evident throughout the book, interwoven with frequent signs of European influence. The Rev. Devil performs a baptism of fire and water in the 8th Town of Ghosts; agents of the colonial state dominate the 10th Town, and schools and churches, not to mention the Television-Handed Ghostess—the strongest of Tutuola's analogies between technology and spiritual power—crop up consistently in his narrator's amazing wanderings. The simultaneity of layered beliefs and realities—of Yoruba stories and religion with Western Christianity and science—are woven together consistently through a series of trials and tribulations, which lead in equal measure to demonstrations of the narrator's courage, faith, and wonderment. Could Eno have imagined that this was Tutuola's psychedelic vision of Britain in Africa? And could the mix of "primitivist futurism" and "futurist primitivism" that guide the LP be read at all in light of Tutuola's cultural mixings? This is an interesting juxtaposition, but one difference is clear: Tutuola's mixings foreground colonialism, whereas Eno's ignore it. "Unrelated wanderings" indeed.

The trope of "unrelated wanderings" also leads to the simple question of what precisely Eno and Byrne were fleeing when they jumped, perhaps more like Alice in Wonderland, into their bush of ghosts. The answer might be that they were fleeing an increasingly technological 1970s pop and rock music that required spiritual revitalization in order to make contact with the world, in order to present pop as less commercial, less banal and Western, and thus more spiritual, profound, and global.

Thus in Eno and Byrne's bush of ghosts, that is, the LP's whole sonic landscape, there are brief encounters with exorcists and radio preachers, African American spirituals, Arabs, and North Africans, who play the role of frightening and wondrous spirits, alive with mysterious power and passion in voice and sound. Yet Eno and Byrne's ghosts remain, quite contra Tutuola, as others under control. For it is the power to embody and incorporate these other powers technologically, to edit, truncate, and caricaturize them sonically, to create them in and as display miniatures—as "loops" to use the technical tape-editing term—that is most clear in the recording's acoustic material constitution.

Most important, all this takes place in an aesthetic space dominated by dance music, by the allure of physical participation and its promise of bodily pleasure. Danceability is what sold pop and rock music, and Eno and Byrne well understood that danceability was the critical step in resignification, the commodity phase where the exotic tease never strips the familiar. Again the anxious question about virtual religion comes into focus: Is *MLBG*, then or now, a simulacrum of increased spiritual contact that masks an unexamined reproduction of increased spiritual distance?

For the looped material we hear in the composition, Eno and Byrne could have used just about anything and the world would not have known the difference. Group vocal "chant" is widespread, recordings of it quite common, and five second loops with maximal textural ornamentation and minimal melodic ambit easy enough to make. So choosing *Qu'ranic* recitation signals something important, namely, the desire to become intimate with particular others through their religious practices, to cozy up to their spiritual power, technologically detach it, cut and splice it, enter into its mysteries via the tape recorder as a musical instrument. This is what Eno referred to, in celebratory mode, as the desire to "graft" culture, to create a new hybrid of "primitive futurism." But put in more anxious terms, the schizophonic detachment performed creates a new tripartite social form. First, spiritual capital is recontextualized in a new sonic object; second, spiritual powers are resignified as hybrid art, technological mastery, and dance pleasure; and, third, ownership politics are elided or masked by autonomous aesthetics.

The regime of value issue is this: in the eyes of the pop music elite, ethnographic recordings are tokens of raw authenticity. But they require civilizing—"development" to use the common international aid metaphor—to become dance-worthy and pop sales-worthy. This is accomplished by schizophonic variations on four historically important techniques common to Western modernist avant-garde engagements with the exotic: decontextualization, incorporation, juxtaposition, and curation (Feld 1996). In the space of the "Qu'ran" track, these techniques combine with Western modernist avant-gardism's reigning ideological principle: anything that's possible is permissible.

The core modernist story here concerns how the aura—the detachable spiritual powers of others—is called upon to replace or renew Western senses of inner loss. The spiritual becomes an index of primal authenticity, a way to invest authentic difference into sound objects that are overtly hybrid and, in their acoustic material form, familiar to Western pop. In "world music" market terms, religion is recontextualized to become value-added primitivism, value-added aura, value-added difference, value-added nostalgia. Religious sounds are key means for incorporating, juxtaposing, and curating spiritual otherness. This is because their key work in resignification is to create a special sense of contact with something imagined to be more primal, integrated, coherent, pure, innocent, and passionate. And, of course, in the most critical contradiction, spirituality is meant to make the product seem less commercial.

Looking back, *MLBG* reveals an originary moment in a critical "world music" story: the industrialization of desire for pleasure participation in spiritual difference. And, since that moment in 1981, any incisive history of "world music" products will indicate how religion has been and remains critical to the genre's market-cycle reinvigoration and niche expansions. For "world music," *MLBG* was a herald of how religion can have a revitalizing effect in pop music, its legacy the creation of a commodity phantom double whose artistic, marketplace, and consumer interests come together as a historical exemplar of the social life, and empire, of schizophonic things.

Note

This essay was first presented as a lecture in early fall 2004 for New York University's Center for Religion and Media, and I am grateful to Faye Ginsburg, the Center's director, for the challenge to write it, and to the audience for their thoughts. Later 2004 presentations, at the Universities of Bergen, Copenhagen, Palermo, and Texas at Austin also produced stimulating conversations. A version of this essay was published in Italian, in 2007, as "My Life in the Bush of Ghosts: la 'world music' e la mercificazione dell'esperienza religiosa," in *Incontri di etnomusicologia: Seminari e conferenze in ricordo di Diego Carpitella*, edited by Giovanni Giuriati, 329–348, for the EM serie Quaderni, Archivi di Etnomusicologia, by Accademia Nazionale di Santa Cecilia, Roma. A companion essay, researched and written together with Annemette Kierkegaard of the University of Copenhagen, is "Entangled Complicities in the Prehistory of 'World Music': Poul Rovsing Olsen and Jean Jenkins Encounter Brian Eno and David Byrne in the Bush of Ghosts," published online at http://www.popular-musicology-online.com/2010. This text adds the story of *MLBG*'s use of Lebanese singer Dunya Yunis's voice, as recorded by Danish ethnomusicologist Poul Rovsing Olsen, the co-editor, with Jean Jenkins, of the LP *The Human Voice in the World of Islam*, for the Music in the World of Islam series. I am grateful to Ole Reitov for reviewing the current version and sharing with me both his correspondence and his Danish radio interviews with Brian Eno from the period of the recording's initial release.

References

Appadurai, Arjun, ed. 1986. *The Social Life of Things: Commodities in Cultural Perspective.* Cambridge: Cambridge University Press.

Byrne, David. 1999. "I Hate World Music." *New York Times,* October 3. http://www.pitchforkmedia.com/article/feature/37176/Interview_ Interview_David_Byrne.

Di Maio, Alessandra, ed. 2000. *Tutuola at the University: The Italian Voice of a Yoruba Ancestor.* Roma: Bulzoni Editore.

Eno, Brian. 2003. "The US Needs to Open Up to The World." *Time,* January 20.

Feld, Steven. 1994. "From Schizophonia to Schismogenesis: On the Discourses and Practices of 'World Music' and 'World Beat.'" In *Music Grooves,* ed. Charles Keil and Steven Feld, 257–289. Chicago: University of Chicago Press.

———. 1996. "Pygmy POP: A Genealogy of Schizophonic Mimesis." *Yearbook for Traditional Music* 28:1–35.

———. 2000. "A Sweet Lullaby for World Music." *Public Culture* 12 (1): 145–171. Reprinted in Arjun Appadurai, ed. 2001. *Globalization.* Durham, NC: Duke University Press.

Foucault, Michel. 1977. *The Archeology of Knowledge.* London: Tavistock.

Myers, Fred, ed. 2001. *The Empire of Things: Regimes of Value and Material Culture.* Santa Fe, NM: School of American Research Press.

Nelson Davies, Kristina. 2002. "The Qu'ran Recited." In *The Garland Encyclopedia of World Music,* Vol. 6, *The Middle East,* ed. Virginia Danielson, Scott Marcus, and Dwight Reynolds, 157–163. New York: Routledge.

Pareles, Jon. 1981. "Does This Global Village Have Two-way Traffic? Review of *My Life in the Bush of Ghosts*." *Rolling Stone,* August 2.

Robertson, Sandy. 1981. "The Life of Brian in the Bush of Ghosts. Interview with Brian Eno." *Sounds,* March, 7. http://www26.brinkster.com/brianeno/index.html?eno_interviews.html-frameHOME.

Rosaldo, Renato. 1989. "Imperialist Nostalgia." *Representations* 26:107–122.

Rushdie, Salman. 1989. *The Satanic Verses.* New York: Viking.

Schafer, R. Murray. 2002. *The Tuning of the World.* New York: Knopf.

Talking Heads Net. 1999. http://www.talking heads.net/bushofghosts.html.

Toop, David. 1995. *Ocean of Sound.* London: Serpent's Tail.

Tutuola, Amos. 1952. *The Palm-Wine Drinkard.* London: Faber and Faber.

———. 1954. *My Life in the Bush of Ghosts.* London: Faber and Faber.

3

A Place in the World: Globalization, Music, and Cultural Identity in Contemporary Vanuatu

Philip Hayward

Theories of globalization frequently speak of the importance of the intersection and interaction of local and global factors. In his perceptive paper, "The Global, the Local and the Public Sphere," Colin Sparks identified three "general classes of theorizing that assign different values to the local/global pair" (2000, 77):

a) "theories of globalization that see it as a generalization of existing, and usually Western, trends [such as] Giddens, who views globalization as the generalization of modernity" (ibid.);

b) theories "that propose a uniform and homogenous process spreading throughout the world [which] destroys the local, at whatever level it is manifested, and replaces it with a single, standard, and usually U.S.-inspired society" (ibid., 78); and

c) theories that identify "a state system under siege" attacked by "abstract forces, notably the world market, acting at a level more general that that of the state" and also "from below" by "other forces relating much more directly to the immediate experience of the population" (ibid., 78–79).

These classes are, of course, Western reflections on globalization understood as originating in the Western world. This picture looks quite different from particular non-Western locations, especially when the focus is on the character and agency of the local rather than on local vulnerability to Western influences. For such locations and societies, the current bundle of energies, networks, and institutions representing late-twentieth and early-twenty-first-century globalization often appear as simply the latest in a longer wave of Western interventions that include missionary religion, economic exploitation, imperial annexation, colonialism, colonial withdrawal, and phases of global militarization.

In discussing this counter-perspective, this chapter considers the manner in which the accumulation of globalizing discourses and practices in the tourist and music industries have contributed to the cultural identity of the modern Pacific state of Vanuatu. It examines, in particular, the manner in which aspects of these discourses and practices have been interpreted and employed by cultural producers wishing to gain a local advantage in the international system which they represent. The discussion does not so much reflect on Vanuatu's position within the world music economy (envisaged as some paradigmatic object-in-itself) but, instead, details local approaches to the tourism and music industries that are the country's points of engagement with modern global initiatives and thereby its place in the world.

Historical Context

The nation of Vanuatu is a small, sparsely populated archipelago in the southwestern Pacific Ocean, some one thousand miles east of the Australian city of Cairns. It is home to a highly diverse population with more than six hundred distinct local languages and a wide variety of cultural practices. The broader region known as Melanesia—of which Vanuatu forms the southwestern corner—was one of the last areas of the world to be brought under European imperial control, commencing in the late 1700s when various islands were visited by Christian missionaries, sandalwood traders, and slave traders, all keen to expand their activities in virgin territories. The slave traders, known as "blackbirders," operated between 1860 and the early 1900s, primarily in recruiting indentured labor to work in the sugarcane fields of northeastern Australia. Foreign intruders were rarely welcome in the islands, and in the early contact years many foreigners were killed soon after arrival. Despite such initial deterrents, a number of European groups managed to establish commercial and missionary enterprises in the early to mid-1800s. During this period rival French and British factions dominated European activity in the islands. This conflict of interest was resolved by a unique—and in many ways untenable—compromise. In 1906 the islands were constituted as an Anglo-French colonial condominium, under the dual name of New Hebrides/Nouvelles Hébrides. This arrangement did not divide the archipelago into separate spheres of interest but rather overlaid the region's traditional societies with two contrasting and frequently fractious systems of law and administration. Not without justification, this period is often referred to as the joint "Pandemonium"—a phenomenon most evident in the capital city of Port Vila, where different populations were juxtaposed in complex interaction with one another. Independence came to the territory in a typically chaotic manner in 1980, with the British administration supporting the initiative and the French actively assisting opponents and regional separatist movements. Despite this shaky start, the country has remained a relatively stable democracy without the severe legal problems that have afflicted neighboring Melanesian nations such as the Solomon Islands and Papua New Guinea.

Over the past forty years tourism—principally from Australasia, Europe, and North America—has emerged as a major element of the national economy. The "Vanuatu" brand combines three main components. The first is the compact, lively, and cosmopolitan capital of Port Vila, with its residues of the Anglo-French condominium and its mingling of islanders from the whole archipelago. The second comprises the overwhelmingly unspoiled and undeveloped rainforest and coastal and volcanic landscapes that mark most of the nation and have proven particularly attractive to burgeoning eco-tourism. The third element is a series of unique cultural practices such as the traditional slit-gong crafting and performances of Ambryn Island, the "land divers" of Pentecost, and the idiosyncratic John Frum movement based in the southern island of Tanna.

The John Frum movement merits special attention here in the context of current market-oriented and other "rationalist" discourses of globalization and advancement, for it represents an aberrant, illogical, and unproductive development. The group's belief system is based on the idealization of Americans who briefly landed on the island in 1942, during World War II, and just as quickly left at the war's end, leaving behind memories of prosperity and good feelings. The belief that America would one day return to bring lasting development and prosperity to the region became centered on a mythical figure named John Frum, an alias for a native of Tanna who, in an existing religious practice that began in the 1930s, would bring Western prosperity to Melanesia. Viewed from another perspective, it can be seen as an inventive attempt to negotiate the bizarre phenomenon of moments of global militarization in the region and its cultural overspill. Given the absence of any conflict in the New Hebrides itself, what is remembered most about this period is the sudden and unexpected nature of the Americans' arrival; the sheer volume of products and technologies they brought with them; the rapid establishment of infrastructures such as roads, buildings, and airstrips; the presence of African American troops interacting with (apparent) equality with Caucasian colleagues; and the Americans greater readiness to engage in social activity with the ni-Vanuatu (indigenous) population. For ni-Vanuatu, contact with Americans between 1942 and 1945 offered an alternative model of the benefits of engagement with Westerners and the nature of interracial relations in general. This experience had an almost fantastical potency, as it was so far removed from the recent memory of coerced indentured labor offshore or subordination to colonial rule in their traditional homeland. This latter aspect forms a key plank of the John Frum movement.

Had the movement been short-lived, it could easily have been pigeon-holed as an idiosyncratic and unstable collision of premodern and modern world systems, but some sixty years after the end of the war, John Frum followers continue to promote their beliefs and play a part in provincial and national politics. Indeed, the appeal of the movement has risen in recent years. Adherents believe, for instance, that their faith has been rewarded by events such as the U.S. government's award of $66 million to Vanuatu, in March 2006, as its first "Millennium Challenge" development packages to developing countries.

Music plays a key role in one of the movement's primary sustaining rituals. Local John Frum communities on Tanna hold regular Friday night socials at, for example, Sulphur Bay and Lamakara, where adherents (and, increasingly, tourists) participate in all-night dances accompanied by guitar-based ensembles performing compositions based on U.S. pop and country songs that were learned, imitated, and reinterpreted in earlier decades. In 2006, when a live recording of the Lamakara band, titled *Songs of John Frum*, was released on CD in Vanuatu, these Friday night performances became part of a modern media environment. Illustrating the manner in which local cultural production has become enmeshed in broader global systems of circulation and validation, a review in the *Vanuatu Independent* highlighted the following aspects of the release:

> Vanuatu is world renowned for many unique features. One is the John Frum Movement on the island of Tanna . . . While thousands of tourists have found their way to Tanna, intrigued to visit the John Frum headquarters, their unique experience among these people can only be found in photos—and in the memories of the visitors . . . Up until now, books have been written about John Frum and thousands of pictures can be found on the internet to show John Frum people, but no recording of the unique music created by John Frum followers has ever existed. Not until Vanuatu Kaljoral Senta (VKS) completed the first CD compilation that is now available for purchase. . . . Recorded live at Lamakara village on the island's eastern coast, the CD carries songs from the John Frum movement describing their identity and you can hear the soul and spirit of the movement in these amazing tunes. (Ligo 2006b, 4)

The complex engagements with modernity, globalization, and Westernization entangled within the John Frum phenomenon, with its music packaged on CDs for domestic and international consumers, illustrate the problems inherent in many of the "general classes of theorizing" about globalization and the global/local interaction given at the start of the chapter (Sparks 2000, 77). Local responses are always more complex and autonomous than Western theories imagine them to be. The remainder of this chapter considers these aspects in the broader context of the development of a national identity in Vanuatu, the role that culture, and especially music, has played in that identity, and the challenges and opportunities raised by globalization.

Developing Cultural Independence

Although independence arrived somewhat abruptly in Vanuatu, it was supported and enabled by a broader cultural shift that occurred in the 1950s and 1960s, when disparate island communities developed a growing sense of their place within an emergent national entity. The lead-up to independence and, as important, the resolution of regional resistance to this, nurtured a sense of nationhood that became more firmly established in the post-independence era.[1] Three vectors were particularly significant here:

1. An increasing awareness of, and travel to, Port Vila (on Efate Island), as the national administrative, educational, commercial, and social center;
2. An increasing use (and eventual standardization) of the locally developed pan-archipelagic pidgin language known as Bislama; and
3. The development of national radio broadcasting, which, in its distinct early form, enabled communication between island communities.[2]

Although there have been a number of scholarly studies on Bislama and the politics of its official adoption and formalization, the most pertinent, spirited, and accessible body of work on this topic took place between the people of ni-Vanuatu, British and French residents, and overseas academics in the pages of the (Port Vila–based) national press in the late 1970s and early 1980s.[3] Certain aspects of this work are also referred to in Lissant Bolton's (1999) incisive analysis of the role of radio in establishing concepts of *kastom* (traditional) culture in Vanuatu. To date however, there have been no substantial analyses of the manner in which the national music culture of Vanuatu emerged in response to new media technologies and international musical styles or of the role of the tourism industry in enabling or inflecting musical style and practice. To address this gap, this chapter focuses on forms of music that have been expressed within industrial and media spaces, including *kastom*, string band, gospel, and local pop/rock/reggae.[4] The concluding sections expand the frame of reference to consider the access Vanuatu music has to the international music market and the kinds of national identities being proffered by those performances that have achieved some degree of international visibility.

Kastom Music and Dance, and Its Relationship to Radio and Tourism

Bolton (1999) explores the modern ni-Vanuatu notion of *kastom* and the manner in which it has developed through, and in relation with, oral history projects, radio, and the activities of the Vanuatu Kaljural Senta (Vanuatu Cultural Center), and he offers a definition of *kastom* as "practices understood to derive from the pre-colonial past" (ibid., 335). William Miles concurs but qualifies this further, deeming the term to refer to a set of diverse indigenous practices that were recently re-conceptualized as an aggregate in order "to incarnate indigenous cultural authenticity in opposition to colonialism" (ibid., 59). In the discussion that follows I use the term *kastom* with these meanings in mind but also consider the extent to which the term has been continually refigured to fit the shifting requirements of the tourism market.

Aside from the prominent institution of Christian congregational music, prior to World War II a minimal engagement was seen with nontraditional music among the ni-Vanuatu population of the region. What later was referred to as *kastom* music was performed throughout the islands, often accompanying dance, and comprised mainly vocal and percussion music, along with other wind instruments in certain locations (see Kaeppler 1998).

Around 1960, prior to the introduction of radio broadcasting in the New Hebrides, a short weekly program of topical items was compiled by three French residents in Port Vila for broadcast through Radio Noumea, in the French colony of Nouvelle Caledonie (in English, New Caledonia) and could be received by radios in the New Hebrides. The program included local music and stories, and was introduced each week by a short song titled "Kavelicolico," sung in the local language by its Ifira Island composer.[5] Bolton notes that the song was so popular that "the program was known, and is remembered, as Radio Kavelicolico" (1999, 339). With the best reception in the north and central parts of the archipelago, the service was a significant promulgator of a nascent national identity, albeit within a Francophone language frame, and was also significant for its diffusion of stringband music. Bolton points out that the program was important in terms of *kastom,* as many ni-Vanuatu perceived that,

> Europeans [largely] disapproved of and discouraged local knowledge and practice. To radio listeners, therefore, the broadcast of indigenous songs and stories represented an affirmation of local knowledge and practice at a period when such affirmation was not generally accepted from Europeans. (ibid., 341)

Musical contact between different regional groups greatly increased in the postwar era, as individuals moved from various islands to the vicinity of Port Vila in order to secure education and employment. In the 1950s and 1960s performances of local repertoires, both within internal émigré groups and in culturally mixed contexts around Port Vila, became a regular occurrence and included *kastom* performers from islands such as Pentecost, who were asked to appear at various ceremonial functions.[6] In another revision of ni-Vanuatu perceptions of Westerners' disapproval of *kastom* practices, *kastom* troupes were increasingly employed to perform for Western tourists and other visitors. Tourism expanded steadily in the late 1960s, and by 1972 it had surpassed copra production as the New Hebrides' major industry, attracting twenty thousand international visitors and bringing in an estimated $3 million yearly.[7] The increasing number of tourists visiting Efate Island provided a ready audience for performances of *kastom* material, transforming traditional community practices into a commercial activity (at least around Port Vila). This phenomenon was regarded with some concern by ni-Vanuatu commentators. In a lengthy discussion, broadcaster and oral historian Gordon Ligo (1974, 8) noted that the remuneration afforded to Pentecost community performers was to some extent positive (in giving émigré Pentecost youth the chance to maintain their tradition away from home) but also noted that, more generally:

> Tourism is ruining the spirit of our ceremonies. As we want money we perform our custom dances and other ceremonies for the tourists to pay to see them. We repeat these so often that we tend to forget their meaning. Our own people do not enjoy these performances any longer. They are just tourist attractions.

Young ni-Vanuatu writer Tony James made similar assertions, identifying the rise of a new urban youth around Port Vila alienated from their heritage:

> What do we know of the culture of our own people? We have no interest in the custom songs of our parents because we think they are monotonous and we prefer European pop music which we have heard in the night clubs.[8] Yes, we pretend to know the dances from our islands and we put our performances for tourists and other Europeans to watch [but] who is to criticise us if we are not singing the songs in the right way or the beat of the drum is wrong? Our grandparents have died and our parents are back in the villages. (James 1974, 8)

These comments are significant, as they represent part of a greater national discourse around the values and role of *kastom* that was under way at the time. My discussions with coordinators and performers in contemporary *kastom* ensembles based around Port Vila in 2006–2007, some thirty years later, revealed similar anxieties but also a strong commitment to maintain *kastom* performance as an important link to traditional regional culture. Whatever the concerns voiced above, the power of the tourist dollar in the low-employment economy around Port Vila has provided a continuing motive for ni-Vanuatu to perform various types of *kastom* material for tourists at hotel venues, at special events, or at "*kastom* villages" set up specifically to provide employment for island youth by representing aspects of their cultural heritage.

The Development of String-Band Music

The arrival of Allied troops in the southwestern Pacific region, in 1941, following the outbreak of conflict with Japan, in addition to prompting the establishment of the John Frum movement and its musical expressions, greatly influenced the development of local music more generally. The establishment of military bases around Port Vila and on Espiritu Santo Island brought ni-Vanuatu in contact with Western musical styles and offered access to Western instruments such as guitars, ukuleles, and mandolins. Some time during and after the U.S. military invasion, a number of ni-Vanuatu learned to play these instruments, and the guitar and ukulele became the instrumental base of the postwar Vanuatu style of string-band music.[9] The string-band style that developed fairly consistently across the islands was based around songs, initially versions of Western material, performed to a standard rhythmic pattern, usually played in (loose) unison by guitars,[10] ukuleles, and a single-string "bush bass," and sometimes additional percussion instruments. The bush bass is similar to a 1950s European skiffle tea-chest bass, but with a moveable neck to adjust pitch. A common feature of string bands until the 1980s was the use of the ukulele to belt a double-time rhythmic pattern (although this rhythmic complexity has diminished somewhat in more recent ensembles). With exception of the Futunese bands (discussed below) the main differences and audience attraction between ensembles from various areas have been the singers' vocal character and skill; styles of songwriting; if used, the local language; and performers' local affiliations. Although some 1980s and 1990s string bands were notable for featuring instruments more common in the immediate postwar era—such as the mandolin used by the Lumbukuti Beach Boys (from Tongoa)[11] or the accordion featured by the Tuki Mere band (from Lele, Efate)—these have represented individual instances rather than local patterns. Similarly, although some observers assert the existence of distinct regional characteristics such as melodic invention and dexterity in guitar parts in Raga Island string bands (Ligo 2005c, 9), a sufficiently detailed analysis of the range of Vanuatu string bands has yet to be undertaken to gauge the accuracy of such assertions. Moreover, a map of any such regional tendencies has still not been developed.

By the early 1960s string-band music was widely performed in informal social contexts around Port Vila, various parts of Shefa province (i.e., central Vanuatu), and, according to some reports,[12] in the national "second city" of Luganville (on Espiritu Santo Island). However, the pan-regional musical style and appeal of string-band music did provide a new vernacular music for displaced islanders around Port Vila and, by association, New Hebrideans as a whole. The latter aspect was enhanced by a development in the mid-1960s that saw named string bands emerge from community contexts and begin to be featured at public events and festivities. One significant occasion was the Nguna Band's performance as part of the British Queen's birthday celebrations in Port Vila in 1964. Other bands that went on to play at social functions for expatriates as the decade progressed included the Vagabonds, from Noume, who performed around Port Vila in 1966. This increased profile for string bands occurred simultaneously with the introduction of national radio broadcasting.

In her radio discussion of *kastom* music, Bolton (1999) also noted that the early 1960s "Radio Kavelicolico" broadcasts featured string-band music. She relates that the chairman of the Port Vila Town Council, Georges Milne, "gathered together some of the young men who worked for the Vila Town Council, who formed a string band that he recorded for the program" (ibid., 357n6). Significantly, given the pan-national nature of the string-band phenomenon (and the similar musical styles developing in other Melanesian locations), the ensemble comprised two musicians from Ambrym Island, one from Ambae and a Fijian (ibid., 357n3). The introduction of institutional radio broadcasting in 1966, in the form of Radio Vila, also gave the style further exposure. The very first program broadcast on the service, for instance, featured a recording by local mandolin player Paul Isono, "playing his mandolin under [a] mango tree" in the city (ibid., 357n6). The service initially only broadcast short slots of news and recorded Western music, but its local information function allowed string bands occasional access. The first performers to profit from this exposure was the Kawenu College String Band, which was employed to record a Bislama song publicizing the 1967 national census titled "Census Day I Cum." Though somewhat retrograde within the emergent style of string-band repertoire,[13] the song proved popular among ni-Vanuatu and expatriate communities and gave the college band a significant profile.

Radio Vila introduced a Bislama topical affairs show in 1968, but the recording of songs by local artists for transmission did not become a regular occurrence until 1976, by which time the service had been renamed Radio New Hebrides to emphasize its national reach and function. As part of an expansion of Bislama content, the station introduced a weekly string-band show and a *kastom* music program. The string-band material recorded for the weekly show proved popular and was soon introduced into other parts of the schedule. By the mid-1970s string-band music was increasingly recognized as a distinct, vibrant local cultural form in its own right, and was the subject of regular feature articles (usually in French) in the (trilingual) newspaper *Nabanga: Hebdomadaire d'information*. A high point of this coverage was the front cover of the December 22 issue, proclaiming "String-Band—la memoire musicale des Nouvelles-Hebrides," with reports within its pages featuring leading ensembles.

The emergence of a new style of string-band music featuring tuned percussion, pioneered by groups of Futunese musicians based around Port Vila and on Tanna in the late 1970s, and the success of these groups in national music contests[14] also invigorated the genre and secured overseas exposure. In the 1980s, after recording a series of albums, the Port Vila–based Fatuana String Band and the Tanna-based Fatuana Mahtua performed overseas.

Commercial Music Recording

Local commercial-music recording began in the run-up to independence when Radio New Hebrides employee Paul Gardissat initiated Vanuata Productions, recording Vanuatu artists and issuing albums on cassette.[15] He continued this work until 1988, releasing close to 150 albums. These have recently reentered the public sphere as a result of a program undertaken by the Vanuatu Kaljural Senta, which was funded by a grant from the European Union Non-State Actors Programme in 2000, and has seen Gardissat's catalogue digitized, re-mastered, and made available (on individual order) through the National Museum. The majority of performances recorded by Gardissat were in the string-band genre (e.g., Noisy Boys and Tuki Mere), gospel (e.g., the Advent and Aore Singers), or the emergent style of rock/reggae discussed below (e.g., Tropic Tempo and Huarere).[16] The audience for these releases were made up of local residents and tourists, the latter providing the only ad hoc channel for overseas distribution of the recordings. Their circulation within the country and their availability for radio broadcast allowed local music to compete with imported Anglophone and Francophone pop releases, and established a vibrant national music industry in Vanuatu, albeit one entirely centered in Port Vila.

Jean Marc Wong, son of a prominent local businessman, bought out the Vanuata Productions studio (in the Port Vila suburb of Agadis) in 1989. After educating himself in music-production techniques and receiving advice from contacts in Australia, Wong began recording music and established Vanuata Productions as the major national recording company, a position it still holds today, having released more than one hundred albums starting with the debut album of the Mangawiarua String Band. During the 1990s he upgraded his equipment to analogue multi-track before moving into digital production in 2005. Although Wong has periodically employed local engineers, such as Benson Nako in the early 2000s, for the majority of this period Vanuata Productions has been essentially a one-man operation, with Wong producing, engineering, mixing, mastering, and—for low-volume releases—duplicating copies (although larger runs have been handled through Australian and New Zealand manufacturers). Currently Wong has a production routine that records a string band in five to six working days and a pop band (usually requiring more editing and overdubs) in twenty to twenty-five working days. In the 2000s aspiring artists have usually approached Wong with demo tapes, recorded on domestic equipment or at the newer independent studio facilities described below.

Vanuata Productions' releases have a direct retail outlet through the family's Chung Po retail store in central Port Vila, and are also distributed wholesale to other Vanuatu retail outlets. The label achieved its peak sales and greatest profitability with a series of five albums recorded by Vatdoro, Vanuatu's first major popular music band to combine reggae and string-band elements in an amplified format. These albums gave the label its largest production runs ever—five thousand copies per album, and, as Wong recalled, four of these sold out completely. Since the mid-1990s the average sales volume per album release has declined considerably, which, Wong explains, is a result of the greater number of competing releases on the market combined with a downturn in the economy and an increase in illegal CD copying (personal communication, May 2007).

Other studios and associated recording labels have operated for limited periods during the 1980s to the 2000s, some of which have been established by foreign musicians or engineers during periods of residence in the country. The first notable example was Vanu-Wespa, established in the mid-1980s by a West Papuan band, The Black Brothers, during the band's residency in Vanuatu that commenced in 1983. The operation was established to record material by the band for release, but during their stay on Efate they also encouraged, recorded, and released material by artists such as the local band Black Revolution. The band's sudden deportation to Australia in 1988 terminated the operation. Another company that operated during 1997–1999 was Ocean Deep, established by Japanese sound engineer and musician Ken Oshika. The label recorded around ten albums, including their highest-selling album, the debut of the gospel band Exodus (1998), before ceasing operations when Oshika departed for overseas.

Among ni-Vanuatu initiatives, the first attempts to create different production options occurred in 1994, when veteran musician John Josiah set up a home studio system under the name Sina, initially working with two-, four-, and eight-track analogue equipment before shifting to digital in the early 2000s. Sina has produced only around a dozen releases to date but has put out material by popular singers such as Reynolds and albums such as Joe Max's *Wok Tugeta* (2004). In 1996 musician and sound engineer Timteo Kalmet also established a home studio at Erakor, an outer suburb of Port Vila. He initially intended to purchase digital facilities but was unable to obtain finance for this and used analogue equipment instead. One of his first productions was the demo tape for Vanessa Quai's song, *I Was Lost,* which was influential in launching her career (more on this below). He produced seven cassette albums under the label Vantrax as a part-time activity, before the pressure of community commitments and his day job caused him to withdraw from active production.

In the immediate post-independence period a local form of rock was pioneered by bands such as Lawa Melenamu and the Fantastix, Asio, Nakavika, and Rainbow. By the mid-1980s a local version of reggae, pioneered by Myster and Gaby Hvew, also emerged. The latter two musical streams have now largely converged into a local style often simply referred to as "reggae" or "Vanuatu reggae." As in the Pacific in general, reggae initially became popular in the 1980s through exposure to Bob Marley's recordings. Indeed, his inspiration, and the Jamaican roots of the increasingly global form of reggae, are still perceptible in Vanuatu, with the Tropic Sounds music shop in Port Vila prominently displaying pirated CDs of seminal Jamaican-roots performers such as Burning Spear alongside African reggae stars such as Lucky Dube. Despite this cultural influence, Vanuatu popular music has been more strongly influenced by Pacific reggae artists, who use a squarer rhythmic structure that does not stress the second and fourth beats, emphases central to standard reggae. Usually featuring MIDI[17] accompaniments and pop-style vocal harmonies, the influence of New Caledonian, Fijian, and Papua New Guinean reggae can be heard in the work of local artists such as Huarere and Naio. Although artists such as Sam Jani (from Pentecost) and Joe Max (from Malaku) have also attempted to meld reggae and traditional local *kastom* rhythms in some of their material, there are no significant stylistic distinctions between Vanuatu reggae and the general form of Pacific reggae. Similarly Tropic Tempo's attempt to incorporate elements of traditional Banks Islands' material, chants, and instrumentation in its 1996 rock/reggae album, *Vois blong ol Bumbu,* remains an exceptional case.[18] Despite this, a strong local perception is that the sounds of Vanuatu performers are distinctly Vanuatu and express a Vanuatu identity.

Twenty-First-Century Vanuatu Music and Its Industrial Potential: The National Sector

Vanuatu's retail music industry is concentrated in a small area of Port Vila but, even so, information on the national providers of recorded material for Vanuatu's consumers is difficult to obtain because of the absence of centrally collected retail data and the high level of piracy in the domestic market. Indeed, few music industry personnel interviewed for this research in 2006–2007 would even hazard a guess as to the possible proportions of piracy, beyond the perception that Vanuatu's recorded material constituted a sizable slice—perhaps a majority—of the national market, with Western, Jamaican/African reggae, and other Pacific artists constituting the remainder. Discounting the Port Vila shops that cater largely to tourists (many of whom specialize in pirated material that undercuts Australian prices for products commonly available there), a sample audit of Port Vila music shops in August 2006 confirmed that the shelf content (which is not necessarily equivalent to the overall volume of sales) is predominantly Vanuatu material, with fewer other Pacific artists represented than was commonly perceived.[19] Along with its dominance as a national retail outlet, Port Vila is the center of the country's recording industry and a magnet for musicians and engineers wishing to develop their skills, careers, and earning opportunities. There has been no recording studio operation outside the capital area to date, and although some tourist operations exist outside the southwestern corner of Efate Island (where Port Vila is located), the live music scene is also concentrated in this area.

The early to mid-2000s have seen a marked increase in the number of recording operations in Port Vila, with the majority using digital recording and production equipment and operating in mostly rented, non-soundproofed facilities in downtown Vanuatu, with several at the rear of the Hebrida retail complex. The most significant of these is Tropik Zound, which commenced its operations in 2005.[20] The company was established by Benson Nako, who had formerly worked as chief sound engineer for Vanuata Productions. Born in Tanna of mixed Tannese and Enka (Papua New Guinean) parentage, Nako is one of the most experienced studio and live-sound engineers in Vanuatu's music industry and has also worked in live sound in Papua New Guinea. Keen to establish a low-cost, high-quality alternative to Vanuata Productions, Nako initially operated Tropik Zound as a studio for recording mastered CDs and cassettes for local bands to release and retail on their own; usually there was a one-week production schedule, with a standard fee of approximately AUD$750 (1 Australian dollar = US$700) per album. In an interview, in March 2006, Nako acknowledged that this was a very low fee, considering the costs for the building rental and maintenance, equipment outlay, and personnel salaries. This strategy of delivering low-cost, high-quality products, he explained, would then inspire musicians to actively seek higher production values, ultimately allowing him to charge higher fees when the production sector matured. Despite attracting praise and support from local musicians for his "fair dealings" and excellent technical quality, the lack of adequate income undermined the operation. Nako ceased recording in mid-2006 and returned to Tanna on an extended break, before re-launching a more commercially attuned studio operation with a partner.

Other operations based in the Hebrida building in 2006–2007 include the Bistaveos Music Video Company (discussed below), which recently diversified into music production. Former Tropik Zound musician and engineer Roy Tarosa also recently established a recording company, the Aelan Saon Studio, dedicated to gospel music, an enduringly popular genre in a country where attendance continues to be high at established Anglican, Presbyterian, and Roman Catholic churches, as well as more recent arrivals such as the Church of Christ and Seventh Day Adventists. Indeed, many prominent Vanuatu performers have emerged from this context, most notably teenage vocalist Vanessa Quai. Other established performers in the gospel genre include solo performer Laisa Boedoro and vocal groups such as the Reunion Singers and the Monument Singers—all of whom, along with gospel artists from the Solomon Islands, were included on the 2005 compilation DVD *Vansolo Gospel Collection Volume 1.*

Individual musicians such as veteran performers Jean Francois Patterson and Maurice Michel have also established low-cost, technically "low-end" home studios for recording and releasing their own material and have also worked on recordings for emerging young artists. Other recording facilities are also currently in development. One of these is planned for an area of the Port Vila suburb of Freshwater that is home to the band Huarere. Originally from Pentecost Island, Huarere emerged as a string band in the 1980s before embracing the Pacific reggae style and—along with Vatdoro—becoming the most popular national exponent of the style. In 1995 the band secured a bank loan to purchase a plot of land in the Port Vila suburb of Freshwater and built houses, a small general retail shop, and a rehearsal space the band occupies and operates. Successful management of their finances and realistic financial planning ensured them credit and credibility with banks, and their studio was installed in 2007.

In addition to the commercial operations discussed above, VKS Productions, an offshoot of the Vanuatu Kaljoral Sentre, also began to release recordings in the mid-2000s. VKS Productions was established in the early 1960s as one of various initiatives by foreign anthropologists and ni-Vanuatu to preserve and document the cultural practices and heritage of the archipelago. One of its most innovative and sustained projects has been to strengthen the linkage between its national center and its regional operations. As expressed on the VKS website: "The Cultural Center in the capital is the tip of a hidden pyramid—most of its activities are in the outer islands of Vanuatu, with living people and cultures."[21] Building on its formative (and continuing) project of preserving and promoting *kastom* culture (of the kind conceived around the period of independence) the VKS has increasingly extended this focus to include what might be termed "modern vernacular *kastom*" practices. Regarding music, their label has released a series of mastered versions of field recordings such as the previously discussed 2006 John Frum Band CD, as well as studio recording projects such as the Aro Lokol String Band's album *Destination* (2005). Although none of these has achieved broad commercial success, they represent an important heritage resource of local origin.

Despite the volume of music produced locally, and the broad national cultural project of early national radio, the two national radio stations, Radio Vanuatu and Nambawan FM98, predominantly play overseas material, including a substantial proportion of Western pop music. The main radio outlet for Vanuatu music is the new Efate-oriented commercial station FM 107, introduced in 2007, which also features a substantial proportion of reggae and world music. Established in 1994, the national television broadcaster, VTBC's most significant contribution to local music culture, occurred in the form of a thirty-minute, fortnightly contemporary music show titled *Pacific Tempo*, initiated in 2002, providing valuable national exposure for Vanuatu performers. Produced, directed, and edited by Jean-Baptiste Calo, the show was popular with viewers before it was canceled in 2005, although, at the time of this writing, it was being considered for reinstatement. The broadcaster also occasionally covers major musical events such as the annual Fes Napuan. Substantially as a result of *Pacific Tempo*'s example, independent video-clip production commenced in 2002, with dedicated operations, including Bistaveos, run by former actor Joe Jeffred and operating, shooting, and editing in one-room premises in the Hebrida building. Clips are shown on TV, either included in programs or as "filler" material in the schedule. A series of compilation DVDs are also available such as Bistaveos's *Eli Koleksen* (2006), featuring clips of Nauten, Joe Max, and Alphongs Jack Kalontano. In 2006 Calo also became an independent video clip producer, immediately securing high-profile commissions including the tracks from Vanessa Quai's *Transformation* album.

There is currently no copyright law in Vanuatu, for although the Parliament passed the Copyright and Related Rights Act in 2000, it has not been implemented and is believed to have a number of limitations, particularly regarding indigenous copyright issues. Piracy, as noted before, is a considerable problem, and pirated CDs and DVDs of major international music are freely on sale in more than fifteen Port Vila retail outlets; Vanuata Productions, however, is not involved in piracy and therefore this has not been a source of income for major local producers as it has for music industry major Chin H Meen in Papua New Guinea (see Niles 1998). Indeed, piracy of Vanuatu releases, through disk burning and tape dubbing, is seen as a significant issue for artists; despite the lack of copyright legislation, some locally produced material now carries prohibitory statements in Bislama advising that illegal duplication will result in legal action as yet unspecified. Piracy of local releases is a particular problem in a market as small as Vanuatu. With a population of around 210,000 and an average per capita income of around AUD$3000 (US$2,750), the economics of production, let alone profitable production, are tight. Newly released Vanuatu CDs retail at around 1,500–2,000 vatu (1 vatu = US$0.01) and cassettes at around 800–1,000 vatu, although newer releases by major artists can retail at a cost 10–20 percent higher. The standard agreement with artists at Vanuata Productions is a 10 percent royalty on wholesale sales. With an average Vanuata Productions sale in the range of five hundred, this eventually means a return to the musician(s) of around 100,000 vatu per CD album released. Newer independent labels offer more flexible arrangements with individual artist. With a break-even figure of three hundred in sales, Wong estimates that only 50 percent of his label's releases returned a profit in 2005 (personal communication, April 2006) and, though difficult to ascertain, the profitability of other independent releases also appears minimal for all but the most popular tier of performers.

Although it had little impact on local production or industry profitability, another exploitation of the country's copyright-free status attracted international attention in the early 2000s. This period saw the international music industry involved in a number of actions against the digital file-sharing networks that facilitated unauthorized reproduction of its copyrighted product. Along with Napster, which was shut down after sustained pressure in mid-2002, the other most prominent unauthorized operation was Kazaa, created, in 2000, by the Dutch company

Consumer Empowerment. Following successful legal action against them by the Dutch music publishing organization Buma/Stemra, Consumer Empowerment sold Kazaa, in early 2002, to an artfully complicated aggregate of companies called Sharman Networks. Sharman was based in Australia, but its perception of Vanuatu as a "copyright haven," safely removed from the legislative reach of Western national jurisdictions, led it to incorporate in Port Vila. The wisdom of this gambit became apparent in 2005, when the U.S. Supreme Court ruled that digital file-sharing networks infringed upon U.S. copyright law (*MGM Studios, Inc. v Grokster, Ltd* [545 US 913]). The Australian music industry exerted similar pressure on Sharman's Australian operation, and in late 2005 the Australian federal court ordered the company to cease providing services to users with an Australian IP address. Although Kazaa's registration in Vanuatu has provided some protection, these court actions severely curtailed its viability, and it is now a minor player in the international digital music industry. But even though Kazaa's inability to resist international pressure, despite its Vanuatu operating base, can be seen as confirming that "abstract forces, notably the world market, [were] acting at a level more general that that of the state" (Sparks 2000, 78–79), the whole legal drama had minimal impact on Vanuatu's national territory. Given the limited access to electricity outside Port Vila, let alone computers or Internet file-sharing networks, the local industry's engagement with national and international markets has primarily been through more traditional products and transactions.

International Markets

Despite widely perceived similarities with musical styles and sensibilities across Melanesia and the Pacific, the export of Vanuatu music to the region, and to a broader international market, remains largely underdeveloped. Vanuata Productions, for instance, has only one established overseas market, in New Caledonia, where Wong has a reciprocal distribution agreement with the Mangrove label. New Caledonia has a number of significant cultural connections with Vanuatu, facilitated largely by its proximity (an hour's flight away) and the shared Francophone heritage. Initial interest in Vanuatu music in New Caledonia commenced after successful tours by, for example, Vatdoro and Huarere in the 1980s; only a trickle of Vanuatu performances followed in the 1990s, however, and so significant connections did not develop until the early 2000s, when the teenage singer Vanessa Quai began an association with New Caledonia's Mangrove Studios.

Quai's career as a gospel, soul, and pop singer has been managed by her father, Nigel, and achieved a series of major boosts through successes in international song contests (in Egypt and Romania). In order to secure a high-quality, internationally marketable sound, Nigel Quai arranged for four of Quai's albums to be recorded at Mangrove, with David Leroy producing the MIDI backing tracks. The albums have been released locally licensed by Vanuata Productions and Mangrove in New Caledonia, thus securing her a considerable market in New Caledonia that she has nurtured through regular concert tours. Interest in accessing other markets resulted in Quai recording a collaborative album with the rising PNG vocal band Soul Expression for Chin H Meen productions in Port Moresby in 2005. Although the PNG collaboration was seen as creatively successful and apparently a medium-high seller in PNG, collaboration with the PNG has not yet yielded any royalty flow. Meanwhile, production in PNG was complicated by the partners' failure to comply with their financial agreements, and so a similar arrangement is unlikely to be repeated. One positive aspect of the collaboration, however, was Quai's meeting with Solomon Islands' reggae rapper Sharzy, who was brought in to appear on Quai's 2006 album *Transformations,* recorded in Port Vila. Vanessa Quai's international profile, and charity work, was officially recognized in 2007 (the tenth anniversary of her performing debut) through an Order of Vanuatu Award, a career retrospective exhibition at Port Vila's Alliance Française gallery, and the publication of a short book on her musical achievements (Hayward 2007).

A number of aspects of Quai's rise merit attention. The first is that her progress in a music scene is a substantial achievement in a nation that remains conservative in terms of gender roles in public life and in an industry almost exclusively dominated by males. Her rise as a national celebrity is also unusual in itself in a country where, as Miles (1998, 178) has identified, there is "a residual resistance, often internalized, against an individual getting too far ahead of the group."[22] Although the Quai family originate from the northern island of Ambae, where this tendency to discourage great success may be less marked than in central and southern Vanuatu, her recent celebrity status, and indeed her whole career, has contributed substantially, both financially and in terms of morale, to her community and religious service, and has elevated her as a multifaceted public celebrity rather than a pop star in the Western mold. Indeed, her shy demeanor offstage and conservative social behavior show her to be something of the antithesis of Western performers such as Britney Spears or various U.S. R'n'B/rap stars whose images adorn the T-shirts of young urban ni-Vanuatu. The Quai family has also been notable for investing Vanessa's profits from her career into enterprises such as a family child-care center rather than emulating the materialist lifestyle of many Western residents of the greater Port Vila area.

Other Vanuatu artists have also achieved lower profiles and some modest sales in New Caledonia, where Vanuatu string-band music now has a certain niche, with a specially assembled Emau Island string band performing well-received concerts in mid 2006. The latter point underlines the fact that string-band music continues to be popular in Vanuatu and New Caledonia, unlike in Papua New Guinea, for example, where many young people perceive string-band music as dated or parochial, favoring local reggae-pop hybrids. Indeed—and somewhat surprisingly— the commercial recording of string-band music has undergone something of a revival in the last decade. Leading Vanuatu journalist Tony Ligo attributes this to cost-related factors, including the prohibitive price of musical equipment and

MIDI or other computer technologies for amplified reggae bands, and the strong presence of string-band music in villages, where many young musicians are present (personal communication, 2006). Thus the prominence of string bands in the contemporary era is one of the Vanuatu industry's most distinctive international aspects.

The most significant project to date outside the Pacific is the Sunshiners, a four-member band and vocal "super group" featuring singers from Huarere (Ben Siro), XX Squad (Jake Moses), Naio (Gero Iaviniau [Naio]) and Krossrod (John Kapala). The band was designed for the European market with a repertoire of well-known 1980s to 1990s Western pop songs in a style combing semi-acoustic string band–meets–Pacific reggae using ukuleles, guitars, tea-chest bass, and tuned bottles, with amplified reggae-band instrumentation. The idea for the project developed out of meetings between John Kapala and members of the French reggae band Mister Gang during the band's visits to New Caledonia in 2002 and 2003. Mister Gang was formed in Paris in 1990 and recorded three albums with a brass-augmented reggae lineup before visiting New Caledonia and recording their fourth album, *Live in Kanaky,* in 2003. Impressed with New Caledonian music and Pacific culture, in general, they decided to collaborate with Vanuatu performers and sent their saxophonist, Feal Cool Jazz, to Vanuatu to work on demo arrangements in 2005. With the assistance of David Nalo, under the aegis of the cultural development organization Further Arts, the performers signed a four-album option with Sony BMG France, with vocal tracks for the first album recorded in Port Vila in 2005 and post-production undertaken in France in 2005–2006. The twelve-track album, titled *Sunshiners,* was released in Europe in mid-2006 and included versions of David Bowie's *Modern Love,* The Human League's *Don't You Want Me Baby?,* and Crowded House's *Don't Dream It's Over.* Accompanied by members of Mister Gang, the band played an extended Western European tour in the (northern) summer of 2006 to promote the album, appearing at high-profile events such as the British WOMAD festival. Though it is too early to assess its market longevity, its success in securing a European deal and publicity for Vanuatu music, even in such a highly hybridized form, is notable. The band's debut performance in Vanuatu occurred during a gap in their European tour and recording schedule, and—indicating the major market orientation of their operation—required a sponsorship from Telecom Vanuatu totaling 1,345,000 vatu to facilitate a performance at Port Vila's Municipal Stadium in April 2007.[23]

Although noteworthy, Quai's successful collaboration with Mangrove and with Sunshiners' European activity in 2006 are exceptions to the predominantly local orientation of ni-Vanuatu artists in the 2000s. This prompted research that resulted in a European Union–funded report, titled "The Establishment of a Regional Network for the Distribution of Vanuatu Music" by David Nalo (2004), under the auspices of Further Arts. Nalo's research combined fact-finding visits to Australia, Fiji, New Zealand, and Vanuatu with practical, market-testing production projects such as arranging for a remix of the Vanuatu-produced *Children's*

Day album by XX Squad produced by engineer Stephane Herve of Mangrove and the production of a promotional clip for the album track "Wun Gud Wan."[24]

Nalo's report concluded that distribution of Vanuatu albums overseas "has proven to be a difficult issue" (Nalo 2004, 4) in the absence of regular appearances by Vanuatu bands in overseas territories and the related low profile of Vanuatu performances in those areas. Interpreting his overall project data, Nalo also advanced the following points:

> In the field of promotion and distribution of its music Vanuatu is in fact competing with the rest of the world, and with the limited resources we have at our disposal it is proving difficult to break into the market. A niche has been pinpointed and this is where Vanuatu and its musicians must concentrate their efforts—the merging of traditional custom music with modern music. It was observed by the Project Manager that all festival and concert organisations were seeking music with original "untouched" sources of traditional influence. This music is largely categorized in the "World Music" section. Vanuatu has some examples of this with past Huarere performances, and the Tropic Tempo album. But there needs to be a more conscious effort to integrate more of our culture into our music. (Ibid., 4–5)

Along with the two examples Nalo cites, it is possible to identify some recent grassroots engagement with this focus in the work of string bands such as Torotua, that have arranged *kastom* songs in string-band style on their debut album *Natano* (2004). A more overtly syncretic ensemble, Kalja Ridim Klan (KRK), was formed in 2004 featuring ni-Vanuatu and expatriate musicians playing guitar and violin along with traditional percussion instruments and offering a mixture of adapted *kastom* songs and original compositions. The band recorded its debut album in 2007 at VKS Studios with the support of Mangrove (and financial support from the Alliance Française for a promotional video clip). Titled *Long Taim Bifo*, referring to the "time before" Western contact, the album attempts to re-present elements of *kastom* music in a contemporary manner without crossing decisively into the Western mainstream exploited by other commercially successful Vanuatu artists. As band member Mars Melto diplomatically expressed it: "Last year was dominated by the Sunshiners breakthrough tour of Europe. This year we want the focus to be on Vanuatu musicians in Vanuatu. We need to build on the successes of our brothers in the Sunshiners" ("KRK Announce Debut Album" 2007, 20).

Musical Identities and Globalization

Over the four decades since national independence, creative and commercial entities have combined to develop a national music sector that operates industrially, albeit with minimal profitability (in most cases) and with its workers in casual or part-time employment. From an economic viewpoint, the Vanuatu industry is a marginal enterprise with minimal prospects of expansion in a national market in which the majority of the population are only partially engaged in a cash economy. Internationally successful New Zealand songwriter Tim Finn once famously declared that trying to make a living from the New Zealand industry was "like being a haemophiliac rabbit dragged through barbed wire backwards" (Pickering and Shuker 1994, 73). Given the far greater size of New Zealand's industry, Finn's analogy for success must be of an even broader magnitude in Vanuatu. This perspective, though largely accurate, does not explain the substantial investments of time and more diffuse "affective engagements" by fans, supporters of particular artists, or ensembles that have generated and sustained a succession of ni-Vanuatu musical recordings and live performances. The author's research into the motivations of musicians, music-business entrepreneurs, and audiences point to national pride and the desire to hear demonstrably national products as an overarching factor expressed by those involved to overcome financial uncertainties and shortfalls.

The success of national performers such as Vanessa Quai and the Sunshiners in international markets obviously appeals to performers struggling to make a living in such an industrially "cramped space" as contemporary Vanuatu. Initiatives such as David Nalo's (2004) Further Arts report illustrate the manner in which the paths to access such markets are being considered and developed by artists and entrepreneurs astute enough to realize that there are no easy or magical routes to global-market success. The usefulness of popular musicians as "brand ambassadors" for Vanuatu tourism has also been recognized through government and commercial support, a factor also noted by various aspirants.

Speaking on behalf of the Tanna-based movement at the launch of the Lamaraka John Frum Band's CD in Port Vila in 2006, Silas Yatan thanked the Vanuatu Kaljoral Senta "for initiating this project to help John Frum to be heard outside of itself—so its message and philosophy is heard not just around Vanuatu but also outside the country." This recognition of the value of promotion and product placement in global contexts by a movement founded on a mystical interpretation of a previous moment of sudden (and unsustained) military globalization illustrates the continuing paradox of Vanuatu's rapid transition to modernity. Engagement with mass-media and global networks developed by Western nations with very different economic and belief systems is not necessarily seen as incongruent with *kastom* culture. Although the community development orientation of national radio in the immediate post-independence period, as detailed by Bolton (1999), has diminished in the market-driven 1990s and 2000s, the national music sector has taken on aspects of that project, albeit with forms of mass-mediated music that are, in most cases, drastically different from established *kastom* culture. Despite their stylistic differences, they reflect a similar motivation with regard to asserting national cultural difference in a global context and combine this with a new aspiration for global-market access and the broader promotion of Vanuatu as a presence in international cultural and economic arenas. In this context, globalization can be understood not as a restriction but as a resource requiring particular product images and contexts to operate, and offering potentials far beyond those of the local market. Although there still may be no "general class of theorizing" to account for such specifically local non-Western engagements with globalization, any credible theory of global activity needs to factor in actual cultural experience.

Acknowledgments

Thanks to Tony Ligo and Ralph Regenvanu for research guidance; to performers and industry figures Jean-Baptiste Calo, John Josiah, Timteo Kalmet, Benson Nako, Nigel Quai, Vanessa Quai, Ray Tarosa, Danny Tetiano, Donald Watu, and Jean-Mark Wong for their insights; to Anne Naupa and the staff at the Vanuatu National Library for their assistance with research for this project; and to Bob White and Denis Crowdy for their comments on earlier versions of this chapter. Research for this chapter was conducted between May 2006 and September 2007 as part of the Australia Research Council Discovery Grant project DP0666232 on the Melanesian Music Industries awarded to the Department of Contemporary Music Studies, Macquarie University, Sydney.

Notes

1. The most notable example of such resistance was Jimmy Stephens's Nagriamel secession movement on Espiritu Santo.

2. These three factors are, of course, extracted from multiple causes but are considered significant in creating a national "public sphere."

3. Most prominent among these was the *New Hebrides News*.

4. Histories of congregational music and Western art music traditions (such as classical and jazz) in Vanuatu are outside my sphere of inquiry.

5. I have been unable to ascertain the name of the composer. Ifira Island is a small island close to Port Vila.

6. One such occasion was a concert for visiting New Zealand tourists in 1965, reported in the *British Newsletter,* October 31, 1965, 7.

7. These are the results of a national survey published in the *British Newsletter,* August 28, 1973, 1.

8. Along with the Western music featured on Radio Vila and in city nightclubs, there were occasional visits by popular music acts from overseas, such as New Zealand guitarist Peter Posa, who performed in Luganville in 1970, and Fijian singer-songwriter Tomasi Epi, who played in Port Vila in 1974.

9. Mandolin playing rapidly declined, however, and only appears occasionally in the later recorded repertoire of post-1960s string bands.

10. The instruments were usually tuned in the standard Western tradition: E–A–D–G–B–E.

11. Anecdotal information suggests that the mandolins used by early string bands were probably loose-strung, playing chord patterns.

12. Several of my research interviewees made passing references to early string-band music around Luganville, but I have not been able to substantiate these.

13. The lyrics were written by expatriate Sue Camden to the tune of the Australian song "Flash Jack from Gundagai."

14. These groups attracted significant national attention by dominating the prizes at the 1978 National String Band Contest and attracting significant press attention (e.g., Garae 1978).

15. See Bolton 1999 for a discussion of Gardissat's important contribution to *kastom* and Bislama radio broadcasting.

16. Gardissat's catalogue, however, also included brass band recordings and the (one and only) album by Aneytium's Vanuatu Bamboo Band.

17. Musical Instrument Digital Interface.

18. The title, meaning "Old Bumbu's Voice," refers to the band's principal source for the traditional material, a female Banks Islander named Bumbu Rubina Wokot. The CD sleeve notes indicate that she celebrated her one hundredth birthday in 1996.

19. This was made plain by price tags indicating the Australian monetary conversion.

20. The name is variously written as "Tropik Zound," "Tropik Zounds," and "Tropic Sounds."

21. http://www.vanuatuculture.org/fieldworkers/050517_fieldworkersprogram.shtml.

22. Several musicians conveyed this view to the author when describing a period during which they had achieved some prominence, only to experience a backlash.

23. The band performed before an audience estimated (by the author and the organizers) to number around 2,500, with each paying 300 vatu for admission.

24. For details of further activities, see Nalo 2004.

References

Bolton, L. 1999. "Radio and the Redefinition of Kastom in Vanuatu," *Contemporary Pacific* 11, no. 2 (fall): 335–360.

Fes' Napuan Organising Committee. 2005. "Report I go long ol Sponsa" ("Report to Sponsors").

Garae, L. 1978. "Music Knows No Barrier—J. Carlo." *New Hebrides News,* December 2, 2.

Hayward, P. ed. 2007. *Vanessa Quai: Linking Vanuatu to the World (A Tribute to Her First Decade in Music, 1997–2007).* Port Vila: VQMF.

James, T. 1974. "Young Generation: As One Sees." *New Hebrides News,* no. 17, July 9, 8.

Kaeppler, A. 1998. "Vanuatu." In *The Garland Encyclopedia of World Music,* Vol. 9, *Australia and the Pacific Islands,* ed. A. Kaeppler and J. W. Love, 688–709. New York: Garland.

"KRK Announce Debut Album and VKS Announces Fest'napuan." 2007. *The Independent,* March 4, 20.

Ligo, E. 1973. "The Advantages of Tourism," *New Hebrides News,* no. 16, June 25, 8.

Ligo, T. 2004. "European Union Helps Local Musicians Tap Regional Market." *The Independent Online,* February 17. http://www.news.vu/en/ae/music.

———. 2005a. "Island Melodies: A Nice Way to Remember Vanuatu." *The Independent* ("This Week in Vanuatu" supplement), January 16, 3.

———. 2005b. "Vanuatu's Leading Studio Goes High-Tech," *The Independent Online,* February 30. http://www.news.vu/en/ae/music.

———. 2005c. "Vatube Stringband Bringing Back Real Rogan Island String-Band Style." *The Independent,* October 2, 9.

———. 2006a. "'Unique Sounds of Emau' in NC." *The Independent,* August 13, 26.

———. 2006b. "John Frum Songs on DVD." *Vanuatu Independent,* April 10.

Miles, W. F. S. 1999. *Bridging Mental Boundaries in a Postcolonial Microcosm: Identity and Development in Vanuatu.* Honolulu: University of Hawaii Press.

Nalo, David. 2004. "The Establishment of a Regional Network for the Distribution of Vanuatu Music." Unpublished reports Further Arts (Port Vila).

Niles, D. 1998. "Questions of Music Copyright in Papua New Guinea." In *Sound Alliances: Indigenous Peoples, Cultural Politics, and Popular Music in the Pacific,* ed. P. Hayward, 123–126. London: Cassell.

Republic of Vanuatu. 2000. "Copyright and Related Rights Act No. 42 of 2000."

Pickering, M., and R. Shuker. 1994. "Struggling to Make Ourselves Heard: Music, Radio, and the Quota Debate." In *North Meets South: Popular Music in Aotearoa/New Zealand,* ed. P. Hayward, T. Mitchell, and R. Shuker, 73–97. Umina: Perfect Beat.

Sparks, C. 2000. "The Global, the Local, and the Public Sphere." In *The New Communications Landscape: Demystifying Media Globalization,* ed. J. Servaes, 139–150. London: Routledge.

4

Musicality and Environmentalism in the Rediscovery of Eldorado: An Anthropology of the Raoni-Sting Encounter

Rafael José de Menezes Bastos

In 1989 Raoni,[1] the chief of the Txukahamãe Indians in Brazil, and Sting, the British rock superstar, traveled to Europe, where they were hosted by government officials, as an initiative to raise funds for the protection of the tropical rainforest and support the rights of indigenous peoples in the Amazon. Following this effort, Raoni participated in concerts and related events in Brazil and overseas, not only with Sting but also with other figures of the international popular music scene.[2] In 1991 Raoni participated in a show with Elton John, Tom Jobim, Caetano Veloso, Gilberto Gil, and Red Crow (a North American Sioux leader), an encounter witnessed by excited fans who believed in the music as much as in the concert's cause (Carvalho 1991), which mirrored that of Raoni and Sting's trip to Europe and was supported by the Brazilian branch of the Rainforest Foundation.[3]

This kind of encounter between artists and activists was not unique, as others had occurred in the region, such as that between Milton Nascimento—the consecrated Brazilian singer-songwriter—and the indigenous leaders Ailton Krenák and Sian Kaxinawá, from the Krenák and Kaxinawá groups, respectively. In this case the Aliança dos Povos da Floresta (Rainforest Peoples Alliance) provided an institutional framework for the event. The Alliance supports ongoing relationships between indigenous peoples and the *seringueiros* (workers who extract rubber from the *seringa* tree), unified by their commitment to protect the environment. As part of the same initiative, Milton Nascimento's concert Txai—which had the same name as the album (Nascimento 1990)—took place in São Paulo in April 1991 before an audience of more than thirty thousand. This concert was also performed overseas and became the centerpiece of Nascimento and Krenák's excursion to the United States, Canada, Europe, and Japan. According to one source, this series of events "sowed fruitful seeds that effectively aided the cause of indigenous peoples and *seringueiros* in the Amazon" (Aquino 1991; my translation).

In encounters of this type, music is the supreme universe of signifiers, with environmentalism as its world of meanings.[4] The music itself denounces the burning down of the "green," then seen by many as the end of millennium Eldorado and the new pathway for indigenous peoples' position in relation to the *caraíbas*.[5] These concerts occurred in a context where the entertainment industry was increasingly important in Brazil, with that nation ranking sixth worldwide in musical production. At the same time, to underline the magnitude and delicacy of this kind of encounter, it is important to remark upon the relationship between these mega-concerts and the question of national sovereignty in the Amazon, especially as the various personalities involved were politically ambiguous. One may observe how these concerts had assumed the identity of political acts, necessarily situated in a global geopolitical context. State representatives, such as the then French prime minister François Mitterrand, who formally hosted Raoni and Sting in 1989, had defended only partial sovereignty in the Brazilian Amazon, a position they also held for other countries in the region. To particular branches of the Brazilian government and in some sectors of Brazilian society, this would signal new efforts at "internationalizing" the region (Passarinho 1991). Backbiting and innuendos inevitably occurred among the different actors, partly because of the mercantilist appearance of the event. In this context the encounters displayed onscreen seemed like commercials, which led to a great deal of suspicion, especially for an event that, from its participants' viewpoint, claimed to be free of political sin.

This chapter aims to contribute to the study of music and contact between artists as well as to the study of the connections between local, regional, and global levels of analysis, especially in the realm of popular music. One may well ask: What do Raoni, the Amerindian "eminent man," and Sting, the Western pop music icon, have to do with these different levels of meaning and practice? The concept of popular music with which I have worked (Menezes Bastos 2000, 2005, 2008b) departs from that proposed by Vega (1966). Briefly put, I contend that popular music (Western in this case) is a musical tradition as old and widespread as Western art music, because phonographic recording is a global process capturing all kinds of music (popular, art, folk, and even "primitive"). On the other hand, popular music in the West is the legitimate heir of Western art music, the universal music of the world system par excellence, in many ways the foundation of its contemporary topology and the irreplaceable codifier of its ideology (Menezes

Bastos 2000, 2005, 2008b). My analysis takes the global aspect of popular music to be just as important as local, regional, and national forms, and not simply supervening (Menezes Bastos 2008b).

The ethnology of the Xinguano Indians constitutes in many ways a reduced model (Lévi-Strauss 1970, 44–47) for understanding the indigenous societies of lowland South America as atomized entities, fundamentally isolated from one another, having lived, from time immemorial, in the southern part of the Upper Xingu region, in Central Brazil. According to this model, the more recently arrived non-Xinguano Indians—among them the Txukahamãe—have been granted little or no explanatory value, since they are seen primarily as incidental to what takes place in Xinguano proper. To an even greater extent, the *caraíbas* only rarely enter this scenario, as they are largely ignored by the ethnological literature concerning the region. Contrary to the impression given by this literature, the Upper Xingu has become, since the eighteenth century, a cauldron for Brazilian history, society, and culture. There are exceptions, however, to this general model of understanding the region. For example, certain studies have shown that indigenous groups in the region are, in fact, involved in large-scale processes of intertribal and interethnic contact and change. Galvão (1953) deserves mention here, even though his research has contributed to some extent to the reification of the Xinguano/non-Xinguano opposition. This opposition—which is important to see as an opposition—is actually part of a complex system of ethnic classifications elaborated by the Xinguano themselves, a system that includes all indigenous groups of the region, as well as many types of Westerners (Menezes Bastos 1978, 1995a, 2006). Here the Upper Xingu is portrayed not as a petrified space (which I have called "Xinguara Paradise"; see Menezes Bastos 1983) but as a dynamic social system only comprehensible through an inquiry that is cognizant of dynamic change and contact. My description of the *Yawari,* a Pan-Xinguano ritual (Menezes Bastos 1990), as well as my historical reconstitution of the area (Menezes Bastos 1995b), paint a seemingly paradoxical picture of the Westerner's invention. In this context desire seems to cling to pain.

In 1981, while I was doing fieldwork among the Xinguano Yawalapití, Raoni was being initiated in Xinguano shamanism under the supervision of Sapaim, a virtuoso shaman and flutist. At that time Raoni was a host in Eymakapúku, the Yawalapití village where Sapaim taught him shamanism and Kanátu—a great phytotherapist—gave him lessons in phytotherapy. Being the great chief that he was, Raoni received all the honors he deserved from the retired chiefs Kanátu and Sariruá as well as from Aritana, the chief of the Yawalapiti at the time. Not long after, Raoni, still under the tutelage of Sapaim, participated in the healing ceremony organized to cure the naturalist Augusto Ruschi, a ceremony sponsored by the Brazil's former president José Sarney. This impressive episode took place in 1986 (the same year as the naturalist's death), when Raoni appeared on the national stage as a prominent indigenous political figure, a cultural mediator who would not be satisfied with a role limited to local politics and sought pan-Kayapó prominence as well as recognition from the Xinguano. In 1987 Sting made his first visit to the Xinguano sanctuary. What exactly was the neo-Eldorado hunter, who would become the prey of Raoni, hunter of the *caraíba*, looking for?

The sixteenth century constitutes the limit of the modern world system, facilitating capitalist economic growth and European imperial colonialism, inaugurated by Portugal and Spain, and soon followed by Great Britain, France, and other Western European countries. During that time the relationship between the Western "We" and the "Other" became consolidated through a new way of imagining the "Other." In this context Western mythical thought is expressed mainly through literature, in which the "Other" is one of its basic themes, most often articulated as a source of astonishment in the face of something wondrous and awesome. Nevertheless, it is from the seventeenth to the nineteenth centuries that I situate the locus of my historical analysis, precisely when myth is transferred to a secondary position in Western literature and when Western art music is consecrated as *kathólon* (from the Greek, "universal") and as the crucial diacritic of modern Western identity (Menezes Bastos 1990). According to Lévi-Strauss (1979), in this period mythical Western thought migrates from literature to music.[6]

Western art music—*the* "universal language," according to its aficionados— is built up as a cultural domain based on various identifiable criteria: acoustic-mathematical (Weber 1944, 1985), aesthetic-philosophical (Hegel 1974), or psychological and sociocultural (Kunst 1959). Compendia and handbooks about Western music history (Brum 1897) are fertile ground regarding the routine use of these criteria. Despite the variation in the criteria adopted in various sources, they all affirm the distinctiveness of this type of music compared to all other types, whether traditional, popular, Oriental, or even the music of ancient societies such as Greece or Rome. As evidence of this, note that the compendia and handbooks under consideration situate studies about Greek and Roman music in the introductory chapters of the text. Starting from this basic premise, they seem to construct myths about origins, using a historical form of expression to justify their conclusions. Thus the identity of Western art music is articulated in contrast to an absolutely unrecoverable past.

From the native point of view, Western art music starts in the medieval age. The sixth century (Gregorian music), ninth (polyphony), thirteenth (*Musica Mensurata*), and fourteenth (*Ars Nova*) represent privileged moments in the demarcation of its inception. This historical context suggests that Western art music, during its early development, was wholly encompassed by the politico-religious establishment. This institutional framework gives liturgical primacy to its music and transforms it into a tool of colonial expansion. The medieval age is the preeminent time-space for the prefabrication of the West in the sixteenth century. In great part, by means of the art of Gregorian chants, the West could incorporate its own barbarians into the Latin-Roman sanctuary (i.e., Slavs, Germanics, Saxons, Iberians, etc.). In this way Western art music is the symbolic counterpart of the invention of Europe in terms of political economy.

But if Western art music, until the sixteenth century, became fully realized as part of the politico-religious establishment, from the seventeenth century on it became increasingly autonomous as the time-space of the sacred. Simultaneously it revitalized Western mythical thought, committed deicide, and was enthroned in God's temple in terms of what Spengler (1973) referred to as the religion of art. This was a universe that enabled the emergence of the free, equal, indivisible, and universal individual. This individualism, inserted in a system where creation became a central value, suffered from a hierarchical or holistic refraction (Dumont 1995) under the tokens of monumentality, progress, interiority, and universality (Menezes Bastos 1995a). From that point on, for Western music—the only Western art form in which classical Greek-Roman memory is not effective—the individual was a "great master" or a "name." He was a creator, *ex-nihilo* as God.[7]

The second half of the eighteenth century witnessed the second European colonialism as well as the Kantian thematization of man, the latter the basic condition for the birth of the human sciences (Foucault 1985). Thereafter something new occurred in the world of Western music. By means of the critical-interpretive score, the *music of the past* was invented. Previously public music presentations had always been centered on the music of the present. Now programs came to incorporate *music of the past* as such, which comprises the central puzzle of the *Musikalische Wissenschaft*. How would one reconstitute this *music of the past,* given that musical notation is by nature more prescriptive than descriptive? As a kind of ethnography, the critical-interpretive score produced this guarded "past," the new "Other." Significantly the phonograph was developed in the late nineteenth century, enabling the consolidation of *vergleichende Musikwissenschaft* in the second and third decades of the twentieth century in Germany and of ethnomusicology in the 1950s in the United States.

Leibowitz (1957) elaborated a theory about Western music that acknowledged chromatism as the motor of change in music history. To him, from the sixteenth-century Gregorian chants to dodecaphonism in the beginning of the twentieth century, a struggle occurred in the vacuum between the evenness of diatonicism and the irregularity of chromatism. Western music theorists from the Medieval Age and the Renaissance fought to retain chromatism in diatonic regularity, assured that the chromatism provoked ethical dissolution. With the invasion of Western art music by profane music, however, the chromatic project increasingly gained momentum. It became even more significant during the Romantic period, almost rupturing in Wagner's expressionism, and reached, at last, its final expression in Schoenberg's dodecaphonism. Following Leibowitz's terms, Western music reached its terminal phase in dodecaphonism, as it could not longer retain the formal elements of its past. Going beyond dodecaphonism would only be possible at the cost of anachronism or chaos, intolerable alternatives in the context of Western rational thought. Leibowitz's theory resembles Adorno's (1974), which portrays Schoenberg as progress and Stravinsky (1882–1971) as recovery.

Notwithstanding, Leibowitz's and Adorno's conception of Western art music may not be considered simply as the work of two individual authors. On the contrary, one can argue that they serve as written renditions of a system of common sense or the culture of the serialist-dodecaphonic aesthetics and poetics. In its second and third generations, this system attains the status of a true apocalyptic manifesto. Western art music has at last met its death! How to move forward, following the *ratio* of its myth-poetics, where there cannot be progress but only repetitions of what was already created, a proposition that is intolerable to the *ex-nihilo* creator? Here the West died once again, typically between the 1950s and 1960s. These years witnessed the consolidation of the linkage of music with the worlds of technology and the market, either within the realms of mass culture or the culture industry (Adorno 1983, 1986).

The expansion of the phonographic market in the United States in the 1920s happened at the same time as the eruption of tourism and the nascent entertainment industry (Graburn 1976). Opera and jazz were then the favorite genres, especially to an economically affluent audience looking for cosmopolitan entertainment or for an identity different from what is possible in the realm of labor. In the following three decades this market was consolidated and became so diversified that it encompassed everything from Western art music to folk music of various ethnic and national origins. Diversification at the production level was followed by a degree of differentiation at the level of consumption. This dynamic separated U.S. markets for music into progressively larger and more numerous slices. Simultaneously Europe's musical scene did not appear considerably different from that in the United States, except for the "invasion" Europe suffered from jazz (Martin and Roueff 2002, 93–104).

In the 1950s the United States was experiencing the explosion of rock'n' roll. In subsequent decades, especially since the Beatles' breakthrough in England and the British invasion abroad, rock music quickly became a global phenomenon. One may even speak of popular music on the jazz-rock axis as a new *kathólon* of the West. In other words, Westernness gradually gained planetary pertinence through its popular music, which became increasingly incorporative. This incorporative capacity was implemented by means of the cannibalization of musical genres from all over the world, especially the musics of the Black Atlantic and even Western art music, which, somewhere along the way, became completely transformed into a trope of the past. The cannibalization of Western music became possible through the appropriation by the jazz-rock axis of its traditional tonal theory. Generally one may say that after the 1960s almost nothing in the musicality of the planet has not been part of a jazz or rock festival (Menezes Bastos 2000, 2008b).

Since the 1960s popular music appears to be most relevant for its communicative function. What seems important in terms of political economy is the all-encompassing nature of its presence in the technological-industrial establishment, at the end of the chain, characterized by the sales potential of music as a cultural product. An important question, then, is what happened to the music of the new West, with its past orientalized and transformed into a machine that positions and withdraws man from a world where symbolic and diabolic reasons converge. In the end, does truth (a glade or a desert) surrender to the empire of the simulacrum?

If popular music in the 1960s can be considered a language of the new Westernness, it is because it points explicitly to a particular universe of meanings and values, namely social engagement. At that time, mainly in the United States, music was intimately linked to the struggle for civil rights and an emerging identity politics, with a never-ending search for its "roots." Music was also associated with pacifism, the contesting of state-based authority and the military-industrial establishment. These struggles were postulated by the hippie movement on one side and the utopia of socialism on the other, both expressing a certain teleology of the dissolution of the bourgeois state, which is seen as the land of true evil. As if confirming John Lennon's well-known dictum, "the dream is over," the 1970s and 1980s abandoned its struggles with a libertarian teleology. So what exactly was over? Was it indeed "the dream" Lennon referred to, which came to be identified as a kind of illusion?

What Lennon attempted to proclaim through his famous maxim was the conviction of musicians and popular music fans that the struggle against the state—for them a true but essentially abominable vigil—should not be undertaken outside the boundaries of the state. Their certainty in this regard would lead to new tactics: now they would use popular music to fight for a land without evil, accomplished, however, within the limits of that evil land itself. In this model, individuals cannot run away from their world but must be completely open to their presence in it.

The last two decades of the past century witnessed not only a remarkable growth in the popular music market but also a visible consolidation of music's technological-industrial complex. This dual phenomenon became apparent especially at the end of the 1980s, coinciding with the end of the Cold War and the dissolution of the Soviet Union in the 1990s. The Green movement, which began in the 1970s with the Stockholm Conference, gradually became established as a world paradigm during this period, providing popular music with a universe of meanings and values sufficiently important and comprehensive for its worldly aspirations, a disposition inherited from the Western music tradition. It is worth highlighting that the entanglement of popular music—which became the universe of signifiers (*signifiants* in Saussurean terms)—with environmentalism, the corresponding world of the signified (*signifiés*), becomes explicit in a system of thought where the First and Fourth Worlds (the latter that of the so-called primitives) are the only worlds that matter. The Second World is dead and the Third has been built as the past ("undeveloped"), the place of a new Eldorado where the green of emeralds gives way to that of trees. Within this symbolic universe, green signals that movement is allowed and red signals the danger of burned forests. Here popular music—along the jazz-rock axis—is a time machine, taking a trip imagined by "natives" whose destination advances toward everything that is primordial, demanding that nature be free of all contamination.[8]

Sting, born in 1951 and named Gordon Matthew Sumner, was the son of a Catholic working-class family from Newcastle, England, who was raised in the world of rock.[9] His Catholic background endowed him with a moral conscience, forever reminding him of the "obligations of life and the existence of heaven, hell, and sin." At the same time he conceives of rock as a hedonistic enterprise that separates one from magic and religion (Sellers 1989, 1–2). The notions of obligation and pleasure are crucial to comprehend the trajectory that led to his encounter with Raoni, which was heavily influenced by these moral principles (Bloch and Dutilleux 1987). English rock, later radicalized by the punk movement, has its roots in the working class, partly because, as a musical genre, it is characterized by youth's protests against the conservatism of class-based social reproduction as well as English society as a whole (Willis 1976). To Sting, the hedonism of rock seems to constitute the genre as a language of protest to the degree that hedonism represents an ethos contrary to conservatism, which, by definition, is a refutation of pleasure. Living in a world dominated by Protestant worship (itself opposed to the "magic" ritualism of Catholicism), he seemed to be exercising a type of citizenship that resists parochialism, always seeking a larger, global perspective.

Sting's musical background was consolidated in the realm of jazz as a stand-up bass player and bass guitar player in training. In 1970 he entered the Newcastle Big Band, one of the most important traditional jazz groups in town, and remained in the group until it split up in 1976. In 1972 Sting founded his own group, Last Exit, in which he attempted to reconcile his roles as instrumentalist and singer-songwriter. Then, in 1976, he moved to London, where he became a member of The Police, a band that became affiliated with the new punk movement until 1979 and cultivated an ethos of protest against the establishment, especially the manipulations of the record industry. Still, the band was never truly accepted by the new punk, which accused the group of being progressive.[10]

The Police scored its first great success with the album *Roxanne/Peanuts* (1978), which was hailed with enthusiasm by music critics and led to the band's first international tour to the United States and Canada. From then on, the band's image resided between new wave, reggae, and ska music. In the 1980s The Police, now an internationally acclaimed group, began to focus on the defense of human rights, with its sights on the Third World—where famine was rampant and children begged on the streets—as a mandatory place to perform (Sellers 1989, 36). The dissolution of the Police began in 1983 but did not actually materialize until 1985, when Sting decided to develop a solo career that would enable him to dedicate more time to global problems such as peace, human rights, and environmental protection (ibid., 74–75). With this goal in mind, he visited the Upper Xingu for the first time in 1987, following an international tour sponsored by Amnesty International. There, in *Eymakapúku,* the Aruak-speaking Yawalapití Indian village, Sting established contact with Raoni, the disciple of Sapaim, a magnificent Kamayurá shaman and master musician who lived in the village. But what was Raoni, hunter of the *Caraíba,* seeking to gain from preying on Sting, hunter of the new Eldorado?

The historical and cultural characteristics of Raoni's and Sting's biographies seem to establish their encounter in 1987 as their mutual fate. Despite their divergent sociocultural backgrounds, the trajectory of both men greatly emphasized the "Other" as a category of value. Sting was experiencing a period of questioning and engagement regarding global issues and social justice, which was emblematic of Raoni's quest. The same may be said of Raoni in relation to Sting. At that time the Txukahamãe chief was seeking Kayapó-Xingu prominence, and so, Raoni's communication with the white world—for him a realm of abundance and inexhaustibility—was also a plausible aim. And so their encounter, though appearing to be casual, was marked by mutual condemnation.

It is important to examine the relevance of each of these disparate universes first by looking at Western popular music refracted through an environmentalist ideology and, second, by exploring the Xinguano social system embedded in its Kayapó-Txukahamãe connection by means of a political culture legitimized through musical mastery and ritual knowledge. To do so involves a game with two sets of rules, as these two worlds will never truly understand each other. In other words, it does not seem possible to approach this encounter as a well-adjusted system of cultural and symbolic representations, because its basic dualism, though eventually intersected by other elements, is irreducible. In what other field and under what rules, one might ask, would such an encounter be possible?

Sheltered by a sort of recalibrated culturalism, some of the literature on the colonial encounter seems to have been amusing itself with precisely this type of counterpoint. This literature appears to be delighted with the conversion of colonial encounter into a modality of exchange on the level of the Theater of the Absurd (whereas "X" does this, "Y" understands that, and vice versa) taking place in the pleasant and refreshing shades of the Garden of Eden. In other words, despite the undeniable appeal of this literature and its occasional descriptive value, it tends to obfuscate the fact that the colonial encounter occurs within a specific frame of inter-societal contact, namely, that the contact is between the West and Third-World indigenous societies. Thus the basis of their encounter involves the cruelty of exploitation and domination.[11]

The point of this chapter is not to comprehend the colonial encounter either as a logical connection between local, regional, global, and sociocultural phenomena or as a third logical outcome derived from their sum. To do so would acknowledge a cultural arithmetic that purportedly was exorcized by the 1960s. This type of encounter is therefore contradictory, even if the colonizer is present in it through a character representing the savage in idyllic and philanthropic ways or on the grounds of humanitarian aid. This mode of representation may take the form of a utopian ideology aimed at an interethnic political alliance, which seems to apply to Sting's case and goes hand in hand with his dissident biography.[12]

In 1989, when Raoni and Sting—the characters of an event that was paradoxical in many ways in relation to a way of thinking about Brazil—traveled around the so-called civilized world for the good of Brazil, national press and other media broadcast detailed discussions about the trip, judging its moral and political motivations. Prosecutors argued that Sting was intervening in Brazilian issues and Raoni was a traitor. Both were also accused of being mercenaries and only self-interested. Following this media attention a popular quip circulated: "We have to Raonize, otherwise we'll be ExStinguished."[13]

What does this impressive word play mean to imply? First, it captures a sentiment through derisive mockery that is built on two puns: replacing "Sting" with "extinguish" (S) and "Raoni" with "reunite" (R). But the sentiment in the statement moves from the universe of derision and comedy toward the world of tragedy, where R and S are drawn as antagonistic toward each other, "either one or the other." Further, the fatal non-equation expressed here is not limited to a mere story of an encounter between two international celebrities. Instead, a subtle, almost inaudible third voice is also present, a "we," which lays down the expression's moral imperative. This voice intones Sting as the representation of death, the extinction to which "we" are damned unless we reunite under Raoni's gregarious primitivism. But at the same time this primitivism is judged as lost, impossible to be regained, under the token of Bergson's aesthetic laughter. I wonder which Brazil ("we") it might be that judges an alliance between the Fourth World and the First World as lethal, in a sense producing an identity that is separate from the two worlds it criticizes. Will it be the voice of "security and development"? Or, like a driver going the wrong way on a one-way street, will it be some leftist voice against imperialism? Or, better still, will it be the Brazilians' Brazil, suspicious of the moralizing foreigner and skeptical of the indigenous warrior?

Lévi-Strauss (1991) made a noteworthy comparison between the Amerindian and Western dyad. In the West the terms describing the dyad are usually couched in terms of identity, whereas Amerindian thought uses terms based on the logic of difference, producing mutual irreducibility. Following this line of reasoning, Lévi-Strauss studied the relations between twins, a remarkable phenomenon among Amerindians, adopting Romulus and Remus as a Western element of comparison. The recurrence of twins in Amerindian thought in terms of the elaboration of "others" at once in conjunction and disjunction offers a significant clue to decipher indigenous perceptions of the encounter presented in this chapter. This observation, I believe, is also pertinent to the theory of the colonial encounter and of power relations in general.

In Upper Xingu, developing a duality to represent an encounter between entities that are necessarily in conjunction but at the same time irreducible is socially, culturally, and politically relevant. A brief review of the literature may confirm this

(Agostinho 1970, 1974a, 1974b; Menezes Bastos 1989). For instance, the second canto of the *Yawari*'s Pan-Xinguano rite (Menezes Bastos 1990) uses this rationale in the mortal combat of *morerekwat*, the "political-diplomatic chief" (characterized by the Jaguar), against *tenotat*, the "pubertal secluded" (a kind of Hawk). The former is manifested in every rite as the incarnation of contaminated power that is socially efficient and productive. The latter has a different type of power: he is absolutely adroit in terms of knowledge, despite his sterility in sociopolitical relations. In the referenced canto of the ritual, *Morerekwat* is defeated because of his stupidity when facing the pubertal secluded's sagacious enticements.

When I first studied the *Yawari*'s canto I was surprised by its extraordinary thematic likeness to the Brazilian Amazonian folk tale "A Onça e o Jabuti" ("The Jaguar and the Turtle") and the famous Brazilian northeastern folk-musical duel between a feline and some other animal such as a turtle or dog (Cascudo 1980). Considering the importance of the similarities found in these three forms, I suggested that a comparison be made between Brazil (of the north-northeastern folk manifestations) and the indigenous people (of whom rites such as the *Yawari* are pertinent either historically or structurally) (Menezes Bastos 1990). Two aspects of this comparison are particularly relevant. One is the vision of power relations as constituents of sociability rather than as coming from outside and assaulting society (Menezes Bastos 2001). The other is the mingling of tragedy and comedy, which points to the fact that "inferior" beings (comedians and their enticements), and not "superior" ones (tragic beings and their truths), work on the principle of sociability. My position is that this Amerindian form of thinking offers an important model for the comprehension of sociability in general, for the knowledge of music and contact, and for our understanding of the connections between local, regional, and global levels of analysis.

Notes

1. Raoni's real name is Ropni, but I use the former, as that is how he is known in Brazil and elsewhere abroad. Similarly I adopt the ethnonym "Txukahamãe" to refer to the group he represents, the Upper Xingu Kayapó, who refer to themselves as Metuktíre.

2. See Menezes Bastos 1996 for a previous version of this paper, in Portuguese. Thanks to Alinne Balduino Fernandes for the initial English translation. Thanks to Bob White for his suggestions for the essay in its current form. For its content I am solely responsible.

3. http://www.rainforestfoundationuk.org/s-index.

4. Following Saussure (1916), I use the English words "signifier" and "signified" as the translations of the French words *signifiant* and *signifié,* respectively.

5. This refers to the broadest meaning of the term "caraíba," briefly defined as the translation of "civilized" (or non-Indian) by the Indians of the Upper Xingu, whose contact language is Portuguese.

6. According to Lévi-Strauss, the following composers mark out this "mythologization" of Western music: Frescobaldi (1583–1643), J. S. Bach (1685–1750), Mozart (1756–1791), Beethoven (1770–1827), and Wagner (1813–1883). Lévi-Strauss's thesis, a sort of coda to his discussion about the relations of myth and music (see 1964, 1971), should be read on

a formal axis (see Menezes Bastos 2008a). See my 1991 paper for Rabelais's elaboration of the myth of the phonograph. I have also written on the topic in 1990, 1991, 1995a, and 2008a.

7. The seventeenth-century musical chronology refers to Monteverde (1567–1643) and to the Venetian opera. In the eighteenth century J. S. Bach (1685–1750) embodied the center of the system. The following important names included Beethoven (1770–1827) and Wagner (1813–1883). Toynbee (1963) revisited Spengler's (1973) review on music as the ideal temple of Western individualism, which is a topic I have also dealt with (Menezes Bastos 1990, 1995a).

8. On the myth of the Eldorado, the Amazonian indigenous kingdom passionately sought by the Spanish in the sixteenth century during the race for gold and sumptuous spices, see Smith 1990. Eldorado's Hispanic saga meets a related Portuguese narrative with Fernão Dias Paes Lemes's search for emeralds.

9. For an authorized biography, see Sellers 1989; see, too, Sting and Dutilleux 1989 for readings about the singer's ideas on indigenous matters, specifically the Kayapó.

10. The punk movement is characterized by its distain for musical erudition or virtuosity, the so-called progressive music, and its conviction that music should be spontaneous. Its discourse emphasizes tonal and melodic simplicity as well as rhythm, lyrics, and intensity (volume).

11. For an example of the literature's most admirable appeal, see Sahlins 1985. Wolf's (1982) model, in my view, is inadequate to explain the colonial encounter, as it does not take seriously the agency of the so-called peoples without history in relation to that of the colonizers, resulting in the neutralization of their intentions and interests. On the notion of interethnic friction, see Cardoso de Oliveira (1972, 1976), whose view, I believe, is based on an acceptable approach to the colonial encounter. In a system of interethnic friction—which, I contend, is the logical but not ontological equivalent of class struggle—one society denies the existence of the other dialectically, portraying the contradiction in this contentious relationship. For an analysis of various traditional anthropological studies of inter-societal contact, see Oliveira Filho 1988; for a general critique on the topic, see Asad 1973; and for a compendium on the subject in Latin America, see Urban and Sherzers 1991.

12. Sting's intention in aligning with Raoni was manifested in his efforts, in 1989, and particularly those of Brazil's Rainforest Foundation, to raise funds in order to mark out indigenous lands. See Brown and Fernández 1991 for a study on the interethnic political alliance and its drastic repercussions during the gunfight in the 1960s in Peru.

13. The original Portuguese phrase, which is difficult to translate, is "A gente tem que se Raonir senão se Extingue." I thank Lux Vidal for alerting me to this expression, which was disseminated in the country as a rumor and whose author is unknown.

References

Adorno, T. W. 1974. *Filosofia da nova música*. São Paulo: Perspectiva.

———. 1983. "O fetichismo na música e a regressão na audição." In *Benjamin, Habermas, Horkheimer, Adorno,* ed. P. E. Arantes, 165–191. São Paulo: Editora Abril.

———. 1986. "A indústria cultural." In *T. W. Adorno.,* ed. G. Cohn, 92–99. São Paulo: Ática.

Agostinho, P. 1970. "Estudo preliminar sobre o mito de origem xinguano. Comentário a uma variante Aweti." *Universitas* 6/7:457–519.

———. 1974a . *Kwarìp: mito e ritual no Alto-Xingu.* São Paulo: Edusp.

———. 1974b. *Mitos e outras narrativas Kamayurá.* Salvador: UFBa

Aquino T. V. 1991. "Travessia do Povo da Floresta no Expresso do Ano 2000." *A Gazeta* (Rio Branco, Acre), April (section *Gazeta Ilustrada*).

Asad, Talal. ed. 1973. *Anthropology and the Colonial Encounter.* New Jersey: Humanities.

Bloch, A., and J. Dutilleux. 1987. "Sting: um guerreiro roqueiro no Xingu." in *Manchete* 1861:4–10.

Brown, M. F., and E. Fernandez. 1991. *War of Shadows: The Struggle for Utopia in the Peruvian Amazon.* Berkeley: University of California Press.

Brum, M. 1897. *Através da música: bosquejos históricos.* Rio de Janeiro: Officinas Gráphicas de I. Bevilacqua.

Cardoso de Oliveira, R. 1972. *O índio e o mundo dos brancos: a situação dos Tükuna no Alto Solimões.* 2nd ed. São Paulo: Pioneira.

———. 1976. *Identidade, etnia e estrutura social.* São Paulo: Pioneira.

Carvalho, B. 1991. "Jobim e Sting Fazem de Tudo pela Floresta." *Folha de S. Paulo,* March 12 (section *Ilustrada*).

Cascudo, L. 1980. *Dicionário do Folclore Brasileiro.* São Paulo: Melhoramentos.

Dumont, L. 1985. *O individualismo: uma perspectiva antropológica da ideologia moderna.* Rio de Janeiro: Rocco.

Foucault, M. 1985. *As palavras e as coisas: uma arqueologia das ciências humanas.* São Paulo: Martins Fontes.

Galvão, E. 1953. "Cultura e sistema de parentesco das tribos do alto rio Xingu." *Boletim do Museu Nacional,* n.s. (Anthropology), 14.

Graburn, N. H. H. 1976. "Introduction." In *Ethnic and Tourist Arts: Cultural Expressions from the Fourth World,* ed. N. H. H. Graburn, 1–34. Los Angeles: University of California Press.

Hegel, G. W. F. 1974. *Estética IV: pintura e música.* Lisboa: Guimarães.

Horkheimer, M., and T. Adorno. 1947. *Dialektik der Aufklarung: philosophische Fragmente.* Amsterdam: Querido.

Kunst, J. 1959. *Ethnomusicology.* The Hague: M. Nijhoff.

Leibowitz, R. 1957. *La evolution de la música: de Bach a Schonberg.* Buenos Aires: Nueva Visión.

Lévi-Strauss, C. 1964. *Le cru et le cuit (Mythologiques I).* Paris : Plon.

———. 1970. *O Pensamento Selvagem.* São Paulo: Companhia Editora Nacional.

———. 1971. *L'Homme nu (Mythologiques IV).* Paris : Plon.

———. 1979. "Mito e Música." In *Mito e significado,* 65–77. São Paulo: Martins Fontes.

———. 1991. *Histoire de lynx.* Paris: Plon.

Macdonald, D. 1973. "Uma teoria da cultura de massa," In *Cultura de massa,* ed. B. Rosenberg and D. Manning White, 77–93. São Paulo: Cultrix.

Martin, Denis-Constant, and Olivier Roueff. 2002. *La France du jazz: musique, modernité et identité dans la première moitié du XXe siècle.* Marseille: Éditions Parenthèses.

Menezes Bastos, R. J. de. 1978. *A musicológica Kamayurá: para uma antropologia da comunicação no Alto Xingu.* Brazil: Funai.

———. 1983. "Sistemas políticos, de comunicação e de articulação social no Alto Xingu." *Anuário Antropológico* 1981:43–58.

———. 1989. "Exegeses Yawalapití e Kamayurá da criação do Parque Indígena do Xingu e a invenção da saga dos irmãos Villas Boas." *Revista de Antropologia* 30/31/32:391–426.

———. 1990. "A Festa da Jaguatirica: uma partitura crítico-interpretativa." Ph.D. diss., Universidade de São Paulo, Department of Social Anthropololgy.

———. 1991. "Phonographic recording as our emblem for the music of the other. Towards an anthropology of the musicological juncture: Vergleichende Musikwissenschaft, ethnomusicology and historical musicology." In *Music in the Dialogue of Cultures: Traditional Music and Cultural Policy*, ed. M. Baumann, 232–241. Wilmhelmshaven: Noetzel.

———. 1995a. "Esboço de uma teoria da música: para além de uma antropologia sem música e de uma musicologia sem homem," *Anuário Antropológico* 1993:9–73.

———. 1995b. "Indagação sobre os Kamayurá, o Alto Xingu e outros nomes e coisas—uma etnologia da sociedade xinguara," *Anuário Antropológico* 1994:227–269.

———. 1996. "Musicalidade e Ambientalismo na Redescoberta do Eldorado e do Caraiba: Uma Antropologia do Encontro Raoni-Sting," *Revista de Antropologia* 39 (1): 145–189.

———. 1999. *A Musicológica Kamayurá: Para uma Antropologia da Comunicação no Alto Xingu.* 2nd ed. Florianópolis: Editora da Universidade Federal de Santa Catarina.

———. 2000. "The Origin of Samba as the Invention of Brazil (Why Do Songs Have Music?)." *British Journal of Ethnomusicology* 8:67–96.

———. 2001. "Ritual, história e política no Alto Xingu: observações a partir dos Kamayurá e do estudo da festa da jaguatirica (Jawari)." In *Os povos do Alto Xingu. História e cultura*, ed. Bruna Franchetto and Michael Heckenberger, 335–357. Rio de Janeiro: Editora da Universidade Federal do Rio de Janeiro.

———. 2005. "Brazil." In *The Continuum Encyclopedia of Popular Music of the World*, Vol. 3, *Latin America and the Caribbean*, ed., J. Shepherd, D. Horn, and D. Laing, 212–248. London: Continuum International.

———. 2006. "Leonardo, a Flauta: Uns Sentimentos Selvagens." *Revista de Antropologia* 49 (2): 557–579.

———. 2007. "Moses Asch's Contribution to American Ethnomusicology or Utility and Toy, Authenticity and Entertainment in a United State: Toward an Anthropological History of Folkways Records." *Vibrant—Virtual Brazilian Anthropology* 4 (2): 83–96. http://www.vibrant.org.br/index.html.

———. 2008a. "Claude Lévi-Strauss e a Música." In *Música em Debate: Perspectivas Interdisciplinares*, ed., Samuel Araújo, 237–248. Rio de Janeiro: Mauad X.

———. 2008b. "Brazil in France, 1922: An Anthropological Study of the Congenital International Nexus of Popular Music." *Latin American Music Review* 29:1–28.

Oliveira Filho, J. P. 1988. *O "nosso governo": os Ticuna e o regime tutelar*. São Paulo: Marco Zero.

Passarinho, J. 1991. "Internacionalização da Amazônia." Statement given to the Parliamentarian Committee of Investigation, according to the article, "Pressões ambientalistas sobre a Amazônia preocupam o governo," *Folha de São Paulo,* June 26.

Sahlins, M. 1985. *Islands of History*. Chicago: University of Chicago Press.

Saussure, F. 1916. *Cours de Linguistique générale*. Paris: Payot.

Sellers, R. 1989. *Sting: a Biography*. London: Omnibus.

Smith, A. 1990. *Os conquistadores do Amazonas: quatro séculos de exploração e aventura no maior rio do mundo*. São Paulo: Best Seller.

Spengler, O. 1973. *A decadência do Ocidente: esboço de uma morfologia da história universal*. 2nd abridged ed. Rio de Janeiro: Zahar.

Sting, and J. Dutilleux. 1989. *Jungle Stories: The Fight for the Amazon*. London: Barrie and Jenkins.

Toynbee, A. 1963. *Estudio de la história,* Vol. 12, *Las perspectivas de la civilización occidental.* Buenos Aires: Emec.

Urban, G., and J. Sherzer, ed. 1991. *Nation-States and Indians in Latin America.* Austin: University of Texas Press.

Vega, Carlos. 1966. "Mesomusic: An Essay on the Music of the Masses." *Ethnomusicology* 10 (1): 1–17.

Weber, M. 1944. "Los fundamentos racionales y sociológicos de la música." In *Economia y Sociedad,* 2: 1118–1183. México, DF: Fondo de Cultura.

———. 1985. *A ética protestante e o espírito do capitalismo.* São Paulo: Pioneira.

Willis, P. 1976. *Learning to Labour: How Working-Class Kids Get Working-Class Jobs.* New York: Columbia University Press.

Wolf, E. R. 1982. *Europe and the People without History.* Berkeley: University of California Press.

Discography

Nascimento, M. 1990. *Txai.* Rio de Janeiro: CBS.

The Police. 1978. *Roxanne/Peanuts.* LP issued by A&M, AMS 7348.

Part 2.

Mediated Encounters

5

"Beautiful Blue": Rarámuri Violin Music in a Cross-Border Space

Daniel Noveck

Although my doctoral research took place in northern Mexico, one of the more illustrative encounters occurred across the border, in El Paso, Texas. I was returning home during a break between grants when a few of my informants happened to be performing in a museum on the outskirts of the city. They came from the Rarámuri community of Coyachique, in the Sierra Tarahumara region of southern Chihuahua, and they were demonstrating the Matachines dances whose music I had been studying. I decided to stop in El Paso to see the performance, but I neglected to tell them of my plans ahead of time. I also didn't know, on my way to the restroom after an arduous drive north from Chihuahua, that they had commandeered the space as an impromptu backstage. Distractedly pushing the door aside, I found myself surrounded by a crowd of Matachines dancers, festooned in bright bandanas and headdresses, jostling for space amid the stalls and cinder block. We stared at one another for a moment and then fell into laughter at the utter incongruity of the meeting, so far from the normal context of my fieldwork in Mexico.

Later in the day, when the performance ended, I drove out to the main route north and stopped at the intersection of Transmountain Road and the Patriot Freeway, just to the west of Fort Bliss. I heard someone call my name, and turned to see a few of the Rarámuri men wedged into the back of a small truck, waving and smiling at yet another strange meeting place. But now they didn't look so cheerful. The driver had put on a CD of Native American flute music, recorded in a new-age style with a gauzy synthesizer wash. Surely he intended to make his visitors feel more at ease, but to Rarámuri ears this must have seemed like the saddest music imaginable. What the driver did not know was that fiddle music, of almost any kind, would have made them feel more at home. The musical moment reflected a larger dynamic. The driver used indigenous music to exoticize the Rarámuris, but Rarámuris have a musical life that revolves around that most iconically European of instruments, the violin.[1] The two sides in this story, Rarámuris and Americans, are thus joined in mutual fascination as well as mis-recognition. Americans define Rarámuris as a threatened culture requiring discovery, understanding, and rescue, using a perceptual frame that marginalizes Rarámuris even as it is meant to help them. Rarámuris, for their part, make folkloric presentations in foreign countries in order to bring home something of value. Yet this requires them to collude in the fetishization of their own practices. That cooperation can easily break down, as the following narrative shows. Yet even so, indigeneity is as much a product as a prerequisite of these interactions. Modernity and its traditional Other are not given categories but interdependent values defined at particular sites.

One of those sites is the violin. Rarámuris play the violin throughout their ritual and domestic life, and much important ritual work could not take place without it. Yet Rarámuris do not see their own form of the violin, the *Rabeli*, as a specifically Rarámuri instrument. They understand it as a subset of a more widely circulating musical form, within which they have crafted a particular style. The violin thus has an ambivalent status in the Sierra Tarahumara, for it is considered both an emblem of European high culture and an icon of Rarámuri particularity. It embodies intimately local, felt, and lived spaces even as it circulates globally in recorded, decontextualized form. As an object, it exists both as commodity and tool, an object in itself and a means to another end. The instrument thus connects the production of indigenous locality with transnational circuits of movement and exchange.

Fiddling, in short, can be thought of as a world music *avant la lettre*. The notion, however, goes against the grain of much of the discourse around world music. As Feld (2000) noted, the literature on world music is generally divided between what he calls "celebratory" and "anxious" frames. World music is perceived as making connections between modern and traditional societies, and these border crossings are appraised either positively (as creativity "without borders") or negatively (as part of the global capitalist juggernaut). But both perspectives take the fundamental distinction between Modernity and Tradition for granted. Close ethnographic description has a tendency to blur that distinction in fruitful ways. Thus, as Stokes (2004) and others have suggested, the problem is best addressed not as a theoretical question but as an ethnographic one: How might music serve as a frame in which such distinctions are claimed and negotiated in the first place?

This chapter poses that question as it narrates the travels of a number of Rarámuri men from their communities in northern Mexico to sites in the United States and Italy, where they perform traditional dances and learn to build violins in the

European style. It finds indigeneity to be a category marked by an array of intersecting beliefs, hopes, and interests, all of which are mediated through the violin. For the anthropologist, most uncomfortably, there is no privileged position as an "outsider" but only one form of situated knowledge among many.

Indigeneity Performed

Once prepared, the men from Coyachique filed down a pathway behind the Wilderness Park Museum, toward a bare patch of ground behind the main building. A circle had been drawn in corn meal, neatly framing a space for performers and spectators, with the Franklin Mountains looming in the background.[2] Orange fiberglass chairs were placed inside the circle for the fiddler and guitarist, and a group of spectators, many of them from the nearby military base, stood neatly arrayed outside the ring. The dance had been presented as a specimen of an untouched Indian tradition, lost in the modernized United States but preserved in the mountains of Mexico. The performance, however, had an opaque and stripped-down quality, as it lacked the festive and broadly religious elements of a Rarámuri fiesta—the altar and crosses made of split saplings, bowls containing food offerings, vats of *tesguino* (a fermented corn beverage), and mingled smells of incense, goat soup, and thick tortillas. The sonic center of the performance was a Rarámuri violin, but it seemed ill suited to the space, its sound dwarfed by the vastness of the surrounding desert. Meanwhile, the mixture of European and indigenous qualities in the Matachines form—a quadrille dance with a Christian background, European costume (bandanas, boots, and crowns), and music supplied by a violin and guitar—clashed with American expectations of untouched indigeneity.[3]

As if to fix the problem, three men rose to address the audience after the first round of dancing. The director of the museum entered the ring first and explained that the Matachines dance is associated with the Virgin Mary and is danced on key feast days in the Rarámuris' ritual calendar. Then the man who had brought the Rarámuris to El Paso, an outdoor adventure entrepreneur named Richard Fisher, described some of the threats to the Rarámuris' continued survival. Finally, a Rarámuri dancer named Ramón stepped forward and explained through an interpreter that the dance expressed the essence of Rarámuri tradition. It was the dance, he said, that makes Rarámuris "who they are."[4] One spectator, a former resident of the Santa Clara pueblo in New Mexico, said that the dance reminded him of the traditional life he had left behind when he adopted a modern lifestyle in El Paso.

Later Fisher offered a slide presentation in the museum in which he extended the narrative of tradition lost and recovered by detailing his explorations of remote canyons in northern Mexico. He elaborated on his earlier depiction of Rarámuris as a people threatened by constant starvation and the encroachment of modernity, but there were telling inaccuracies in the account. He described Coyachique, the home community of the Rarámuri performers, as a town with "no church or state presence," even though it indeed has both a state-supported school as well as an old church.[5] He listed the construction of a road to the community as a threat to its existence, even though the road was championed in the community by Fisher's main ally there, a renowned violin maker named Patrocinio López.[6]

Fisher, in short, presented an essentialized portrait of Indian life in the Sierra Tarahumara that justified his own interventions. Rarámuris countered with their own construction of indigenous locality but in a more subtly coded way. During the dance, the Rarámuri fiddler made prominent use of a tune called "Semati Siyoname." The tune has an anthemic quality for Rarámuris. It was composed by Erasmo Palma, a renowned musician from the culturally important community of Norogachi, and it is perhaps the only violin tune that can be heard at Rarámuri fiestas throughout the Sierra Tarahumara. The title can be translated as "beautiful blue" or "beautiful sky," and it can be read as a play on "Cielito Lindo," or "beautiful sky/heaven," an old and much beloved Mexican Mestizo ballad.[7] But whereas the "beautiful heaven" of the Mexican title refers figuratively to a beautiful and desirable woman, the Rarámuri title re-imagines this as a beautiful place, experienced from a Rarámuri vantage. The title "Semati Siyoname," then, engages with Mestizo nostalgia and machismo but reframes it in terms of a Rarámuri imagery of beautiful communities embodied in fully realized Rarámuri localities, or beautiful places. As a popular tune disseminated on the regional radio station, this may have been the one Rarámuri fiddle tune that could effect that imagery in trans-local terms.

Traveling Objects: The Italians, the Church, and the Violin

The semiotic flexibility of the violin therefore made it central to the articulation of two linked but competing worlds of value. Americans used it to simultaneously glorify and marginalize Rarámuris, while Rarámuris responded with their own imagery, even if this was done in a typically non-confrontational way. But if Rarámuris used the musical capacities of the violin, Europeans and Americans tended to focus on its materiality. In the Sierra Tarahumara the violin symbolizes the cultural value of the European, and this paradoxically gives it resonance as a metonym of the indigenous. I noticed this when I visited the late Father Luis Verplancken, S.J., in his study in the center of Creel. Padre Verplancken was widely revered in the Sierra for his work developing water resources, education, and health services for Rarámuris. He was also a guiding force in the founding of a crafts store in Creel's central square, just next to the bank and the train station. The store buys crafts from Rarámuris at reasonable prices and sells them to benefit the mission clinic.

After catching up on news, Verplancken mentioned that an interesting violin had recently turned up in the possession of a Rarámuri man near Cerocahui. He thought it must have come from the early Jesuit missionaries to the Sierra, and he was eager to show it to me. After vanishing for a moment into a back room, he returned with a black, wooden case, elegantly shaped, with a brass handle attached to an arched top. As he extricated the violin from the box, it was immediately evident that the instrument was a European factory model, probably from the early twentieth century. Telltale signs marked it as inexpensive: the purfling on the top was not inlaid but had been painted on and the varnish was not of especially high quality. The top of the violin was cracked, and it had lost its tailpiece, which someone had inventively replaced with a shaped piece of cow horn fastened to the end peg with thick wire. The tuning pegs were similarly hand-carved, but Verplancken had replaced these with factory-made pegs, keeping the old ones in a small plastic bag. Inside, the instrument bore one of the false Stradivarius labels that are ubiquitous in older European violins.

That last detail affirmed its pedestrian roots. This was a store-bought violin that, like so many, had been purchased or bartered for by a Rarámuri. But Verplancken was unfamiliar with the fine points of violin valuation, and he was intrigued. "How else," he asked, if the instrument did not come from missionaries, "could a Tarahumara have gotten hold of a violin like this?" In a world of notably mobile Indians and circulating objects, then, Verplancken assumed that this violin was anomalous—an object whose presence implied some kind of intervention by outsiders. In short, the violin implied a history in which the church served as caretaker and enlightening force for isolated Indians who were innocent of the wider world.

It was this symbolic resonance of the violin that underlay a plan to bring Rarámuris to Cremona, Italy, the storied birthplace of the modern violin, in order to learn the techniques of modern violin making. An advance group had arrived in Creel in early 2001, comprised of prominent citizens of Cremona who were committed to promoting the town's legacy. The group was headed, or at least funded, by a businessman named Giovanni Carotti, a wealthy man who traveled with a personal assistant. He had made his fortune after the Second World War by cornering the Italian market in industrial valves. Also with the group were the director of the school of music in Cremona and the mayor of Cremona at the time, Paolo Bodini. The director of the music school was an accomplished violinist, and he had brought with him a violin recently completed by Bissolotti, a renowned violin maker working in Cremona.[8] The Italians sought to integrate Rarámuri practices of making and playing the violin into a European story about the instrument and its universality. Verplancken and the Italians concurred with each other in valuing the cultural wealth of the Sierra and its material embodiment in objects of art. They worked together, each reinforcing the other's imagined universes of value. But the expectation of commonality could also serve as a source of tension.

The first meeting took place at the mission store in Creel in April 2001. As I arrived at the store I met Patrocinio, who had spent the night at the nearby Posada de

Creel, a creaky wooden structure fronting the train tracks. Patrocinio referred to it by its old name, the Hotel Chávez, conjuring a time when the hotel was owned by the Creel *ejido,* and was cheaper and friendlier to Indians. Patrocinio seemed happy to see me; I sensed that he was slightly nervous and appreciated the presence of a more or less trusted gringo. The group congregated outside the mission store, where Verplancken introduced Patrocinio to Senor Carotti. Pointedly Verplancken asked Patrocinio how many children he had and how many he might have lost. It was an awkward moment, placing one of the more anguished episodes in Patrocinio's life on display before a group of strangers (he had lost an infant son, in the clinic just a block away, some years previously). But Verplancken was clearly intent on demonstrating the omnipresence of Rarámuri poverty.

After greetings, the group retired to a room behind the mission store that served as a concert hall for Romayne Wheeler, an American pianist living above the Rarámuri community of Munérachi. The meeting convened around Romayne's piano. Patrocinio had brought with him two violins, recently made and carefully wrapped in white cloth for the journey up from Coyachique. Once out of their wrappings, the group began to examine the violins. They were small by Rarámuri standards, conveying the sense that Patrocinio was copying European violins. This was, in fact, the way he had learned his craft. But these violins had outlandish peg heads, with a swooping, snakelike figure doubling over itself. For Patrocinio, these were a point of pride, displaying his mastery and inventiveness. For the Italians they had the opposite effect, pegging the violins as craft-store curios. Their disappointment was palpable.

The Italians hovered over perceived errors in execution—a messy seam between the fingerboard and neck, pencil marks here and there, an uncarved block of wood for the bridge which was, in any case, placed too far back on the body, well out of line with the notches on the f-holes. They were dismayed over the lack of a sound post or bass bar. Their greatest discomfort, however, was with the bow, a simple stick strung with local horse hair. No serious music, I could sense them thinking, could be played with such a crude apparatus. I tried to defuse the tension by suggesting that these construction techniques belonged to a different way of thinking about violins. These were, after all, *rabelis,* as Rarámuris called them, more akin in their construction to medieval instruments than to the modern violins first perfected in Cremona. This had little effect. Eventually Patrocinio performed some Pascol tunes to demonstrate the violins' sound. He looked uncomfortable as he played, glancing at me often as if for reassurance.

Finally the more delicate issues came to the fore. A longtime donor to the mission clinic in Creel, Carotti had decided to invite Rarámuris to Cremona to learn the art of violin making at the place the Italians thought of as its source. Verplancken had volunteered Patrocinio López for the cause, as his reputation as a leading maker of Rarámuri violins for the tourist market was by now well established. At length the Italians came to the point of the proceedings, extending an invitation to Patrocinio to live in Cremona for a year, where he would study at the International School of Violin Making. Patrocinio seemed interested in the proposal, as he enjoyed his reputation as the most highly regarded violin maker in the Sierra, and such an invitation only cemented his claim to the title.

There were misgivings about the idea, nonetheless. An Austrian anthropologist in the room whispered to me, "This is bad. It's just rich people who want to use their money to make themselves feel good." It was an obvious point but perhaps too simplistic: Patrocinio had been dealing with this type of situation for many years, and he clearly knew what he was doing. It seemed just as patronizing to assume that he needed the protection of outsiders. Still, the director of the music school worried about the distance between Patrocinio's traditional craft and the fine art of Cremonese violin making. He pulled me aside to ask if I thought it was worthwhile for Patrocinio to participate. "Do you think he will really learn something in Cremona?" he asked. "I mean, his violins . . . it's not art, it's just their tradition." I replied that Patrocinio's violins were unusual in that he copied European designs. He might learn something from the exposure to a European shop. "Above all," I said, "you should ask him."

The question was put to Patrocinio, and he accepted the offer to come to Cremona. Scheduling issues, however, proved to be a sticking point. The idea had been to bring someone to Cremona for a whole year, but this was unthinkable for an average adult Rarámuri, both practically and emotionally. Thus, when Patrocinio explained that he could only leave for one month because he had to take care of his family, further consternation ensued. If the purpose was to produce a Rarámuri violin maker, then it would surely be defeated by such a trivial stay. This was an awkward moment, as it hinted at the inconsistencies of the project: Was the intention really to train a Rarámuri man as a violin maker, or was this simply window dressing for more common, philanthropic aims (Carotti's support of the mission, educating an "underprivileged" Indian, etc.)? Having made so much of the former, it was unseemly to suggest that ulterior motives were at work.

Carotti skirted the issue by offering to buy Patrocinio's violins. Patrocinio named a price of 3,000 pesos each—about US$300 at the time. Verplancken interpreted the price to Carotti, who seemed stunned and vacillated until Patrocinio lowered his price to 2,500 pesos. Carotti countered with an offer of 2,000 each. Patrocinio assented but added that he would only accept that price because they had invited him to Italy. He would sell them the violins at a discount, he declared, as a sign of friendship. It was a magnanimous gesture that immediately put Patrocinio on the higher ground.

When the meeting adjourned we were all invited to a small building next door in the church compound, where Verplancken had something he wanted to share with Carotti: a trove of colonial-era paintings that had been rescued from the garbage during the renovation of an old mission church in Cusárare, not far from Creel. The paintings were of eighteenth-century vintage, competent although not spectacular examples of colonial religious art. Some contained striking, even haunting images of saints and biblical characters. One stood out in particular: about a century older than the others, it was a portrait of two young Spanish nobles, a brother and sister, standing together in an alcove decorated with floral designs. The painting had a special quality and immediately captured Carotti's attention. He began to prod Father Verplancken to sell him the portrait. This went on for some time, during which the Father's normally placid surface grew perceptibly ruffled. Far from being salable objects, these paintings were part of the cultural patrimony of the Sierra and of Mexico itself (Weiner 1992).

The disconnect that had opened up around the violins seemed to grow wider. Verplancken meant to impress the Italian magnate with the cultural riches of the Sierra, but Carotti, an outsider with little time for such details, had failed to grasp the point. This was a disappointment for the Padre, but, as his resistance became apparent, Carotti seemed only more intent on wresting the work of art from the collection. At one point during the exchange Paolo, the mayor of Cremona, turned to me and whispered, "You know, Carotti is an extremely rich man. If Verplancken named a price of a million dollars for that painting, it wouldn't be a problem." The painting, in any case, stayed where it was. The group moved across the street to the church on the central square in Creel, where the director of the music school took advantage of the space to give an impromptu concert on his Cremonese Bissolotti violin. We sat quietly in the pews and listened.

In the end the decision was made to bring Patrocinio to Italy, albeit for the shorter period. The trip was planned for a year hence, which was just enough time for the various arrangements to be made. The plan had one unforeseen but fateful ramification: because Patrocinio had been invited, the sponsors of the Italy trip had set themselves on a collision course with Richard Fisher, the North American entrepreneur responsible for organizing the museum performance in El Paso, Texas.

Terms of Exchange: The Canyoneer and the Repartimiento

As an object of art, and as a musical instrument and symbol, the violin could provide the occasion for sending Rarámuris to foreign places as representatives of indigenous Mexican culture. But this was not the only kind of value at work. Rarámuri men embarked on these journeys, in part, to help feed their families. There was a more material problem, in other words, of producing and reproducing Rarámuri localities as generative spaces. Somewhat surprisingly it was the American entrepreneur, Richard Fisher, whose activities addressed this issue most directly, and perhaps most effectively, from a Rarámuri point of view.

If the Rarámuris have achieved some kind of public fame in the United States over the past two decades, Richard Fisher has played no small part in generating it. Fisher has been working as a tour guide in northern Mexico and the southwestern

United States since the early 1970s. His early "canyoneering" business was the subject of an essay by the mountaineering writer Jon Krakauer (1990), who portrayed Fisher as an avid adventurer and intrepid back-country guide. In the course of one of those trips Fisher met Patrocinio López of Coyachique, and formed a lasting partnership with him. In lectures and publications Fisher cultivates the persona of a Victorian explorer, comparing himself to the Norwegian explorer Carl Lumholtz, who traveled through the mountains of northern Mexico in the late nineteenth century (Lumholtz 1987 [1902]).[9]

Fisher gained notoriety in the 1990s for bringing Rarámuris to elite "ultra-running" races—cross country races in which contestants run for vast distances in rough terrain, often above tree line in the mountains of the western United States. He earned a reputation as a difficult figure by signing flamboyant publicity deals (with Nike Shoes for instance), inviting disruptive film crews to races, and jealously guarding the Rarámuri runners from contact with the press or even other participants. Because of the resulting ill-will toward Fisher, Rarámuri runners eventually became unwelcome at these events. According to at least one devoted runner I interviewed, Fisher had corrupted the spirit of the sport, although at least some of the rancor stems from the fact that Rarámuris began to win races. In 1994, when Rarámuri runners were allowed to wear their tire-tread sandals instead of running shoes, they took first, second, and fifth place. The winner that year was a fifty-five-year-old Rarámuri man from Panaláchi.

When running became impossible, Fisher turned to folkloric performances and museum lectures. His trips involve a set of exchanges that bring tourists and goods into the Sierra, and take Rarámuri dancers and performers out. The key moment of exchange happens at distribution points on the canyon bottom— *repartimientos,* as Rarámuris call them—where food and goods are exchanged, in a sense, for the Rarámuri performers. Rarámuri men are selected for these journeys not only for their ability to dance or play music but also for their comportment (the ability to refrain from getting drunk) and their dress (their traditional appearance).

The dance performance in El Paso, in October 2001, was preceded by one such exchange. Early in the morning Rarámuris filtered down the hillside of Coyachique to Coyaina, the terminus of the trail leading to Coyachique and a designated spot for exchanges between Rarámuris and various kinds of *Chabochis.* Once the crowd had gathered at Coyaina, Patrocinio López took charge of the proceedings, standing next to a large red cattle truck owned by a trusted Batopilas businessman, Erasmo Paredes. The truck was loaded with many sacks of corn, along with other commodities including soap, lard (*manteca*), cooking oil, and one large can of sardines for each family. Paredes, a *chabochi* (non-Indian) who was trusted and respected among Rarámuris, had carried the goods from Cuauhtémoc that morning. Having made his delivery, Erasmo sat against the rocks across the road with the other Rarámuris who had gathered in the shade and read a newspaper he had picked up in Creel. Patrocinio worked with an assistant named Jaris, who kept track of the distribution with a list. The two men went through the list according to each commodity, reading out the names of the men and waiting as they or their wives came to pick up the goods.[10]

This process seemed to go on for hours; the wind picked up, died down, and picked up again. The shade shrank against the rocks by the side of the road, until the crowd of people seeking refuge in it could move no closer together. As the afternoon stretched on people became hungry, and they began to open the cans of sardines they had received, eating them for lunch. Fisher himself was nowhere to be found, and people wondered aloud about his whereabouts. Some hours later he arrived in a white van with a photographer and another assistant in tow. Dressed stylishly in southwestern hat, silver jewelry, and Converse sneakers, Fisher posed for photographs. Most of these were with Rarámuri women and children, with the delivered food always figuring prominently and opulently in the background. Others would complain later that it was only the "friends of Fisher," however, who received such benefits.

In time the musicians and dancers assembled at the bottom, dressed traditionally as Fisher requested, although Ramón V. was dressed in a clean white T-shirt, black jeans, huaraches, and a baseball cap. He carried a small knapsack and two violins in a sack, which he planned to sell in the United States (Ramón is a talented violin maker, but because he sees himself as holding a lower status than Patrocinio López, he makes his violins slightly smaller in size). Soon the men filed into the van, and they were off. Fisher drove them to Creel that night, and the next day they crossed the border into the United States.

Confrontation

On this occasion problems arose that exposed the deeper stakes in the project. Many of the difficulties began when Patrocinio elected to stay behind. He had begun to tire of the voyages, and for some time he had professed a desire to stay at home with his family and return to farming. The trips to the United States relied heavily on his skills, and so without him things did not run smoothly. According to men who recounted the events on their return to Mexico, they were treated poorly when they reached Tucson and worked, as they often did, on Fisher's property. They claimed that they were paid more for the work than what they could earn doing the equivalent work in Batopilas but less than the rate for such labor in the United States. The real indignity was that they had not been fed well; each day began with oatmeal, which they consider a beverage. This was not enough to sustain them for a day of work, particularly for people who are accustomed to a high-protein breakfast of beans and thick tortillas. Adding insult to injury, they were dropped off on their return in the highland town of Creel, some four hours by bus to Coyaina and the trail to their village. That meant that they had to pay bus fare to get back to Coyachique, cutting another 160 pesos out of their promised pay. When I spoke with people during the fiesta of Doce de Diciembre of that year, the Rarámuris of Coyachique were quite angry. One prominent member of the community told me that they were going to exact revenge: "You'll see—we're going to screw (*chingar*) that Fisher."

When Fisher returned to the area in February 2002 he had to mollify the disaffected Rarámuris of Coyachique and negotiate the terms of the Italy project without making his interest too evident. The first of these he handled with aplomb. Fisher brought nineteen sheep with him from the United States as a gift to the families in Coyachique, and he promised a further shipment of twenty or thirty tons of corn, although the mission to deliver it was later aborted when he arrived on a Sunday and could not purchase the grain. The sheep seemed to infiltrate Coyachique and earned the nickname "the friends of Ricardo [Fisher]," which seemed to refer both to the sheep and to the people who had received them. The sheep refused to pen up at night with the Rarámuris' goats, forcing their owners to make special enclosures, an unwanted expense of time and resources. But Fisher had nonetheless demonstrated his mastery of the *Noráwa* relationship by maintaining a balance of exchange.[11] With the delivery of the sheep all complaints seemed to cease. The earlier negativity about Fisher magically vanished, and when he planned a new trip to the United States all those who were invited were happy to go along.

Ramon and Valentin go to Italy

Fisher, however, had now learned about the trip to Cremona, and the unavoidable logic of the situation was that if Patrocinio were to go, Fisher would go along with him. Patrocinio had, in fact, expressed a desire to remain at home, in keeping with his general mood at the time, but with Fisher's return to the Sierra he suddenly became animated about the trip. Fisher also wanted to change its terms. Instead of going as a pupil, which Fisher considered exploitive, he thought Patrocinio should go to Italy to teach *them* about Rarámuri life. Such a plan, of course, would require Fisher's help, but when I bumped into him on a side trail in Coyachique and asked if he would go, too, he demurred. His intentions became clear enough some time later, when the mission office in Creel received a newsletter from his organization, Wilderness Research Expeditions. The letter contained a solicitation for funds to send Patrocinio to Italy to study violin making. The trip was naturally well funded already, and Verplancken, inferring that Fisher intended to use the money himself, became incensed. He immediately phoned Fisher to rescind the invitation, telling him "you've spoiled it for Patrocinio and for yourself." Fisher responded with a fax complaining that Patrocinio, an "international public relations personality," was being treated like a child. The next time I saw Fisher, he compared the trip to the colonial-era practice of kidnapping indigenous people in the Americas and sending them to Europe as curiosities, where they often fell ill and died.

Verplancken, for his part, washed his hands of both Fisher and Patrocinio, whom he considered to have become too arrogant. He turned instead to two anthropologists, myself and Anapaula Pintado Cortina, for help in finding a replacement. The two of us had strong reservations about participating, but avoiding the issue seemed worse. At least in this way we could have a hand in the process and act as advocates for the Rarámuri men. With this in mind I suggested Ramón Figueroa of Bacuséachi, a man who relished the prestige that came with his renown as a violin maker, and who was adept at defending himself among Mestizos and Gringos. Ramón had made a number of attempts to go to the United States, only to be turned back at the border for lack of proper documentation. Anapaula asked Ramón's cousin, Valentin, a violin maker who lived in Coyachique and had always been overshadowed by Patrocinio's fame. In contrast to Ramón, Valentin was a tall, gentle man, a talented craftsman with a keen eye for the aesthetics of a violin but little facility in dealing with foreigners.

As with the journey to the United States, the practicalities of the trip were central. Like Patrocinio, Ramón agreed to go to Italy with the proviso that he only travel for one month—more than that, and he feared that his family would go without food and needed items.[12] Padre Verplancken agreed to the terms and planned the trip for the following Spring. After Semana Santa, however, it was moved ahead without warning in order to accommodate the Padre's schedule, and it was expanded from four to eight weeks. The Padre would take the men to Italy personally, and they would return with Romayne Wheeler, who happened to be performing in Italy during the spring. After Cremona they would travel to Rome, wait for Romayne to finish, and then return to Mexico four weeks later than he (and I) had promised.

Suddenly Ramón and Valentin were to leave in a matter of days. The church hastily delivered food to the men's families, but it turned out to be insufficient: one costal each of corn, beans, and potatoes, the latter apparently partly rotten, for a family of five or six for a period of two months. The church seemed to assume that since Rarámuris were subsistence farmers, they lived only on what they grew, when in reality Rarámuri households depend on a number of store-bought products. Ramón traveled to Creel to complain, saying that his family could not survive on the supplies, and would also need coffee, sugar, lard, oil, soap, and dried milk. The Padre agreed to bring another shipment of goods to Ramón and Valentin on the day they were to leave for Italy. The plan was unworkable, however, and so Anapaula and I had to deliver the food ourselves, after taking Ramón and Valentin to Creel to meet the Padre. The two men would have to leave home without seeing for themselves that their families were provided for.

The difficulties played on existing tensions around race and respect. On arriving in Creel we checked in with the mission and were sent to the clinic for dinner. We were served in a small back room reserved for Rarámuris, with a sliding window through which the food was passed from the kitchen. Ramón and Valentin complained that the beans tasted rotten. After dinner we were shown our living quarters for the night—rooms in the mission compound behind the mission store. After Ramón noticed that he and Valentin had been offered a much dirtier spot than the two anthropologists, we all shared a single house. Thinking that the Rarámuris were being infantilized, I said to Ramón, "They're not really treating you like men." "No," he replied, "they treat us like animals."

In the morning we presented ourselves at the office of the Padre, on a side street off the central plaza of Creel. Verplancken welcomed the two men and explained that they would spend six weeks in Cremona, and then another ten days or so sightseeing in Rome. With great animation, the Padre explained, they were going to be able to see the house of the Pope, "La Casa del Papa!" At this point Valentin, who had been silent and pensive throughout the proceedings, leaned over to Ramón and whispered, *"Rilowi bitéachi?"* ("The house of the *potato?*").[13] The two shared a private laugh as the Padre looked on uncomprehending. Both Ramón and Valentin had expressed a desire to return home rather than see Rome, but the Padre persevered, arguing that the Vatican was an important place and it would be a great honor for the Rarámuris to see it.

We drove to Chihuahua City the next day and dropped off one of Ramón's daughters at the home of a Mestizo family, where she worked as a maid. In the evening Anapaula and I met Padre Verplancken for dinner at Ricky's Tacos, and I expressed my reservations about the trip. We offered to go to Italy ourselves so that we could bring Ramón and Valentin back home with us if necessary. The Padre stiffened: unwittingly I was questioning his judgment. Pushing on anyway, I explained that I was worried that the Italians would not appreciate the Rarámuris' approach to the instrument. The Padre countered that they ought to learn "proper building techniques" so that their violins would sound better. I made things still worse when I made the anthropological point that the Rarámuris' violins sounded great to them just as they were. At this the Padre appeared to give up on us, and we departed with a strained cordiality.

Verplancken was gracious nonetheless when we met in the airport the following morning. We brought Ramón and Valentin from their hotel, arriving early to avoid extra stress, and secretly gave each of them 500 pesos as spending money for their journey. Once they were checked in, the tickets cleared, and baggage passed down the conveyor belt, we bade them farewell. I patted Ramón on the back and assured him that all would be well, as he headed through the metal detector and into the waiting lounge behind the Padre, the long hulk of the airplane filling the window at the back end of the room.

In the end our worst fears never materialized. Neither Anapaula nor I found money to go to Italy, as we had hoped. We called numerous times from Batopilas to assure them that there were no problems at home, and brought one of Ramón's daughters to Batopilas so she could speak with him on the phone. The men brought back photographs: Ramón and Valentin sitting in the back lot of the school with various friends they had made, drinking beers and looking relaxed; strange photos of them in their room at Carotti's house, where they were locked in at night, surrounded by medieval tryptichs; Ramón playing the fiddle for Carotti's guests in a restaurant in Cremona, in his Bacuséachi clothes, looking like the prize primitive on display; Ramón and Valentin in ill-fitting Western clothes, having gained weight from copious rich food and little exercise, standing by the ocean near Rome.

Their return was marked by a photograph published in the largest city paper, *El Diario de Chihuahua,* showing the two Indians holding their violins, just back from their voyage to Europe. "After eight weeks at the International School of Violin Makers in Cremona," the caption read, the two *indigenas* had returned to the state of Chihuahua. Because the reporter had gotten his information from a man who had been feuding with Padre Verplancken throughout the course of the project, the newspaper article had a pro-government slant. "The state government financed the Tarahumaras," the article read incorrectly, "who now charge as much as 500 dollars for their violins." Curiously Valentin was listed only by his family names, whereas Ramón's full name was given, even including a first name that he did not use. This reflected the personalities of the two men; I could easily imagine the conversation with the reporter, Ramón happily giving his full name, while Valentin secreted himself behind the smokescreen of his reserve, no doubt exasperating the reporter.

Their reminiscences about Italy were limited and typically concerned the pragmatic. The men had befriended a Mexico City native who was a student at the school, and he helped them immeasurably with their work. This seemed to be decisive in making their experience worthwhile. They most enjoyed the relaxed time in the back of the shop in Cremona, drinking beers and chatting. They had nearly completed two violins and carried these back with them to the Sierra. In Cremona they were visited by an American man who was a donor to the mission in Creel. He generously purchased high-quality violin-making tool kits for Ramón and Valentin. The sets, which cost around US$1,500 dollars, were useful, as they could be applied to other tasks besides making fine violins. But Ramón said that he had worried constantly about his family's well-being, and he was relieved when he returned home to find that all was well in Bacuséachi.

Conclusion

The aim of this chapter has been to venture an ethnographic description of a social space and describe how a number of actors negotiated its problems and possibilities. This was a field defined by an imagined divide between the modern and the traditional, the civilized and the indigenous, the Euro-American and the Indian, in which the meanings of those terms were variously interpreted by multiple agents, with differing aims and agendas. Because of its multivalence and mobility, the violin served as a linchpin, bringing these divergent intentions into a common frame. Ensnared in a web of cross-cutting agendas, each actor ended with imperfectly realized goals.

The role of the violin in this case suggests that many of the special qualities claimed for world music as a genre of popular music developed since the 1980s are, in fact, much older, and that the grounding of world music discourse, both among proponents and detractors, is equally problematic. Modernity, in general, is neither steamrolling its cultural others nor establishing a utopian space of expressive equality through music (Erlmann 1999; Slobin 1993). Both assessments miss a more foundational problem, namely, that these analytic categories are already implicated "on the ground" as political and cultural categories informing the actions of people we seek to understand. Capitalism, in other words, helps to produce the very spaces it then cordons off as Other (cf. Chakrabarty 2000). This process is negotiable at certain points, according to different kinds of value, and the negotiations are central to the expressive practices we seek to understand. Thus music does appear to be an increasingly important space where the difference is made audible, so to speak, and negotiable. The problem, however, should be addressed ethnographically rather than solely in theoretical or epistemological terms.[14] My approach has been to suggest that a musical instrument can be a key site in such dynamics, because it has a "social life" (Appadurai 1988; Turino 1983; Dawe 2001). Objects, signs, and musical forms (Bauman 1990; Steiner 1994; Feld 2000) can circulate among different fields or "regimes" of value, producing these fields and their borders in the process (Myers 2001).

It is precisely this multivalence and mobility that makes the violin a linchpin here. For the Catholic Mission in the Sierra, the violin was metonymic of a continuing attempt to "improve" and "civilize" Rarámuris while valorizing their more positive cultural attributes.[15] But in attempting to represent Rarámuri cultural (and spiritual) wealth to outsiders, and to legitimate the Mission as benefactor along the way, the Catholic cleric ends up reproducing the paternalism of the Church, as well as its more subtle racism, in the Sierra. For the Italians who came to Mexico under the auspices of the Church, the violin embodied the universal value of European high culture, such that the Rarámuri approach to the instrument could only hold a subordinate position, even as they sought to foster awareness of Rarámuri traditions and their ties to Europe.

A central problem for anthropologists stems from their location in a discourse about folk music and the violin.[16] As a practical matter they become brokers, as they attempt to mediate a series of fraught relationships between church, state, capital, and Rarámuris. The practical issues challenge theoretical concerns: deconstructing the essentialism of Fisher's enterprise, however tempting, is somewhat beside the point, as Rarámuris themselves have little interest in the truth value of Fisher's representations but care more about how they might be made productive from their point of view.[17] It is difficult indeed for anthropologists to escape an underlying complicity, as Appadurai (1996) has described it, in producing an image of the local, even as they attempt to serve as advocates for Rarámuris against institutionalized racism in its various forms.

For the Gringo entrepreneur, the violin became problematic insofar as it undercut his trenchantly, if hypocritically, anti-colonial discourse. Fisher posed as the true ally of the Rarámuris, even as his explicit identification with Victorian explorers revealed a certain imperialist nostalgia (Rosaldo 1989). The scheming of the entrepreneur, in this case, is a manifestation of what Feld (2000) characterizes as the "politics of exploration": to represent difference while relying on the very machinery that homogenizes and "primitivizes" the Other, pre-digesting it for consumption "at home." As Feld suggests, "like other sites of discovery, this one provokes the same anxious question: Is world music a form of artistic humiliation, the price primitives pay for attracting the attention of moderns, for gaining entry into their world of representation?" (ibid., 166).

The Rarámuris' use of the violin complicates the question: humiliation from one angle could resemble success from another. Hence, in Italy, learning to make a violin was less important than the journey itself and the chance to valorize Rarámuri traditions on a world stage, both of which could be converted, on returning to the Sierra, into greater prestige and perhaps greater wealth for one's own family. In El Paso Rarámuris could use the violin to make a subtle riposte to the dominant discourse of indigeneity on display at the museum. In this sense it reflected a more pugnacious stance, which came to light as Rarámuris conflicted with Fisher over the terms of their pay. The violin fits into an ethos of "*chingando al Gringo*"—essentially playing the system to invert its terms. By redefining themselves as culturally valuable they blunt their own domination as "blacks" and "animals." Rather than do away with the language of racial domination in the Sierra, Rarámuri men may only want to claim its efficacy for themselves.

Perhaps surprisingly, then, the Rarámuris might respond to Feld's query in the negative. Although Rarámuri voices appear muted in this narrative, one might ask why they participate in the first place. I suggest the answer lies in the effort of Rarámuri musicians to make local places as generative matrices, as locales that are reliably and productively "Rarámuri." This in itself is a contradictory endeavor, for it requires an engagement with the wider circulations of signs, commodities, and people. Hence, for Rarámuri men, the violin is metonymic of a more general aim of labor: to convert barren land to food, to claim the powers of "the colonizer" and reuse them in the making of productive local spaces, and, in the process, to make themselves Rarámuris (Noveck 2007).

Notes

1. I use the words "fiddle" and "violin" somewhat interchangeably in the chapter. The instrument is essentially the same; the terms reflect different approaches to playing it.

2. At the time this looked to me like an affectation, locating the Rarámuris in terms of North American indigenous groups, but a similar device was used to bound the dance

space in the dances for the Año Nuevo celebrations in Munérachi later that year. Lime was used instead of corn meal, however, since the latter would have been perceived as a waste of food.

3. Iannielo (1988) draws suggestive parallels between figures in Easter processions in the Italian Tyrol and the Matachines figures as danced in the Sierra Tarahumara. See also Acuña Delgado 2008.

4. When Ramón left Coyachique for El Paso he was dressed in clean and well-fitting Western clothing—jeans, T-shirt, baseball cap. Now, in the United States, his dress was impeccably traditional.

5. The church was built on the river, far below Coyachique, for the convenience of visiting priests from Batopilas. Rarámuris of Coyachique walk down to the church for the winter cycle fiestas held there, dance through the night, and then hike back up in the morning. When one Rarámuri teenager painted a map of the region on a rock face behind his house, he represented Coyachique with an image of its church.

6. The road has since been built in Coyachique.

7. The Spanish word *cielo* means both "heaven" and "sky."

8. At the time of this writing, Bodini is a national senator representing Cremona in Rome.

9. One of Fisher's numerous tourist publications placed Lumholtz's photo and biography on the final page, beside an equivalent biography of Fisher.

10. This is a generally important role in Rarámuri exchanges, such as running races.

11. A *noráwa* is a special or preferred trading partner

12. It turned out that Ramón had a long-running feud with a neighbor, so his worries partly concerned the safety of his family in his absence.

13. Valentin was playing on the similarity of the Spanish words for potato and Pope, *papa* and *Papa*.

14. Both Tsing (2000) and Stokes (2004) make a similar point, if from a different vantage, on the problems of ethnography given the conditions of global capitalism.

15. It is important, however, not to generalize this example to include the church as a whole. Speaking of the relationship between the Catholic Mission and the Rarámuris, Padre Javier "Pato" Avila once told me that "they've taught us more than we have taught them."

16. The aim of this essay is not to claim a privileged position for the anthropologist but rather to avoid the "ritual dissociation" with which some anthropologists approach other "outsiders" in the field (Rosaldo 1989, 107).

17. In the sexualized racial language of the Sierra, Rarámuris are not against "screwing" in itself but simply prefer not to be on the receiving end.

References

Acuña Delgado, Angel. 2008. "Matachines Tarahumaras. Reinventando la Tradicion." *Revista de Antropologia Experimental* 8 (2): 29–39.

Appadurai, Arjun. 1988. *The Social Life of Things: Commodities in Cultural Perspective.* Cambridge: Cambridge University Press.

———. 1996. *Modernity at Large: Cultural Dimensions of Globalization.* Minneapolis: University of Minnesota Press.

Bauman, Richard, and Charles L. Briggs. 1990. "Poetics and Performance as Critical Perspectives on Language and Social Life." *Annual Review of Anthropology* 19:59–88.

Chakrabarty, Dipesh. 2000. *Provincializing Europe: Postcolonial Thought and Historical Difference*. Princeton, NJ: Princeton University Press.

Dawe, Kevin. 2001. "People, Objects, Meaning: Recent Work on the Study and Collection of Musical Instruments." *Galpin Society Journal* 54:219–232.

Erlmann, Veit. 1999. *Music, Modernity, and the Global Imagination*. Oxford: Oxford University Press.

Feld, Steven. 2000. "A Sweet Lullaby for World Music." *Public Culture* 12:145–171.

Iannielo, Cristina. 1988. "Il Carnavale a Comelico Superiore." *Mondo Ladino* 12 (1–4): 77–135.

Krakauer, Jon. 1990. *Eiger Dreams: Ventures among Men and Mountains*. New York: Lyons and Burford.

Lumholtz, Carl. 1987 [1902]. *Unknown Mexico; Explorations in the Sierra Madre and Other Regions, 1890–1898*. Vol. 1. New York: Dover.

Myers, Fred R., ed. 2001. *The Empire of Things: Regimes of Value and Material Culture*. Santa Fe, NM: School of American Research.

Noveck, Daniel. 2007. "Playing Places: Indigeneity in the Rarámuri Violin." Ph.D. Dissertation, University of Chicago.

Rosaldo, Renato. 1989. "Imperialist Nostalgia." *Representations* 26:107–122.

Slobin, Mark. 1993. *Subcultural Sounds: Micromusics of the West*. Hanover, CT: Wesleyan University Press.

Steiner, Christopher Burghard. 1994. *African Art in Transit*. Cambridge: Cambridge University Press.

Stokes, Martin. 2004. "Music and the Global Order." *Annual Review of Anthropology* 33: 47–72.

Turino, Thomas. 1983. "The Charango and the 'Sirena': Music, Magic, and the Power of Love." *Latin American Music Review/Revista de Musica Latinoamericana* 4 (1): 81–119.

Weiner, Annette B. 1992. *Inalienable Possessions: The Paradox of Keeping-while-Giving*. Berkeley: University of California Press.

6

World Music Producers and the Cuban Frontier

Ariana Hernandez-Reguant

In the 1990s Cuban music experienced international visibility not seen since its prerevolutionary heyday in the 1940s and 1950s. This time, however, what triumphed in the world's major cities was not the latest dance craze emanating from the island but the traditional music of yesteryear—with a contemporary bent. Unlike in the earlier era, the music industry's major companies were not responsible for this popularity. This time, it was the work of small independent labels that combined their profit imperative with a mission, and a passion, to bring a diverse soundtrack to a booming multicultural Western world. The most famous Cuban music album of the decade, Ry Cooder's *Buena Vista Social Club,* introduced Cuban sounds in many homes already familiar with other musics from around the globe. This time, indeed, Cuban music was not marketed in Latin dance circles but within world music networks, framed within the intersecting histories of Cold War politics, market trends, and developments in the cultural industries both in Cuba and abroad.

In the early 1990s the opening of Cuba's economy to overcome the post-Soviet crisis intersected with the development and expansion of the world music industry. At that time the cosmopolitan multiculturalism then in vogue in the cities of the First World provided a market niche for the emergent independent labels devoted to the recording and marketing of non-Western and fusion sounds for Western ears. African music was first, and then Cuba opened up just at the right time. But as U.S. and multinational corporations shied away from operating on the island, in compliance with a three-decade-old U.S. embargo, the field was left to small enterprises from Europe, Latin America, and elsewhere with few stakes in the United States. These companies were marked by extreme flexibility, autonomy, and mobility, catering to increasingly segmented and specialized audiences. In

111

foreign lands these labels were represented by individual producers who, whether they owned the label themselves or worked freelance, had the independence required to act decisively far away from home. These individuals, rather than aloof corporate executives, came to be seen as the faces of the global economy in many parts of the world. It is their stories this chapter seeks to unravel. In showing their enormous impact in the international marketing of Cuban popular music in the 1990s and beyond, their professional trajectories provide a lens into cultural commerce and globalization as more capricious, fragmentary, and fortuitous than is usually presented.

There was something unique about the way in which these music producers operated in foreign lands. They were neither anthropologists nor members of a diasporic community with long-standing ties to the particular place but nor were they tourists or business travelers with no emotional attachment. Always in search of new frontiers, these producers were the contemporary equivalent of old colonial traders, who merged their love of music and adventure with a determination to succeed in a crowded and increasingly fragmented market. They fit the definition of "cultural brokers" developed by Steiner (1994) for African art dealers and intermediaries, who would both coach the producers and guide the prospective publics. In this case, they provided the world music industry with an imprint of both connoisseurship and progressive politics, and pursued a balance between cultural altruism and the need for profit. They were invested in marketing a cultural authenticity that only they were able to retrieve, yet often imposed the collaboration of Western musicians and arrangers in order to achieve a sound that would at once be exotic and recognizable. They thrived on cultural difference, making a living as both cultural brokers and business intermediaries, translating Cuban culture and music to their home audience and skillfully dealing with various socialist and capitalist bureaucracies. Yet they also presented themselves as artists, not only because they may also have been musicians but because their individual instinct, sensibility, and talent was the basis for their ability to set trends and select art that appealed to, and thus shaped, the cultural tastes of global urban middle classes hungry for new products.

In Cuba they cultivated an image of cosmopolitanism, adapting to local ways and using their individual charms as well as their foreign citizenship strategically to acquire social capital and successfully navigate the cumbersome Cuban bureaucracy, always distrustful of foreigners' motives. These producers often displayed a vague sympathy for the Cuban revolutionary regime so that their business would be perceived there as friendly, but they were not so politically committed as to alienate prospective buyers back home. Simultaneously outsiders and insiders, they constituted a particular kind of cosmopolitan subject, one that wanted to lay low and blend in. To borrow from Ulf Hannerz (1990, 241): "They want to be participants, or at least, do not want to be too readily identifiable within a crowd of . . . locals in their home territory. They want to be able to sneak backstage rather than being confined to front stage areas." Unlike anthropologists, however, they sought to take advantage of their foreign status, turning their mobility and multinational business contacts into capital while in Cuba. For instance, they relied on their privilege as foreigners in Cuba during the Special Period, when a double economy kept most Cubans in dire poverty while allowing foreigners to maintain a high standard of living. At the same time they prided themselves on their insider knowledge, gaining recognition at home as Cuba experts abroad, while achieving status in Cuba as sympathetic entrepreneurs who would help launch Cuban arts into the international arena.

As they progressed from making musical compilations out of existing Cuban catalogues to coordinating original recordings, some of these producers developed sentimental ties with the island and returned often. They became fascinated with the music, culture, and society of a country that had just opened its doors to foreign entrepreneurship, and they learned to negotiate with the cumbersome, unpredictable Cuban socialist bureaucracy and its associated legal regime in ways that large corporations would not—and not just for fear of U.S. sanctions but because they found it more profitable to leave that work to the independents and, if anything, step in at a later stage. This is not to suggest that independent producers would be assured success. In fact, those who specialized almost exclusively in Cuban music, and who established offices in Havana, were not as successful as those who maintained their autonomy from the Cuban bureaucracy and eventually moved on to other frontiers around the vast world.

This chapter offers a historical tour through the kinds of engagements that foreign producers, linked to the emerging world music industry, developed with Cuban music and the Cuban socialist infrastructure since the mid- to late 1980s, leading to the smashing success of *Buena Vista Social Club* in the world market at the end of the nineties. On the one hand, their prior musical and business experience in other parts of the world, most notably West Africa, determined the type of sound that would become internationally recognized as Cuban as well as the marketing images associated with that sound. On the other hand, their modus operandi as small-business entrepreneurs, artistic curators, and cultural brokers inspired a new generation of music producers in Cuba who were able to impact the development of a state-owned yet flexible industry out of a stale top-down socialist bureaucracy that chastised the role of cultural intermediaries. The following pages detail these developments, from music producers' encounter with Cuban sounds in Africa to their licensing, recording, and marketing of Cuban music in the 1990s.

Cuban Music and World Music

The market for Cuban music shrunk dramatically during the early years of the Cuban Revolution. U.S. labels and music editors, which controlled the sector up until then, left Cuba, and, since 1961, a trade embargo against the island closed the United States to the import of Cuban music, recorded or live. Spain, historically, had been another important outlet, but its fascist government was not sympathetic toward the new Cuban regime. Furthermore, the nationalization and bureaucratization of the music industry by the revolutionaries did not help matters. Cuban-made records hardly found international distribution beyond small solidarity organizations and exceptional licensing agreements with sympathetic labels. The Finnish Love Records was probably the most effective. Thanks to Finland's privileged relations with the communist bloc, it diversified its large catalogue, comprised mostly of Finnish rock and protest-song music, with materials from those countries, including Lenin's speeches. Throughout the 1970s Love Records licensed several LPs from Cuba's state label EGREM and also issued new recordings by Cuban groups playing in Finland such as Omara Portuondo (in 1974) and Paquito d'Rivera (in 1976).[1] Overall, between the early 1960s and the mid-1970s, international tours beyond the socialist countries or pro-communist and solidarity events were few and far between for Cuba's traditional music ensembles. Only sporadically, the most famous bands from the prerevolutionary era, such as the Aragon Orchestra, continued to tour internationally, beyond the socialist bloc.

For a few years, in the second half of the 1970s, a thaw in U.S.–Cuban relations during the Carter administration facilitated musical exchanges between the two countries. Many U.S. jazz, rock, and salsa musicians traveled to Cuba from 1977 on and jammed with local musicians there, often producing collaborative recordings. Dizzy Gillespie played a key role in bringing American musicians to Cuba, including Stan Getz and Ry Cooder, and bringing Cuban jazz musicians to Europe and the United States, raising the interest of the majors in the industry.[2] U.S. music critics, television producers, record executives, and musicians were able to visit as official guests of the state music company EGREM, which treated them to numerous auditions and jam sessions (Palmer 1988). In 1979 the CBS-sponsored Havana Jam Festival brought a wealth of American pop musicians to Cuba, including Billy Joel, Kris Kristofferson, Weather Report, and the Fania All Stars—without its prime singer, Cuban exile Celia Cruz—to play with Cuba's foremost bands such as Irakere and the Aragón Orchestra (Rockwell 1979). At the same time Cuban groups traveled to the United States, typically under the banner of cultural exchange.[3] This rapprochement was short lived, however, as the Reagan administration curtailed exchanges and reestablished hostilities. In addition, loud protests, commercial boycotts, and picket lines on the part of Cuban exiles threatened the careers of the Latin musicians who had played in Cuba and scared off others from doing so, as well as intimidating the audiences for the Cuban bands that ventured into the United States during these years.[4]

Africa was where Cuban dance music maintained a steady popularity, particularly in the former French colonies. Since the 1920s Cuban son music had often been mimicked by local musicians, and the Cuban dance craze of the 1940s and 1950s influenced an entire generation of musicians and dancers throughout the region, consolidating a long-term fan base; Abidjan and Dakar, for instance, became known as strongholds for Cuban dance music (Steward 1999). The EMI-issued GV collection of hundreds of 78s Latin music recordings from the *Gramophone* and *Victor* catalogues was sold throughout West Africa until the late 1950s and were played profusely at local stations. Most important, Cuban music shaped the development of national music in many countries, from Congo to Senegal (Shain 2002; Steward 1999; Topp Fargion 2005; White 2002). After the Cuban Revolution, Cuban music, as well as New York salsa, was issued by local labels from Congo, Mali, and elsewhere. Cuban orchestras like Jorrin (in 1965) and Aragon (numerous times through the seventies) toured the continent to great acclaim, playing in the best venues, and receiving a personal welcome from presidents such as Sekou Touré of Guinea and Marien Ngouabi of Brazzaville, who claimed to be their fans (Bonet 1972; Marrero 2001).[5]

The African policies of the Cuban Revolution further ensured Cuba's cultural presence in the region. In particular, growing numbers of Cuban-educated African students returned home with the latest sounds and dance trends from the island. Specifically those who studied music contributed to the development of an Africanized Cuban sound in their respective countries. This was the case, for instance, of a group of Malian musicians who spent eight years in Cuba from the mid-sixties on, and who, under the leadership of the flutist and composer Boncana Maiga, formed the dance orchestra Maravillas de Mali, which was immensely popular in the 1970s in many parts of West Africa. At the same time entrepreneurial producers from Africa often traveled to Cuba in order to license and reissue Cuban recordings in their countries, as well as to produce new ones. One of these was Ivory Coast producer Raoul Diomandé, who was in Cuba in 1979 when Fania All Stars played there. Inspired by their energy, he piloted the formation of a similar Areito All Stars (Areito was Cuba's main record label) with the idea of launching the group in Africa. The band included jazz players Arturo Sandoval and Paquito d'Rivera, as well as traditional musicians such as Rubén González and Pio Leyva (the latter featured in the *Buena Vista Social Club* project in the 1990s). They recorded several albums, and although they never made it to Africa, their improvisational work has been remembered since and was recently remastered and reissued by Nonesuch, the same world music label that distributed *Buena Vista Social Club* in the United States (Sweeney 2001). Through the 1980s and 1990s African music labels such as Sonodisc as well as West African independent producers continued to distribute or license Cuban LPs, which often garnered gold records for Cuban musicians, including Barbarito Diez and Pio Leyva, both very famous in the region.[6] In the early 1990s the New York–based Africando, with Boncana Maiga among other African and Caribbean musicians, was the latest incarnation of the African fusion of Cuban music (Steward 1999).

Many European producers, journalists, and travelers became familiar with the contemporary sounds of Cuba precisely in Africa, not only because of the wide circulation of Cuban music there but also because of the Cuban substrata to much

African popular music. African clubs and DJs in Paris and other European cities also contributed to the popularization of Cuban dance music in Europe, as they would play it along with the latest hits from the continent.[7] It was only a matter of time before the African music boom in the early 1980s would pull Cuban music along, offering it alternative channels to those foreclosed by the multinational Latin music industry. Specialty record stores like the London-based Sterns began to carry Cuban materials, often issued by African labels, as well as Latin music from the United States.[8] As world music began to take hold as a marketing category, Cuban music was included within it, no longer confined as a "tourist curiosity in hidden-away racks."[9]

Britain, and especially London, home to most of the emerging world music labels, became a hub for Cuban music.[10] As a result of earlier contacts between British musicologists and journalists, such as Lucy Durán, and Cuban institutions, like the Center for Music Development (CIDMUC), London became an important post for Cuban bands.[11] Indeed, the broad array of musicians playing in Britain since the mid-1980s on, often sharing the stage with African groups at world music festivals throughout the continent, included traditional groups (Celina González and Septeto Nacional de Ignacio Piñeiro), dance orchestras (Los Van Van, Rumbavana, and the Orquesta Revé), standard son groups (Sierra Maestra), and Afro-Cuban folk and fusion ensembles (Sintesis, Los Muñequitos de Matanzas, Afro-Cuba, Lázaro Ros, and Carlos Embale) (Sweeney 1989b).[12] For some of them, these tours resulted in new recordings, either live or in studio, with European independent labels.[13]

A 1989 newspaper article credited "the recent heightened profile of Cuban music in the UK" to "a small number of enthusiasts who have succeeded in prising out of Havana a number of groups regarded by the Cuban authorities as insufficiently sophisticated and international to represent Cuba in the West" (Sweeney 1989c). Indeed, until this time the Cuban cultural apparatus had been more concerned with promoting "high" culture, as evidence of revolutionary education, than popular music. Although, at least since the late 1970s, protest songs (Nueva Trova) and jazz had enjoyed institutional support, popular music, including rumba and son, was marginalized until the tourist and cultural industries grew and created a demand for it. In the 1990s the opening of new clubs and hotels, the revamping of the EGREM monopoly to facilitate its international operation, and reforms in travel restrictions and labor laws all provided opportunities for a new generation of music graduates to play both at home and abroad.

In the United States, too, Cuban popular music began to enjoy some media exposure in the late 1980s, thanks both to the emerging world music industry there and to a fortuitous 1988 amendment to the U.S. embargo, allowing for the circulation of Cuban cultural materials including live and recorded music, provided that their goal was eminently educational and cultural rather than commercial. While music licenses were permitted, this was not the case for new recordings if they entailed paying royalties to Cuban residents. It was thus possible to distribute original Cuban recordings in the United States as long as they were issued abroad by a non–U.S. party. These limitations did not help raise the interest of the majors, leaving the sector to small entrepreneurs linked to the new world music scene, mostly in college towns and cosmopolitan cities like New York and Boston. Hence, although Cuban music was not played on Spanish-language radio for commercial and political reasons, it was regularly featured in independent stations throughout the country as well as on National Public Radio's *Afropop* show, which started in 1988 and was initially devoted to music of Africa for an urban Anglophone audience—later adding the African diaspora.[14] The Cuban musical connection with contemporary, rather than traditional, African music was often highlighted by concert critics as well. For instance, when Havana's Cabaret Tropicana show was presented in the United States, the *New York Times* explained that the project was undertaken by a promoter who specialized in African music and had become interested in it while in Zaire through his acquaintance with the Cuban ambassador there. In referring to the show's aesthetics, however, the journalist lamented that they were "closer to Las Vegas than to Lagos" (Pareles 1988a, 1988b).

This distance between Las Vegas and Lagos—between North America and Africa—was precisely what the early world music productions were aiming to bridge. Though not denying Cuban music's roots in Africa (see Pacini Hernandez, 1998), they chose to emphasize, instead, African music's roots in Cuba. These producers, that is, took contemporary African music as a starting point, tracing a genealogy back to Cuba as its source. Unlike historical musicologists typically interested in tracing the African influences in Cuban music, these world music producers found inspiration in the identification of Cuban elements in African pop fusion. Thus, while Cuban music was incorporated into African grooves, back in Cuba it maintained the reputation of having national authenticity. In this way world music marketing differed from that of the Latin music industry in proposing a different type of globalization. While Latin music traditionally stressed hybridity and transnationality as markers of a pan-American community whose borders were to be overcome, world music proposed a mosaic-type map where national differences were upheld rather than blurred through the particular interactions and hybridizations between forms. This was, in any case, the starting point for a foray into Cuban music as world music.

The Producer as a Musical Curator

A 1985 LP titled *Viva el Ritmo, Cuba Baila* was the first to appear in the emerging world music context. It was issued by a new British label, Earthworks, mostly devoted to compilations of contemporary musical genres from Africa. The founder of Earthworks, South African expatriate Donald "Jumbo" Vanrenen, had become familiar with Cuban music in Africa and also through the Love Records catalogue.[15] The album's musical selection included dance tracks by Cuba's most popular bands (Son 14, Los Karachi, Irakere, and Los Van Van, among others), all licensed from the Cuban state music company EGREM. Both liner notes and cover art presumed an audience new to Cuban music and yet politically progressive. The commentary included general information on the specific musical genres represented (e.g., guaganó, conga, and rumba), while leaving out the names of the musicians and composers, the specific instrumentation, and other recording data. The album's front cover featured a photograph of a small-town parade of men in straw hats playing acoustic guitars and handheld percussion instruments—an image altogether unrelated to the recording itself. In turn, the back cover featured the slogan "Venceremos" ("We shall win"), referring to the Latin American revolutionary struggles for justice and independence, along with a note crediting the support of the Britain-Cuba Resource Center, an international solidarity organization devoted to promoting "understanding of the Cuban Revolution and friendship between the people of Britain and Cuba," and dedicated to, among other things, coordinating brigades of British volunteers to work in building projects and rural harvests in Cuba.

Viva el Ritmo sold relatively well, all its thousand copies, and inaugurated a string of similar compilations on the same and other labels. They all featured eclectic selections, statements in favor of solidarity with Cuba, and didactic liner notes.[16] This preference for musicological information over the usual minutia of recording and musicians' lineups, of interest to music buffs, hinted at the neophyte character of its prospective buyers as well as world music's own bias against recognizing individual authorship of traditional music (see Feld 2000).[17] Instead, these productions assigned a central role to the music producer, normally employed by the label and unrelated to the musicians in the recording. In a sector where the creation of stars out of non-Western musicians with often unpronounceable names seemed daunting, the music producer began to figure prominently as both a music connoisseur and cultural broker, who could garner the public's confidence. Following on the footsteps of musicians such as George Harrison and Paul Simon, who, respectively had made Indian and South African music intelligible to Western audiences, Peter Gabriel in Britain, David Byrne in the United States, and Santiago Auserón in Spain introduced their fans to Cuban music. Although in some cases they collaborated with Cuban musicians to produce hybrid sounds, they all worked, as both musical curators and cultural intermediaries, to present Cuban music in its original form to a wide audience.

A compilation of songs by Cuba's Orquesta Revé was one of Real World's earliest releases, set to coincide with the band's 1989 European tour. The label had been founded one year earlier by Peter Gabriel with the goal of disseminating music from the five continents, which for cataloguing purposes were divided into nine color-coded regions: Africa, North America, South America, Asia 1, Asia 2, Oceania, the Caribbean, Europe, and the Indian Subcontinent. The label's marketing presented music as a sort of global energy brought together by a mosaic of local particularities. In the Revé album, for instance, Elio Revé had wanted the cover to display the band's picture (Sweeny 1989a), but, instead, it featured a NASA photograph capturing a light spectrum over the Pacific Ocean "just before sunrise," suggesting a transcendental immensity in which the music participated. The liner notes, in tune with Earthworks' practice, were written by experts and abounded in the specific history of the changüí, the genre played by Revé, and its African and Caribbean connections.

At about the same time Luaka Bop was founded in the United States by former Talking Heads singer David Byrne as a vehicle to present to his fans his own music as a solo artist, as well as the international music he liked—which Byrne carefully labeled as "ethnic," not "folk" (Morris 1991). After recording a Talking Heads album, *Naked* (1988), in collaboration with African and Caribbean musicians, Byrne released *Rei Momo* (1989) on his new label, in collaboration with Latin musicians including Cuban exile singer Celia Cruz, Tito Puente, Ruben Blades, and others. These collaborations generated an interest in African and Latin American music, which would lead to several compilations of licensed music from various countries, beginning with Brazil, and continuing with three albums of Cuban music, released in the early 1990s.[18]

The first was an anthology of Silvio Rodriguez's protest songs, which received mixed press reviews for their outmoded support for socialist movements and did not sell very well (Billboard 1991). The two that followed, *Dancing with the Enemy: Dance Hits from the '60s and '70s* (1991) and *Diablo al Infierno* (1992), were compilations of songs by different bands and did much better: the first was hailed by *New York Times* music critic Peter Watrous (1992) as one of his favorite twelve albums of the year. Although these albums did not openly support the revolutionary regime, they included statements in favor of cultural exchanges with Cuba. For instance, in the text on the back cover of *Dancing with the Enemy,* the question was posed as to whether music could be communist or capitalist, while *Diablo al Infierno* contained a plea to reestablish communication with the Cuban people, at the time suffering the hardships of the Special Period:

> Now is a time of tremendous creativity as well as tremendous suffering in Cuba. You can feel the electricity in the street. A new generation has come of age and is feeling its way as best it can. It's articulate, literate, passionate, and fiercely musical.

The novelty, for a U.S. release, was to be found in the third album, *Diablo al Infierno* (1992), which included the latest hits from the island and not all licensed from previous recordings: some actually were recorded live by Byrne's associate and *Afropop* field producer Ned Sublette.[19] Hence Byrne and Sublette did not merely deal with the Cuban bureaucracy long-distance but spent time in Cuba traveling and seeking to understand daily life on the island and to grasp the music that moved young people.[20] Their choices were guided both by their own observations in the field and a preconceived notion of how the final product should sound. According to Byrne (Luaka Bop n.d.):

> The Cuban govenment was pretty helpful—it's their record label after all. . . . They assumed at first we'd want all the "classics"—Beny Moré etc—but we were interested just as much in the little side roads that this music occasionally took. The a capella rhythm section of Grupo Vocal Sampling and the cool doo-wop sounds of Los Zafiros . . . and anything with a wah-wah, an early synth sound or Farfisa organ was of special interest.

Byrne and Sublette, both accomplished musicians, saw themselves not only as music curators, even though at that point their role consisted in selecting existing music rather than shaping a sound in the making. They also viewed themselves as leaders of taste, and also cultural intermediaries, seeking to shape audiences' sensibilities back home with regard to other cultures—in fact, Luaka Bop's website included a merchandise page with all sorts of ethnic items for sale. Byrne's label indeed continued along that path, building an extremely diverse world music catalogue. In contrast, Ned Sublette went on to found his own label in New York City, Qbadisc, devoted exclusively to Cuban music, mostly EGREM licenses. He returned to the island many times, establishing a lasting collaboration with Cuban musicians and producers, organizing U.S. tours for Cuban groups, and consolidating a reputation as one of North America's leading experts on Cuban music. Yet his label did poorly, as it did not transcend the small circle of diehard Cuban music fans.

Around that time, in Spain, the leader of the iconic pop band Radio Futura, Santiago Auserón, had been interested in traditional Cuban music for years (de la Nuez 2006). He first went to Cuba in 1990, and with the help of Cuban musicologists he licensed material from EGREM for a series of CDs on traditional Cuban son.[21] Recalling the success of previous compilations on other Spanish labels, Auserón was able to convince a multinational company, Ariola-BMG Spain, to produce what would have been a series of fourteen albums, under the title of *La Semilla del Son* ("The Seeds of Son")—all consisting of material licensed from EGREM.[22] The first was a double compilation of assorted Cuban traditional groups like Matamoros, Beny Moré and Compay Segundo (including the latter's version of a song, "Chan Chan," that *Buena Vista Social Club* would make internationally famous). The recordings, however, sounded more like musicological finds than contemporary sounds that could appeal to young people, and the label discontinued the series. Nonetheless the popularity of Cuban music began to take off. A number of traditional Cuban music concerts and festivals took place over the following years.

For instance, in 1994 a week-long flamenco and son festival brought traditional son groups from Cuba to Sevilla, in Southern Spain, including Omara Portuondo and Compay Segundo, whose vitality and advanced age astonished audiences and the press (Cantalapiedra 1994). At the same time many Spanish rock, pop, jazz, and flamenco musicians began to collaborate with Cuban musicians and experiment with fusion sounds—including Auserón himself, under the stage name Juan Perro.[23]

All these works effectively paved the way for the later success of Cuban music in Europe and the United States. They also reinforced the role of the musical producer as both an artist and a connoisseur; all the aforementioned producers were musicians and had deep knowledge of the music they were presenting to the public. They were also cultural intermediaries as well as intuitive trend setters who opened new ground rather than merely following a predictable marketing path. Their main hindrance was not rooted in their artistic and business instincts but in the political realities of U.S.–Cuban relations, whose underpinnings they tended to underestimate.

When Jumbo Vanrenen (from Earthworks) signed Cuba's prime dance band Los Van Van on behalf of Mango Records (the world music division of Island Records) for several albums, he did not think that the Latin music industry would actively impede their dissemination. Los Van Van's first album with Mango, *Songo* (released in LP in 1988 and in CD the following year), was recorded in studio in London with one of Latin music's most famous recording engineers, Jon Fausty. Yet the band was not allowed to tour the United States, and one roadblock after another impeded the album's distribution, air play, and media access. Without entrée to the North American Latin music market, sales were slow, and the relationship between the label and the band was severed. Making matters worse, the musical exuberance of Cuban dance music was too difficult for neophyte European dancers who preferred U.S. salsa—a problem that other labels encountered years later when seeking to commercialize timba music in Europe.

The main option for labels still interested in commercializing Cuban music was to continue to license existing Cuban recordings and, if anything, remaster them to obtain a higher-quality sound. According to Sweeney (1993), eighty to one hundred such licensing agreements were signed in 1991 and 1992 alone. But the repertoire was limited, and sometimes the same materials were licensed to more than one label. A few courageous entrepreneurs initiated a working relationship with the Cuban bureaucracy and with record bands there, and in some cases opened offices in Havana, with varying degrees of success. By the end of the decade, those who set up shop in Cuba and whose catalogues focused exclusively on Cuban music—usually popular dance music—had gone bankrupt. Only those who came and went, and whose catalogues were not solely focused on Cuban music, ultimately succeeded.[24]

From Field to Studio

By 1990 producer and musicologist Eduardo Llerenas had a two-decade-long experience with field recordings of rural and indigenous music in Mexico and the Caribbean, and he had made a dozen trips and many more field recordings of traditional music throughout Cuba. Like other ethnomusicologists before him, he was able to obtain the support of the Center for the Development of Cuban Music (CIDMUC).[25] But, unlike others, he returned again and again, embodying the transition from ethnomusicology to world music in terms of both modus operandi and marketing goals (Feld 2000). His first record label was Musica Tradicional (Traditional Music) and was a home-based operation to issue the musical archive he had accumulated over the years. There Llerenas released his first Cuban album, a double CD of traditional son music from the central and eastern regions of the island, accompanied by erudite liner notes he wrote himself. Shortly afterward, in 1992, he founded Discos Corason with his new wife, Mary Farquharson—whom he had met at an African music festival. Farquharson, a British promoter of African music, had been an active player in world music circles in 1980s Britain, cofounding the World Circuit label (which later produced *Buena Vista Social Club*). Corasón, based in Mexico City, sought to produce music from Cuba, Mexico, and the African diaspora, but rather than focusing on the creation of stars, it sought to achieve an imprint sound that would appeal both to purists and urban consumers with eclectic tastes. According to Llerenas, "people go looking for Corasón, and not for the artists."[26] That particular sound stemmed from the producer's criteria, which was exerted during the studio sessions. For instance, in his Cuba work, Llerenas, in order to maintain a distinct and consistent sound, typically used the same studio and worked with the same recording engineer.

The label's location in Mexico City allowed it to skirt the political issues faced by its Anglo-American counterparts. It also made the label's approach less parochial than that of some of the European and North American world music labels, because in this case the audience did not need to be educated about remote cultures. Liner notes were substantial and included musicological descriptions and in-depth historical background, yet they did not appear naïve to the most erudite buyers. They also included information that experts would appreciate, such as musicians' lineups and studio recording data. In addition, the covers were discreet, with no need to scream out a product that relied on the quality of its content. Corasón's first Cuban album—Cuarteto Patria's *A Una Coqueta,* which included Eliades Ochoa's version of "Chan Chan" later re-recorded in *Buena Vista Social Club*—was released in 1993, and between then and 2005 the label issued more than twenty original Cuban albums and its catalogue had expanded to include not only Mexican and Cuban music but African and Gypsy as well.[27] It also had become World Circuit's distributor in Mexico—all of which strengthened Corasón's reputation within the world music sector. Corasón was uniquely able to carve a market niche not only in Mexico but in Europe and the United States as well, where it had a fluent distribution.

Meanwhile two projects of a different sort, also born out of the world music experience, attempted a more radical intervention—the Vieja Trova Santiaguera and the Buena Vista Social Club. These newcomers sought to regenerate Cuban traditional music in one stroke by repackaging it for new audiences in Europe and elsewhere. Both projects involved forming new bands with traditional musicians, something that would not have been possible a few years earlier because of strict Cuban labor laws that treated musical bands as labor units and made it difficult for a musician to switch bands or start a new one. In both projects, the producer had an instrumental role in crafting a new sound for an old music. Both were multimedia enterprises, combining audio releases with international tours, accompanying publications, and full-length documentary films. Most important, they created a sentimental narrative, fostering empathy for the musicians and a longing for the period the music re-created. Because the music was traditional and the musicians of advanced age and ostensibly out of fashion, the story of how their collaboration came about re-created a kind of nostalgia that was not for the consumption of the Cuban exiles who famously dwelled on it but precisely for those who had never known it but wished to imagine it in all its purity.

The second of these projects, Buena Vista Social Club, topped every element of the first. Whereas Vieja Trova Santiaguera remained a modest affair, Buena Vista sold millions of albums around the world. The two projects were similar in many ways: both entailed rounding up old musicians to play old standards; both stressed nostalgia, authenticity, and survival; and both relied on the strong command of a non-Cuban producer. Only Buena Vista, however, conformed to the world music guarantee of quality by using a well-known musician to produce the music (and later a well-known filmmaker), linking Africa and the African diaspora in its marketing, and having a solid distribution and promotion network.

Production as Performance

The Vieja Trova Santiaguera project took off in 1993, when a Spanish entrepreneur, Manuel Domínguez, saw in Cuban music the opportunity to save his struggling business and launch a new world music record label, Nubenegra. Santiago Auserón's collection, although discontinued by the label, had been well received by the press. Domínguez had experience with Cuban music from his years as manager of a folk music label and believed that the Spanish market was ripe for a major Cuban act.[28] With the help of an associate, he rounded up five traditional musicians from Santiago de Cuba—all but one had already appeared in Llerenas's earlier releases—and formed a new band, Vieja Trova Santiaguera. The band's first album was recorded in Havana and consisted of well-known standards, since the men had an otherwise limited repertoire (Domínguez 1998). The following year the band traveled to Spain and subsequently toured Europe, an experience documented in the film *Lágrimas Negras* (Herman Doltz 1997).

In Europe these musicians circulated in world music circles and were marketed as "living legends," anachronistic survivals of a bygone era that audiences now had the opportunity to witness. Their concerts opened with a brief biography of the musicians, highlighting their advanced age and humble beginnings in manual trades unrelated to music such as masonry and carpentry, upon which "the public would break into applause upon hearing such great biographies" (Domínguez 1998). In the film this contrast between their obscure lives in Cuba, where they were hardly recognized, and their acclaim in Europe's main concert halls translated into a superimposition of images and sounds, always stressing a rags-to-riches trajectory that almost did not happen. As Domínguez (1998) pointed out, these men were nothing in Cuba. There was no interest in their music to the point that even in a festival honoring traditional son music in their very home town, their faithful renditions were unappreciated in comparison with the contemporary experimentation of younger bands. Adding insult to injury, after a concert all vehicles were put to the service of younger musicians and their electric equipment, and the elders had no choice but to hitchhike home dragging their heavy instruments in the middle of the dark night. Thanks to European altruism and solidarity, these men were saved from oblivion in the eleventh hour. The story had all the necessary ingredients to elicit sympathy: the innocence, humility, and gratitude of the old men, the absence of any political context, the emotionality of the music, and the uplifting portrayal of old age.

Despite this imagery, the Vieja Trova Santiaguera project, as noted above, did not launch the musicians, the film producer, or the filmmaker to stardom. The film, for instance, was not distributed commercially, and eventually all the musicians returned home to their previous lives. The whole operation was a very low-budget affair. Domínguez was broke and could barely afford the musicians' food, in Europe or in Cuba. During recording sessions in Havana, for instance, Domínguez (1998) recalls that the elderly musicians were merely fed sugary water for breakfast and just a few shots of rum to help them get through the day. When traveling through Cuba they stayed in the inexpensive Communist Party hostels where Domínguez sneaked in without paying, and in Europe they shared rooms and traveled in old battered vans, which left their aging bodies sore and tired. Eventually one of the musicians left the group, and after producing two more CDs the project slowly died out. Subsequently Domínguez was able to sign two other Cuban groups for his label: the traditional son group, also from Santiago, Septeto Santiaguero, and the singer Omara Portuondo, who had collaborated with the Vieja Trova Santiaguera project and appeared singing duo in "Lágrimas Negras" and the bolero "Veinte Años," as she later did in *Buena Vista Social Club*. She would ultimately leave Nubenegra to join World Circuit, the *Buena Vista Social Club* label.

Thereafter the Nubenegra catalogue moved on to the music of other countries and continents, slowly building up a solid and diverse catalogue for a Spanish audience. Despite the modesty of this enterprise and marketing reach, Domínguez had introduced an approach akin to that in the pop and rock indies tying the music to an image and a narrative but also signing certain groups for more than one album, looking to build up a name. Following on his footsteps another label proved that his intuition had been right. It only needed the resources to go bigger.

Nick Gold, director of the London-based world music label World Circuit, knew that Cuban traditional music could have far greater sales.[29] According to World Circuit's website, he knew of Cuban music's enormous popularity in West Africa "from recordings by bands such as Orchestre Baobab . . . and from talking with such musicians as Ali Farka Touré.[30] Although the label was mostly devoted to African music, it had issued three Cuban CDs, two licensed from EGREM and the third recorded in London with the son group Sierra Maestra, led by Juan de Marcos.[31] Gold had also kept up with developments on the island through colleagues in the world music milieu such as Duran, Llerenas, and Farquharson. He was also familiar with Domínguez's Vieja Trova Santiaguera project—after all, the world music industry was a tight community of familiar faces gathered around a couple of small journals and trade fairs. In 1996, coached by Lucy Duran and Juan de Marcos (both with experience in Cuba and Africa), Gold decided to produce an album with Cuban and Malian musicians to be recorded in Cuba. He then enlisted Ry Cooder, a trained ethnomusicologist with a long history of collaborative recordings with musicians from around the world, including the famous Malian kora player Ali Farka Touré—a world music Grammy collaboration produced by World Circuit.[32] Cooder had been to Cuba previously as a member of Dizzy Gillespie's 1977 crew and at the time was collaborating with bassist Orlando "Cachaito" López and singer Pio Leyva, among others, in a recording for the Irish band The Chieftains' *Santiago* album, which went on to receive a world music Grammy award in 1997.[33] Thus unlike Domínguez and other earlier world music entrepreneurs, Gold hired a specific producer for this project, not only to curate the musical selection and oversee the arrangements but to actively collaborate in its performance and recording.

As reported on World Circuit's website, the African musicians never arrived in Cuba owing to "a saga of lost passports" (McGuire and Gold, n.d.). With the EGREM studios rented for two weeks, Cooder had to manage with what he had. In addition to the musicians already hired—such as Eliades Ochoa and Barbarito Diez, both very popular in Africa—de Marcos quickly rounded up a few others who were retired and therefore available, including Compay Segundo, Ruben Gonzalez, and Ibrahim Ferrer. The resulting album, *Buena Vista Social Club,* consisted of well-known Cuban standards, some of which had been recorded in the same version and the same or similar lineup by both Llerenas and Domínguez; these included Eliades Ochoa's very personal rendition of "El Cuarto de Tula" and "Chan

Chan," and Omara Portuondo's heartfelt interpretation of "Veinte Años."[34] But distinct in this album was Ry Cooder's intervention with his slide guitar, along with the minimal percussion played by his son, Joachim, and the mix achieved by the recording engineer Jerry Boys, who had worked with the Beatles and the Rolling Stones.[35] The resulting product, a contemporary packaging of traditional sounds, was a huge success.

Released in the summer of 1997, the album was marketed to a world music public that listened to National Public Radio and read the *New York Times* and the *New Yorker,* and for whom *Buena Vista Social Club* was the first Latin album they ever bought (Gonzalez 2000). In the United States the album was ignored by Spanish-language radio (Valdés 1999). Nonetheless, it quickly climbed the Billboard charts, and within three months it had sold 1.5 million copies worldwide—including the United States where it was distributed by Nonesuch. That year it received a Grammy Award as Best Tropical recording, further boosting sales. Meanwhile Ry Cooder had convinced Wim Wenders to join him in Havana to film the recording of a follow-up album.[36] *Buena Vista Social Club,* the film, followed *Lagrimas Negras* in terms of approach (emphasizing the musicians' age and humble pasts) and narrative devices (interlacing flashbacks to their quaint Cuban environment and the world's concert halls), including similar scenes such as the elders' awkward arrival in the big city (in one case London and in the other New York) and Omara Portuondo's emotional duo. Wim Wenders's signature, however, ensured the film's circulation. In just its initial three-month run in U.S. art houses, it grossed $38 million. An Oscar nomination in 1999 ensured its worldwide commercial distribution and subsequent DVD release.

The film furthered World Circuit's marketing discourse. The participating musicians were presented as treasures on the verge of extinction that, thanks to Ry Cooder and Wim Wenders, were given the chance of their lives: their last possible opportunity to find fame and applause. Most important, it emphasized the central role of the music producer as a rescuer of disappearing cultures as well as a broker between the cultural producers located in remote places and their publics in the world's metropolis. The film was not an ethnographic documentary but instead a road movie—and not only because it was produced by a company named Road Movie Filmproduktion. Rather than providing historical, political, and socioeconomic context about the culture of Cuba, it focused on a main character who was also the narrator: Ry Cooder. The story was presented from his perspective, and it was to him that the musicians he discovered narrated their lives. As final credits roll over the group's final encore at Carnegie Hall, it is Cooder who is the last to leave the stage, basking in the farewell given him by acclaiming New York audiences.

In both the film and the associated marketing campaign, any contentious issue was avoided. Political references to the Cuban Revolution or the U.S. embargo were minimized, and potentially controversial subjects such as race relations were hardly mentioned, even though the very title of these productions, *Buena Vista Social Club,* referred to a segregated venue for Afro-Cubans in the 1950s. In *Buena Vista,* references to the Afro-Cuban past are minimal, and blackness is "positive" and "embraceable," to quote Hélan Page (1997, 102*)*. In various television interviews, Ry Cooder compared singer Ibrahim Ferrer to cross-over crooner Nat King Cole and the entire group as a bunch of Louis Armstrongs, thus stressing not only their virtuosity but their ability to transcend social and cultural differences. The allusion to race was therefore oblique, with the narrative emphasis placed instead on age (Tush 1998). Old age place these men in an earlier era from which they had not quite awoken—Wenders, for instance, in explaining that they would not recognize the image of John F. Kennedy, claimed that they were living in a sort of bubble or time warp. Their pre-capitalist lives brought them a humanity and an innocence that was endearing to the jaded Western audiences. Singer and composer Compay Segundo, for instance, born in 1907, was described by Cooder as a "nineteenth-century man," whose mind and aesthetics were formed before radio existed, just as Havana was described as a city untouched by commercialism (Koppel 1999; Newshour with Jim Lehrer 1999; Rose 1999).[37]

As was the case with the Vieja Trova Santiaguera, the point was to allow Western audiences to enjoy Cuban music without necessarily having to turn aesthetic enjoyment into an ideological statement. In other words, it allowed them to reinvent a relationship with the island based on a sentiment that Moreiras (1998, 31) has termed "an orientalism of the heart"—a phenomenon of empathy in which "an entire class of Latinamericanist solidarity workers and left-wing intellectuals, as well as melodramatic citizens in general, are indicted at the level of affect." Within this framework, Cuba was presented as inhabiting a sort of "timeless eternal"—to use Said's expression. Even as Havana, by the mid-1990s, was inundated by tourists, traffic, dance bands, and entrepreneurs seeking to beat the absent embargo-abiding U.S. companies, the film production notes (1998) described the island as "an exotic place sealed off from the ultra-noisy world where most of us live," and both Wenders and Cooder, in interviews with the press, referred to Havana as living in a time warp, and to the musicians as a dying species from a purer yet vanishing era (Watrous 1999).

The Cuban musicians went on to record solo albums with the World Circuit label, while Ry Cooder moved on to other ventures, not without having to pay a fine to the Treasury Department for breaking the embargo.[38] But the legacy of *Buena Vista Social Club* endured. The album kept on selling. By 2005 the initial release had sold five million copies worldwide, and the ninety-some-year-old Compay Segundo had become a household name in many countries.[39] For audiences around the world unfamiliar with Cuban music, *Buena Vista Social Club* defined the sound that would count as properly Cuban.[40] In Cuba, too, the production was not without consequence. Although initially resented in music circles for its focus on ruin and decay, and its indifference toward contemporary musical and social developments, it nonetheless led to a revalorization of traditional son music. Unlike dance genres preferred by the island's youth, such as timba, traditional son was uncontroversial (its lyrics were innocuous and its aesthetic prude), in addition to having an obvious export potential. Inseparable from the album was the new recognition bestowed to the musical producer as an artist in his or her own right. Hence, in Cuba, a small state-controlled infrastructure of musical production and commercialization was refashioned following the model provided by world music in terms of the centrality awarded to the music producer. Thus, despite a socialist tradition that did not valorize the work of cultural intermediaries, the musical producer's work became fundamental, not only in curatorial terms but for its creativity and intuition. The musical producer, not the musician, was ultimately responsible for an imprint sound that would appeal to audiences around the world.

Conclusion

Through the 1990s the world music industry, mostly based in Europe and North America, expanded its reach to the most remote regions of the world. It marketed traditional sounds to urban audiences and fostered musical collaborations between Western and non-Western musicians. What was peculiar about this apparent globalization story was that it required the fragmentation and autonomy of its actors in order to circumvent the numerous roadblocks imposed on the circulation of cultural commodities, from international sanctions and country-led embargoes allegedly geared to promote democracy in foreign regions to the quick turnover of cultural and entertainment fads among the world's urban consumers. In this context, the intervention of the world music industry in a small state-controlled Cuban music infrastructure resulted in two important developments. The first concerned the definition and conceptualization of Cuban music in the world. Specifically, a by now standard Black Atlantic narrative of musical circulation which situated Africa at the genesis underwent a significant reformulation, for Cuban music came to be presented not so much as an heir to ancestral African sounds but rather as an inspiration to contemporary African dance music. The second and related development was the central role assigned to the musical producer. As shown throughout this chapter, for music buyers, the musical producer, more than the armchair music critic, became a leader of taste and the guarantor of quality in a very crowded market where most consumers would otherwise feel unable to discriminate. But that was not the whole story. For musicians and music professionals worldwide, these independent producers, despite their frequent financial struggles and risky propositions, were ambassadors of an expanding capitalism that, contrary to expectations, did not have to be corporate. It was these men, and not anonymous corporate addresses, who, in these contexts, came to be seen as the faces of the global economy.

Acknowledgments

I am indebted to David Cantrell, without whose generosity this research would have been cumbersome. I also thank the following individuals for their assistance: Joaquin Borges Triana, Daniel Brown, Simon Broughton, Cary Diez, Jan Farley, Trevor Herman, Eduardo Llerenas, Krister Malm, Owen Marinas, Albert Reguant, Ole Reitov, Rick Shain, Robert Urbanus, Donald A. "Jumbo" Vanrenen, Bob White, and Bladimir Zamora.

Notes

1. The EGREM LPs that Love Records licensed included albums by Irakere, Sara González, and Carlos Puebla. The label closed down in 1979, but much of its catalogue has been reissued on CD by Siboney Records. I thank Jumbo Vanrenen for bringing this label to my attention.

2. Between 1977 and 1985 Dizzy Gillespie visited Cuba on several occasions, the first time with Stan Getz, David Amran, Ry Cooder and other North American musicians. His 1985 participation in Havana's jazz festival was documented in the 1989 film *A Night in Havana* (dir. John Holland).

3. These included the rumba group Los Papines, which played in museums and other specialized venues in 1977, and Cuba's National Ballet, which performed at the Kennedy Center in Washington, D.C., one year later (West 1977; Jackson 1978).

4. The salsa band Típica 73 had to disband after a trip to Cuba because of boycotts and pressure from the industry (Geronimo 1979). In 1983 salsa star Oscar D'Leon, after playing at a Varadero festival, managed to salvage his career by publicly apologizing on his return to the United States, but, as a result, he fell out of favor in Cuba and his music was banned from the radio (Mosquera 2007). For an account of the picketing and protests by anti-Castro demonstrators at a New York concert by the Aragon Orchestra, see Rockwell 1983. In the 1980s Emilio Vandenedes's Los Angeles KXLU show was one of the few that played contemporary Cuban music. After 1988 Miami's Ediciones Vitral, owned by left-wing radio personality Francisco Aruca, licensed and distributed Cuban recordings "from secret locations" to a clientele of young Cuban migrants (Branch 1991).

5. The Aragón Orchestra toured Africa in 1971, 1972, 1973, 1977, and 1978, including Benin, Cabo, Verde, Congo Brazzaville, Egypt, Guinea Conakry, Guinea Bissau, the Democratic Republic of Congo, Mali, Senegal, Sierra Leone, Tanzania, and Zaire (Marrero 2001). Similarly U.S.-based salsa bands, including Johnny Pacheco, the Orchestra Broadway, and Fania All Stars (with Celia Cruz) toured Africa during the 1960s and 1970s to massive and devoted audiences (Steward 1999).

6. Sonodisc distributed the Cuban Areito label in France and Africa in 1985–1986. One such producer was Ivory Coast–based Daniel Cuxac. In 1990 he presented Barbarito Diez, Pio Leyva, and others, with gold records garnered in West Africa. See Granma International (1990). See also Shain, this volume.

7. Jumbo Vanrenen, personal communication, August 2007.

8. Robert Urbanus, owner of Stern Records, personal communication August 15, 2007.

9. Trevor Herman, personal communication, August 20007.

10. By then Cuban jazz music had a regular presence in the city. Personnel from the famed London club Ronnie Scotts normally attended Havana's Jazz Festival, and Cuban bands like Irakere had been playing there regularly since 1985, when the club had a nine-week festival devoted to contemporary music from Havana, which included Arturo Sandoval, Chucho Valdes and Irakere, and Gonzalo Rubalcaba (Williams 1985). Some of their performances were recorded and commercially released. For a detailed account on the development of world music networks in Britain, see Farley 2001.

11. Since the late 1970s British musicologists, journalists, and promoters such as Jan Farley and Lucy Duran had been traveling to Cuba (Jan Farley, personal communication January 25, 2008). Duran had family links to the island and was able to conduct research on son music under the auspices of the CIDMUC (Duran 1989). She later facilitated British tours for Cuban groups. The CIDMUC was headed by East Germany–trained musicologist Olavo Alén, who provided support for many foreign ethnomusicologists during these years.

12. A BBC documentary, *What's Cuba Playing At* (Dibbs 1985) further exposed the music of the island to the British public.

13. Some of these albums include Gonzalo Rubalcaba's *Giraldilla* (CD Messidor 1989), recorded in studio in Munich; Chucho Valdés's *Solo Piano* (CD Blue Note 1991), recorded in studio in London; Irakere's *Live at Ronnie Scotts* (CD World Pacific 1991); Los Muñequitos de Matanzas's *Cantar Maravilloso* (CD Globestyle 1990); and Sierra Maestra's *Son Highlights of Cuba* (CD Wergo 1993).

14. For a history of the *Afropop* show, see http://www.afropop.org/multi/feature/ID/119/Raven+radio+memoir.

15. The following paragraphs are based on e-mail correspondence with D. A. Vanrenen (July 31–August 6, 2007).

16. The Earthworks label, later part of Virgin, issued two more compilations of that sort, the CD *Sabroso!* (1987), with an eclectic selection similar to that of the 1985 LP, and *Cuba Fully Charged* (1993), devoted to high-energy salsa and timba music. In addition, the British label Globe Style, known for its African music releases, issued several compilations of Latin music, including an album dedicated to the Ritmo Oriental Orchestra, licensed from EGREM (*Ritmo Oriental—Is Calling You*, CD ORB 034, 1988).

17. The same bias had been present for years in ethnic arts in Africa and elsewhere. See Price 1989 and Steiner 1994.

18. See Farley 2001 for a description of the types of collaborations between Western and "world" musicians in early world music recordings.

19. In 1989 the documentary *Roots of Rhythm,* narrated by Harry Belafonte, as well as its accompanying CDs, included both previously released licensed material and live recordings conducted in Cuba (*A Carnival of Cuban Music,* CD Rounder Records 1990; and *Cuban Dance Party,* CD Rounder Records 1990). See Rosow 1989 and Duran 1991.

20. This information comes from an interview with David Byrne posted on the Luaka Bop website: http://www.luakabop.com/label/cmp/main_banner.php3 (accessed August 7, 2007). In 1990 the production company for Robert Redford's film *Havana* (1990) negotiated with EGREM to license the film's soundtrack—probably the first time that a

major Hollywood studio undertook such negotiations with a Cuban state company since the revolution. (The film, however, did not obtain permissions to be shot on location.)

21. I owe this information to Cuban journalist Bladimir Zamora (personal communication, July 26, 2007), who collaborated with Auserón in this enterprise.

22. In Spain, in the mid-1980s, the *new* flamenco label Nuevos Medios licensed a double LP by singer Bola de Nieve (LP 63-010). Later in the 1990s it issued similar compilations with licensed material by singer Maria Teresa Vera (CD *Boleros Primordiales*, 1992), and Beny Moré with Trio Matamoros (CD *Sangre Conga*, 1992). In 1990 Nueva Trova singer Carlos Varela released *Jalisco Park* on the Manzana label, which subsequently opened an office in Cuba and developed a substantial catalogue of new recordings by various Cuban artists.

23. In 1995 Auserón, under the name Juan Perro, issued the CD *Raices al Viento* (*Roots to the Wind*) on BMG. The album was recorded in Havana in 1994 with the participation of Cuban musicians such as Compay Segundo. Before then, Galician bagpipe player Carlos Núñez collaborated with the Vieja Trova Santiaguera, later including them in a fusion album (*Brotherhood of Stars*, CD RCA Victor 1997).

24. Tumi Records was a case in point. For more on these labels, see Hernandez-Reguant 2002.

25. In 1989 a group of Finnish musicologists carried out an expedition into Pinar del Rio province, along with their CIDMUC colleagues, and recoded traditional music in situ. These recordings were not released until 1997, during the post–Buena Vista boom. (CD *Pinareño. From the Tobacco Road of Cuba*. Germany: Piraña Records).

26. Interview with Eduardo Llerenas, July 20, 2007.

27. Its first Cuban release, technically, was a double CD of original recordings by various traditional son groups in 1990, but that was on his label Musica Tradicional before Corasón's founding (Eduardo Llerenas, personal communication).

28. Manuel Domínguez, e-mail communication, July 8, 2001.

29. In 1993 Gloria Estefan topped the charts both in the United States and in the United Kingdom, where she went platinum, with *Mi Tierra* (*My Land*), an album of traditional Cuban music. She was accompanied in the U.K. by the London Symphony Orchestra.

30. http://www.worldcircuit.co.uk/#About.

31. The first CD was a 1987 album by Cuban country music singer Celina González (Fiesta Guajira, licensed from EGREM and digitally remastered) and the second, in 1993, was Ñico Saquito's *Good-bye Mr. Cat* (an original 1982 EGREM recording that included Eliades Ochoa, who later participated in *Buena Vista Social Club*). Sierra Maestra's album followed in 1994 (CD *Dundunbanza!*)

32. CD *Talking Timbuktu* (World Circuit 1994).

33. http://www.thechieftains.com/discography/disc_santiago.asp.

34. She was, in fact, under contract by Nubenegra at the time, which raised some conflict between both labels (Domínguez, personal communication, 2001).

35. I owe this observation to Jan Farley, personal communication, 2007.

36. The enormous success of the album prompted the label to produce a series of sequels led by each of the participants in the original recording. Most of them sold very well. Compay Segundo's *Las Flores de la Vida*, for instance, sold one million copies (in a country of forty million), even before it was released in the United States (Granma 2000).

37. Radio was introduced in Cuba in 1922.

38. Ry Cooder also appeared in Juan de Marcos's *Afro-Cuban All Stars* album (1997), which was released three months before *Buena Vista Social Club*.

39. Compay Segundo's 2000 album *Las Flores de la Vida* (World Circuit) sold one million copies in Spain alone (a country of forty-five million) (Granma 2000).

40. http://www.billboard.com/bbcom/yearend/2005/news/passing_artist.jsp

References

Billboard. 1991. *Album Review: Silvio Rodriguez. Los Clásicos de Cuba 1.* April 13, 66.

Branch, Karen. 1991. "Firm Sells Culture Direct from Cuba." *Miami Herald,* May 28, 1991, B1.

Cantalapiedra, Ricardo. 1994. "Cuba y Andalucía unen sus culturas musicales." *EL PAIS,* January 1. http://www.elpais.com/articulo/cultura/ESPAnA/CUBA/CUBA/Cuba/Andalucia/unen/culturas/musicales/elpepicul/19940801elpepicul_13/Tes/.

Chanan, Michael. 1999. "Play It Again, or Old-Time Cuban Music on the Screen." *New Left Review* 238.

De la Nuez, Ivan. 2006. *Fantasía Roja.* Barcelona: Mondadori.

Dibbs, Michael, dir. 1985. *What's Cuba Playing At?*

Domínguez, Manuel. 1998. *Pura Trova* (liner notes). Madrid: Nubenegra.

Duran, Lucy. 1989. "In Pursuit of Son." *Folk Roots* 67:30–33.

———. 1991. "A Carnival of Cuban Music: Routes of Rhythm Vol. 1." "Cuban Dance Party: Routes of Rhythm Vol 2." *Ethnomusicology* 35 (2): 292–296.

Farley, Jan. 2001. "The 'local' and the 'global' in popular music." In *The Cambridge Companion to Popular Music,"* ed. Simon Frith, Will Straw, and John Street. Cambridge: Cambridge University Press.

Feld, Steven. 2000. "A Sweet Lullaby for World Music." *Public Culture* 12 (1): 145–171.

Gerónimo, Roberto. 1979. "Tipica 73 triunfa en Cuba." *Latin NY,* January, 60–61.

González, Fernando. 2000. ". . . And Back Again." *Boston Globe,* December 24.

Granma. 2000. "Disco de Diamante" para Compay Segundo." November 9.

Granma International. 1990. "Gold Records." October 21, 7.

Hannerz, Ulf. 1990. "Cosmopolitans and Globals in World Culture." In *Global Culture,* ed. Mike Featherstone, 237–252. London: Sage.

Herman Doltz, Sonia, dir. 1997. *Lágrimas Negras.*

Hernández-Reguant, Ariana. 2002. "Radio Taino and the Globalization of the Cuban Culture Industries." Ph.D. diss., University of Chicago, Department of Anthropology.

Holland, John. 1989. *A Night in Havana. Dizzy Gillespie in Cuba.* DVD Docurama.

Jackson, George. 1978. "A Pair of Stylized Cuban Premieres." *Washington Post* June 9, B3.

Koppel, Ted. 1999. "The Story of the Buena Vista Social Club." ABC Nightline transcript. ABC News, June 25.

Luaka Bop. N.d. Interview with David Byrne.

Manuel, Peter. 1991. "Latin Music in the United States: Salsa and the Mass Media." *Journal of Communications* 41 (1): 104–117.

Marrero, Juan Gaspar. 2001. *La Orquesta Aragón.* Havana: Jose Martí.

McGuire, Dave, and Nick Gold. N.d. "The World Circuit Story." http://www.worldcircuit.co.uk/#about (accessed May 2, 2008).

Moreiras, Alberto. 1998. "Global Fragments. A Second Latinamericanism." In *The Cul-*

tures of Globalization, ed. Fredric Jameson and Masao Miyoshi. Durham, NC: Duke University Press.

Morris, Chris. 1991. "Byrne's Luaka Bop Imprint Expands Its Musical Turf." *Billboard,* October 26, 9

Mosquera, Raul. 2007. "Tipica 73." http://www.laconga.org/tipica73.htm (accessed August 13, 2007).

Newshour with Jim Lehrer. 1999. Transcript. November 16.

Pacini Hernandez, Deborah. 1998. "Dancing with the Enemy: Cuban Popular Music, Race, Authenticity, and the World Music Landscape." *Latin American Perspectives* 100, 25 (3): 110–125.

Page, Hélan. 1997. "'Black Male' Imagery and Media Containment of African American Men." *American Anthropologist* 99 (1): 99–111.

Pareles, Jon. 1988a. "For the Tropicana, a Long Mambo to a U.S. Tour." *New York Times,* May 15, sect., 39.

———. 1988b. "A Survey of Cuban Song, in Tropicana Revue." *New York Times,* May 20, C3.

Price, Sally. 1989. *Primitive Art in Civilized Places.* Chicago: University of Chicago Press.

Rockwell, John. 1979. "Havana Jam." *New York Times,* March 5, p. 13.

———. 1983. "Concert: Cuba's Orquesta Aragón." *New York Times,* July 17. http://www .nytimes.com/1983/07/17/arts/concert-cuba-s-orquesta-aragon.html (accessed June 3, 2011).

Rose, Charlie. 1999. "Interview with Ry Cooder and Wim Wenders." Video. September 17. Available at http://www.charlierose.com/guests/ry-cooder.

Rosow, Eugene, dir. 1994 [1989]. *Roots of Rhythm.* DVD Docurama.

Shain, Richard M. 2002. "Roots in Reverse: Cubanismo in Twentieth-Century Senegalese Music." *International Journal of African Historical Studies* 35 (1): 83–101.

Steiner, Christopher B. 1994. *African Art in Transit.* Cambridge: Cambridge University Press.

Steward, Sue. 1999. *!Musica! Salsa, Rumba, Meringue, and More: The Rhythm of Latin America.* San Francisco: Chronicle Books.

Sweeney, Philip. 2001. *The Rough Guide to Cuban Music.* London: Penguin.

———. 1989a. "Interview: Havana Party: Philip Sweeney Talks to Cuban Musician Elio Reve, Leader of the Successful Salsa Band Orquesta Reve." *The Independent* (U.K.) June 9, 19

———. 1989b. "Music Culture Bazaar. The Womad Festival in Morecambe." *The Independent* June 20, 14.

———. 1989c. "World Music Variety Is the Salsa of Life." *The Independent.* July 7, 17.

———. 1993. "A Bare-Bones Music Trade Feeling Its Way in Cuba." *Billboard,* March 20, 1.

Topp Fargion, Janet. 2005. "Out of Cuba: Latin American Music Takes Africa by Storm." CD (liner notes) *Out of Africa.* TSCD927. London: Topic Records.

Tush, Bill. 1998. "A Look at Grammy Award Winner Ry Cooder." CNN *Showbiz This Weekend.* March 7.

Valdés, Alicia. 1999. "It's Not Latinos Responsible for Buena Vista Social Club's New Rise." *Los Angeles Times,* August 14.

Watrous, Peter. 1992. "The Pop Life; Top 12's, or So." *New York Times,* January 1.

———. 1998. "An Angel Calls Back the Music of Old Havana." *New York Times,* July 1.

———. 1999. "Capturing a Cuban Sound Before It Could Die Out," *New York Times,* June 6, sect. 2, p. 22.

West, Hollis I. 1977. "Los Papines: Performing with an Afro-Cuban Beat." *Washington Post,* August 4, D12.

White, Bob. 2002. "Congolese Rumba and Other Cosmopolitanisms." *Cahier d'études africaines* 42 (4), 168: 663–686.

Williams, Richard. 1985. "Reassessment Time." *The Times* (London), no. 62199, July 25.

7

Trovador of the Black Atlantic: Laba Sosseh and the Africanization of Afro-Cuban Music

Richard M. Shain

The phrase "world music" originally arose in the 1980s as a marketing tool to clear a space for non-Western music in "First World" record/CD stores. Over time it entered academic discourse as a monolithic label for global cultural flows. According to this model, new communication technologies such as records and radios promote the global dissemination of Western music. This dissemination stimulates the creation of new music forms, and some of this exotic music finds its way to the industrial West where the media machine transforms it into a consumer good to be sold locally and internationally. Most writing on world music assumes that this model is universally applicable but with a few allowances for local cultural particularities and economic disparities. Few scholars of world music, however, consider the extent to which a Western spatial perspective shapes their global cultural atlas. Just as maps produced in Europe make Europe look larger and Africa smaller because they are drawn from a European vantage point, so, too, do advocates of the world music spatial model assume an asymmetrical dyadic relationship between "major" northern cultures and "minor" southern ones. As a result, researchers too often present world music as either a manifestation of "McDonaldization" (Ritzer 2010, 1996) or as an example of an emerging global village.

The life of the Senegambian Afro-Cuban singer Laba Sosseh challenges this rigid, Western vantage point and undermines many of the facile suppositions on world music scholarship. Sosseh, from the 1960s until his death on September 20, 2007, devoted his time to expanding musical exchanges between the two developing regions of West Africa and the Caribbean by skirting the usual international circuits of cultural exchange. In the 1960s and 1970s he championed a more authentic Cuban style of performing Afro-Cuban music in Africa. In the 1980s he reversed direction by pioneering the spread of an Africanized salsa to the United States and the Caribbean. In his last years he attempted to introduce his style of Cuban music to Communist Cuba itself. Sosseh's career charts an artistic trajectory outside the world music paradigms of globalization and imperialist culture. An assessment of his work leads to a spatial reorientation of dominant world music models and restores agency to non-Western performers.

Sosseh's success raises questions about the demographics of global music publics and the roles played by Western cultural influence and economic dominance in molding world musics. As Timothy Taylor persuasively points out in another chapter of this book, world music audiences, from a North American or British perspective, overlap with classical music publics, sometimes even poaching from them. The world music group, though small, is highly educated, cosmopolitan, and prosperous. Taylor's insight illuminates the position that world music performers such as Senegal's Youssou N'Dour have come to occupy in contemporary U.S. culture. N'Dour regularly appears in classical music halls such as the Kimmel Center in Philadelphia and Carnegie Hall in New York, and is the subject of major articles in newspapers including the *New York Times* and the *Philadelphia Inquirer*. One of the record labels he has recorded for is a part of the Time/Warner media empire, which has ensured that his work gains widespread exposure and respect. In 2004 he even won a Grammy Award for the "Best Contemporary World Music Album," a rare honor for an African artist.[1] Although it would be easy to see N'Dour's ascendancy to world music stardom in North America as archetypal for an African performer,[2] Sosseh's career demonstrates that N'Dour's audience has not been the only public for world music in North America. The anticipated audience for Sosseh's music in the new world was not comprised of "armchair" middle-class travelers or cultural studies theorists. Instead, throughout the 1980s, his music targeted Spanish-speaking, working-class listeners who then made him a minor star on the New York–Miami salsa club circuit. While a class-bound Carnegie Hall perspective renders Sosseh invisible, his achievement in the Americas, from an African perspective, is comparable to N'Dour's and perhaps even more remarkable.[3]

Sosseh's career also contradicts the argument that economic structures of dominance always determine the direction and nature of transnational cultural flows and that pervasive Western influence is always at the heart of world musics. Although Sosseh was knowledgeable about music from France, Britain, and the United States, he dedicated his life to music from the impoverished island nation of Cuba. His devotion to Cuban music had little to do with Cuban economic activity in the Senegambian region, which during his lifetime was minimal. It had even less to do with politics, as Sosseh had no interest in the Cuban Revolution and the ideologies it spawned.[4] Like the Hausa-speaking audiences in Northern Nigeria that love Indian film musicals, Sosseh found his creative inspiration in cultural materials far removed from the major global centers of economic exchange (see Larkin 2008). When Sosseh migrated to the United States in the 1980s, he was reversing the supposed flow of cultural influence from West to East and North to South, bringing his brand of Afro-Cuban music to the Hispanic United States from West Africa.

Indeed, Sosseh's career inverts much of the conventional wisdom about world music. By looking at his life on both sides of the Atlantic, it becomes clear that world music can come from unexpected places in unanticipated ways. Sosseh's music had its roots in a South-South dialogue that underscored cultural difference and local identities. His work demonstrates that globalization does not inherently produce cultural homogeneity. Alternatively, non-Western communities can deploy communication technologies (records, cassettes, and radio) to create forms of counter-globalization that rather than promote Western cultural hegemony resist it.

Laba Sosseh and the Cubanization of African Popular Music

Before examining Laba Sosseh's initial project of Cubanizing African popular music, it is useful to understand the different ways Africans and North Americans have understood and used the nomenclature for Cuban-based musics. In North America "Afro-Cuban music" refers to a number of musical genres including rumba, son, and guaracha that have their origin in the musical practices and religion of the Cuban population of African descent.[5] Performers from other ethnic backgrounds or nationalities in the Caribbean basin, however, can be considered bona fide Afro-Cuban musicians such as Miguelito Valdes (a Cuban of mixed Mayan and European descent), Tito Puente (a nuyorkrican, or New York Puerto Rican), and Johnny Pacheco (a Dominican). Latin music generally refers to the musical traditions of the Hispanic Caribbean that includes musics of non-African origin such as *Bolero*. Salsa, a much contested term, is an Afro-Cuban music first introduced in New York by Puerto Rican, Dominican, and Cuban émigrés after the Cuban Revolution that also incorporated rhythms from the Pan-Hispanic world (*jaropo* from Venezuela, *cumbia* from Colombia, and *plena* and *bomba* from Puerto Rico).[6] It has since become an international phenomenon that took root in South America, Asia, and Europe as well as Africa.[7] In present-day francophone West Africa, the terms "Afro-Cuban music," "salsa," and "Latin music" are interchangeable. Younger performers and audiences are aware of the specific and distinct meanings attached to these terms in the Caribbean and the United States but still prefer to interchange them simply for convenience. Increasingly salsa has

replaced the other two terms in popular usage, although Sosseh remained ada-
mant to the end of his life that he was *not* a salsa musician. In this chapter I follow
West African practice, if not Sosseh's, and reflect contemporary Senegalese usage.

Other pioneers of Latin music in Africa included Joseph "Grand Kalle" Ka-
basele and Tabu Ley "Rochereau" Ley in the Congo, Boncana Maïga in Mali,
Salum Abdallah and Cuban Marimba in Tanzania, and the great guitar bands in
Sekou Touré's Guinea such as Balla et Ses Balladins, but Sosseh differed from his
contemporaries in his loyalty to Cuban tradition, even when public taste shifted
in the 1970s.[8] Sosseh located his fount of authenticity *outside* Africa, in Cuba itself
and in the *barrios* of Latin New York, whereas other African performers such as
Franco (Luambo Makiadi) of OK Jazz in Kinshasa, either through encouragement
or state-sponsored coercion, found cultural authenticity in re-embracing their indigenous musical roots.[9] Sosseh incorporated African elements into his music: he
sang in Wolof, the dominant language of Senegal, if it helped him reach a larger audience, or he incorporated African rhythms into his work, if he felt it highlighted
the African roots of Cuban music. However he never incorporated an innovation
in his music at the expense of what he considered a true "Cuban sound."

For Sosseh and many of his generation, the Afro-Cuban sound was a music of
liberation, a tool for fashioning new identities and behaviors.[10] He and his public considered Afro-Cuban music the essence of elegance. Even more important,
Cuban music represented a cosmopolitanism rooted in the Black Atlantic, as opposed to Western Europe, and a form of resistance to European colonialism. That
Cuban music was dance music for couples, often linked with nightclubs, further
enhanced its appeal for Sosseh and other Senegalese. The music epitomized a new
form of sociability that contributed to the foundation of a modern postcolonial national culture. Embracing Latin music allowed Sosseh to be modern and African
at the same time while resisting the hegemonic pull of Francophone and Anglophone culture.

By the time Sosseh heard modern Cuban music as a child in the late 1940s, it
had already been circulating around Senegambia for a generation. In 1930 RCA
Victor released "El Manisero" ("The Peanut Vendor") by the Cuban bandleader
Don Azpiazu and his Havana Casino Orchestra.[11] The record was a surprise hit in
the United States, and by 1931 it had reached Africa.[12] Its impact was immediate
and lasting, especially in Senegal. Many Senegalese Latin ensembles still have this
song in their repertoire. The success of "El Manisero" prompted RCA, in 1933, to
distribute its Latin American G. V. Series[13] that featured such Cuban ensembles
as Septeto Habanero and Trio Matamoros.[14] Marketed in Francophone West Africa by the Compagnie Française d'Afrique Occidental, the records were heard in
Senegal at a number of venues. Senegalese who were born during this era recol-
lect growing up surrounded by Afro-Cuban music in their parents' houses, at the
market, and on the street. For many, it was the sound of modernity.[15]

Despite Senegal's sensational reception of Afro-Cuban records, their availability was limited at first and their price remained high. As a result, Latin music circulated largely to a limited consumer group in major urban areas. This changed significantly in 1939, however, when Radio Dakar, the first Senegalese radio station, went on the air as part of Radio Afrique Occidentale Française. The station was set up to promote the interests of the French, not to serve Senegal's indigenous population in any meaningful way, and, unlike its counterparts in Anglophone Africa, it avoided playing African music for many years (Gibbons 1974; Larkin 2008). All programming was initially in French and, in fact, originated in France. The station's main function was to broadcast propaganda and official information, but it also played dance music to entertain the personnel of the French colonial regime. Along with the tangos, boleros, and beguines so popular in Paris during this period, Cuban music figured prominently in the station's playlist, reflecting the perennial French enthusiasm for Latin culture.[16] The station's relatively strong signal served to familiarize many Senegalese with the Afro-Cuban sound after World War II.

Until the 1950s Senegalese only knew Cuban music through these recordings and radio broadcasts. In the postwar period, however, Senegalese musical groups began to perform covers of Afro-Cuban music. These bands went through a long apprenticeship to approximate a Cuban sound. Initially, they played Afro-Cuban music note for note, chord for chord, and word for word by listening to records repeatedly. The Spanish lyrics of Miguel Matamoros and Ignacio Piñero, two famous Cuban composers, were delivered with feeling, even though performers could not understand or correctly pronounce them. By the early 1960s, however, Senegalese musicians began to learn Spanish and master Cuban musical forms, putting their own artistic signature on them. Laba Sosseh played a major role in this professionalization of Latin music performance and recording.

Sosseh was born on March 12, 1943, in the Half Die section of Banjul (then Bathurst), the capital of Gambia, into a notable *griot* family.[17] Growing up, he remembers hearing Cuban music all around him.[18] He was especially attracted to such early son groups as Sexteto Habanero and Septeto Nacional. Like many of his generation, he learned to sing Afro-Cuban music (and Spanish) by singing along with 78-rpm discs as an adolescent. By the time he was twenty he had become a professional musician, performing with a number of local bands including the Harlem Jazz Band and Rock a Mambo. These bands became increasingly in demand as Gambia prepared for its independence celebrations in 1965.

As part of these celebrations the Dakar impresario Ibra Kassé and the Nigerian saxophonist and bandleader Dexter Johnson, then residing in Dakar, came to Banjul. Kassé and Johnson were among the foundational figures in African Afro-Cuban music. Kassé was one of the first African nightclub managers in Dakar, and as Senegal approached independence, he thought it would be a good idea, for both business and patriotic reasons, to launch an ensemble of African musicians to play at his new club, the Miami. He assembled his new orchestra, the Star Band, by raiding talent from already existing bands such as Guinea Jazz and Tropical Jazz. Its Pan-African personnel made it unique among major African orchestras of the period. Nigerian, Ghanaian, and Guinean ensembles during this era mostly consisted of citizens from each nation. In the Star Band, by contrast, the musicians came from Anglophone, Lusophone, and Francophone Africa and hailed from at least four countries.[19] When Kassé heard reports of an extraordinarily gifted young Gambian singer, it was no surprise that he tried to recruit him for his ensemble.

Dexter Johnson was the cynosure of Senegalese audiences during this period. He exemplified for them everything a "modern" entertainer should be. Little is known about his early career, except that he reputedly was born in or near Ibadan in Nigeria and was active in the Lagos highlife scene during the 1950s. According to the Senegalese musical historian Garang Coulibaly, he migrated to Dakar from Liberia in 1957 and tried to win over audiences there to this calypso and jazz flavored music, which was then so popular in Anglophone West Africa.[20] The Senegalese and French listening public, however, showed little interest in highlife, and his band attracted few fans. Johnson then joined forces with the Guinean guitarist Papa Diabaté, first in Guinea Jazz and then in a group of their own. The Johnson-Diabaté collaboration, although artistically and commercially successful, was short-lived. In 1958 Diabaté returned to Guinea to help his newly independent country create a national ensemble. By this time the Senegalese regarded Johnson as the best "modern" instrumentalist in Dakar. When Kassé wanted to form his all-star band, Johnson was the logical choice to lead it. In Sosseh, Johnson found a musician who shared his drive for a higher level of professionalism in Senegalese popular music.

Impressed by Sosseh's singing, Kassé and Johnson invited Sosseh to relocate to Dakar and become a member of the Star Band.[21] Sosseh accepted the offer and soon was rehearsing with Johnson six days a week. Johnson had a sophisticated harmonic sense, and playing in his band was regarded by many Senegalese musicians as an unparalleled opportunity for advanced musical training. Sosseh remembers Johnson as an agreeable person who was uncompromising only about achieving technical precision in music.[22] The two quickly established a musical rapport, and together their performances at Kassé's Miami Club helped initiate a more stylistically authentic Latin music in Senegal.

This more *típico* approach entailed revamping the band's repertoire, moving away from the polite ballroom rumba style in favor of a tougher *conjunto*-influenced sound that stressed more rhythmic and technically complex instrumentation. Until Sosseh and Johnson's innovations, the songbook of Senegalese bands reflected an orientation toward what the Senegalese call *variétés*—a potpourri of Latin, French popular music, calypso, and even rhythm and blues. A standard set randomly jumped from genre to genre with little alteration in style. Sosseh and Johnson distilled this mélange down to primarily its Latin numbers. Simultaneously they abandoned the polite, easy listening approach associated with much of the hotel lounge music of this period.[23] Their new sound was more kinetic and pulsating, the Senegalese equivalent of the Cuban *conjuntos* of Arsenio Rodríguez, Chappotin, and Cheo Marquetti. Sosseh's vocals retained their traditional Senegambian grace but adhered more scrupulously to *clave* than other Senegalese singers had done up to that point, an emphasis that remains important in Senegalese Afro-Cuban music performances today. By emulating the slightly nasal tone characteristic of many Cuban singers, he also brought Senegalese Afro-Cuban music into closer stylistic alignment with Cuban practice.[24] Johnson and Sosseh demanded greater virtuoso technique and more accurate renditions of Cuban musical mannerisms from their colleagues, especially in their percussion section, than was usually the case in Dakar. They insisted that their drummers differentiate between African and Cuban rhythms, never combining the two as is often done in Senegal. The *congueros* were to stay strictly in the Caribbean tradition. If African rhythms were called for, they were to be played on the *tama* (talking drums), not on any other instrument in the ensemble. Aided by the spread of government radio stations to rural areas with programming that stressed salsa, these modifications ushered in a new era in Senegalese music, where Cuban music dominated popular taste both among Western-educated elites in Dakar and St-Louis, as well as the youthful general public in the countryside.[25] Sosseh soon became one of the most sought after singers in Dakar. Before long his reputation spread throughout Francophone West Africa as a result of the broadcasts of his work throughout the region and tours by his band.

From National to Transnational Star

Despite his burgeoning fame, if other changes in the 1960s had not altered the popular-culture landscape in Africa, Sosseh would have remained just a notable performer in a small West African country. His rise fortuitously coincided with the emergence of an African show business that was regionally rather than locally based. The growth of this new economic and cultural phenomenon was fueled by the advent of an African-based recording industry and the emergence of transnational entertainment entrepreneurs such as Daniel Cuxac and Aboudou Lassissi, who recruited talent throughout Africa and aggressively marketed their products regardless of postcolonial national boundaries. These impresarios saw in Sosseh and his Africanized Cuban music a cultural commodity whose appeal could transcend ethnic, religious, and national divisions, and even compete with imports from abroad such as U.S. soul and rock music. They urged him to migrate to Abidjan in Ivory Coast, which by the late 1960s, along with Kinshasa in the Congo and Johannesburg in South Africa, had become one of the three commercial centers of the African entertainment industry.

Sosseh needed little convincing. Abidjan at this time was one of the most cosmopolitan and international cities in Africa with a rapidly growing entertainment sector. Sosseh was aware of the success that his colleague, Dexter Johnson, had been enjoying there since 1968. When Johnson, wanting to take advantage of his spreading renown, had left Dakar and relocated to the booming capital of Ivory Coast, his arrival caused a stir. Almost immediately he had access to some of the most important figures in Ivorian society, including President Houphouët-Boigny himself. His band played at some of the most exclusive venues in the country, and both money and fame quickly came his way. By the end of the year Sosseh decamped to Abidjan and plunged into the Ivorian music scene. He organized an ensemble, the Super International Band of Dakar, and, like Johnson, rapidly became a celebrity. He was to remain at the highest echelons of the Ivorian entertainment world, becoming one of West Africa's first recording stars, until he departed for the United States in the 1980s.

The African entrepreneurs who made Abidjan a show business hub initially made their fortunes by distributing records, mainly Latin music, to the rapidly expanding West African market, gradually pushing aside the Lebanese merchants who had controlled this lucrative sideline. They invested the profits from this activity in the promotion and management of artists and in staging ever larger concerts.[26] They soon realized that the increasing number of Africans owning phonographs was a huge untapped domestic market for records geared specifically to African tastes. By the 1970s two enterprising Africans, the Senegalese Daniel Cuxac and the Nigerian-Ivorian Aboudou Lassissi, had established record companies. Cuxac's DC Productions mostly compiled erudite collections of classic Cuban music that were distributed both regionally and globally. Lassissi's Sacodisc International, by contrast, specialized in recordings of musicians from all over West Africa, with an emphasis on African salsa. Sosseh, who already knew Cuxac from Dakar, eventually became a featured artist with Lassissi's record label.[27]

Initially Ivorian recordings were made and pressed in Paris. By 1974, however, a sophisticated recording studio had been set up in Abidjan, and the lower costs of recording at home stimulated the growth of Lassissi's company. In 1977 Sosseh made his first album for Sacodis, "Lassissi présente le formidable Laba Sosseh— Special Liwanza Band" (LS 5-77). The record was an artistic and commercial triumph and made Sosseh a star throughout West Africa and beyond. For reasons that are unclear, Sosseh was slow to capitalize on his success and return to the recording studio. For the next three years he performed frequently in Abidjan and elsewhere, maintaining his status as a champion of an authentic style of Cuban music.

Given the favorable conditions for performers there, musicians flocked from all over Africa to play in Abidjan's clubs and record in its state-of-the-art studios. Live music of many types was everywhere. but Latin music was especially prevalent. Wealthy Ivorians were great aficionados of Cuban music and sponsored local tours of their favorite New York Latin artists. They paid these musicians well and treated them with considerably more respect than they were accorded in the United States.[28] As a result, U.S. salsa performers commonly spent extended periods in Abidjan.

The Cuban singer and bandleader Monguito (Ramón Quian), who eventually incorporated Laba Sosseh into his orchestra, found the atmosphere in Abidjan particularly welcoming. Born in Cuba, Monguito played with the Conjunto Modelo before migrating to New York after the Cuban Revolution. In New York, between 1962 and 1966, he worked with Orquesta Broadway and Johnny Pacheco's *pachanga* band, two celebrated Latin ensembles. In 1967 he branched out as a soloist, part of the famous Fania roster. By the mid-1970s, when his career had declined somewhat in the United States, he began to commute regularly between New York and Abidjan, where he was revered. Given the high status and great popularity that both he and Sosseh enjoyed in Abidjan salsa circles, it seems inevitable that the two would meet. Proximity alone, however, does not explain the intense bond the two established. Monguito's contemporaries regarded him as the "blackest" of all Afro-Cuban salsa vocalists in the United States. Sergio George, who produced one of his records in the late 1980s, said:

> If salsa had black music, Monguito was it . . . I meant "black" as in its simplest, most raw form, just focusing on the Afro-Cuban percussive element . . . It was similar to Africando[29] in a way, but, of course, before that record was done.

Playing with Sosseh provided Monguito with an opportunity to situate his "blackness" in an explicitly African context. Although a number of jazz artists such as Randy Weston were involved in similar enterprises of racial re-definition during the same period, it was exceedingly rare for a Latin musician to do so (Moore 1997; Arsenio 2006; Clarke and Thomas 2006). For his part, Sosseh was eager to use Afro-Cuban music as a tool to be both African and modern in a culturally globalized world. The two projects intersected and, in the late 1970s, they began to perform together, although it is unclear as to when and how their artistic collaboration started. The artistic partnership worked so well that Sosseh became an ad hoc member of Monguito's band. Aboudou Lassissi saw a rare business opportunity in this unique ensemble that straddled the Atlantic. He agreed to finance a recording session in New York with Sosseh and Monguito's band. Sosseh was eager to make the trip. Ivorian musical taste was beginning to change, and Latin music was losing some of its popularity in Abidjan.[30] Sosseh knew that with his fluent English and mastery of Spanish he was well prepared linguistically to adjust to U.S. society and take advantage of the commercial opportunities for an Afro-Cuban musician in New York.

In 1980 Sosseh left Abidjan for the United States, where he was to remain for eight years. He immediately felt at home in New York, reveling in the city's size and ethnic diversity. Twenty years after his stay, he remembered its neighborhoods and restaurants in specific detail and with pleasure. New York also had a music industry infrastructure with recording studios, record companies, radio stations, and a network of salsa clubs that was unparalleled in Africa. With its pan-Hispanic community of Latin musicians, the city offered him the chance to expand his vision of Afro-Cuban music beyond what was possible in Senegal or Ivory Coast.

Laba Sosseh's time in New York ushered in the most productive phase of his career. During his stay in the United States he endeavored to bring African and Caribbean music back into collaboration with each other. He and Monguito recorded four LPs together. The first of these, *Salsa Africana, Vol. 1: Monguito El Unico and Laba Sosseh in U.S.A.,* made in 1980, has been the most influential (LS 26-80). The music reveals that a four-century conversation has been taking place across the southern Atlantic and not simply a one-way transmission of artistic influence. The recording recognizes and celebrates the artistic differences between the Cuban Monguito and the Gambian Sosseh that arises from their distinct historical experiences. Together their music is a "stream laden with . . . many colliding temporalities" (Attali 1985) that powerfully evoke the continuities and disjunctures of the Black Atlantic. It charts an alternative model of globalization, powerfully analyzed by Paul Gilroy (1993) in his book, *The Black Atlantic,* that takes the tropical societies of the South as its reference points and largely bypasses the industrialized powers of Europe and North America.

According to Sosseh, he and the Cuban-American and Puerto Rican musicians he recorded with faced few obstacles in discovering a common musical language, a tribute to his mastery of Afro-Cuban musical forms and the other musicians' openness to new ideas.[31] Under Sosseh's tutelage, the Caribbean-American salsa instrumentalists on the recordings were able to achieve an African lilt in their playing. Sosseh was not overly articulate about his working methods, but he likely interacted with Monguito and his musicians in the same way that he instructed young Senegalese Latin musicians in the years before he died. Sosseh, a master of every instrument in an Afro-Cuban ensemble, would stop a band abruptly upon hearing something that did not seem right. He would then approach the offending musician and demonstrate precisely the sound he was looking for, sometimes waving his walking stick for emphasis. His method, both stern and humorous, was also highly effective, judging from the results.[32]

The records that resulted from this trans-Atlantic encounter are a convincing *bricolage* of "Fania"-salsa brass arrangements, Cuban percussion, and Senegambian melodies. Despite its uniqueness and cultural significance, the project went unnoticed by the musical and academic worlds in the United States and the Caribbean, although it was well received in Latin music circles and given extensive radio airtime. African audiences and connoisseurs were quick to recognize its impact, especially in Senegal and Ivory Coast, where its influence was immense. The sales were impressive and supposedly attained "Disque d'Or" status.[33]

During the same period Sosseh signed a contract with SAR music company of Miami, run by the Cuban-American singer Roberto Torres. Sosseh recorded two albums for the label, in 1981 and 1982. Both intensified his Africanization of Afro-Cuban music. On one album cover Sosseh is pictured on the Brooklyn Bridge, wearing a beautifully embroidered African gown, a perfect visual image of what he was trying to achieve on his recordings for Torres's label. Working with the Cuban-American SAR musicians who had no previous experience with African music,[34] Sosseh recorded albums for the U.S. Latin music market that sounded as if they could have been made in Abidjan or Dakar. He wrote nine of the twelve songs and ensured that the material had African tempos and musical textures. The music is in $\frac{4}{4}$ time, like most salsa, but the rhythm is much more like an African "shuffle" or a Colombian *cumbia* than a Cuban *guaracha*. The records were a minor commercial success in the Latin music market and circulated widely around the Caribbean basin. They especially appealed to Colombians, so much so, in fact, that in 1987 Joe Arroyo, one of Colombia's most famous singers and band leaders, "covered" one of Sosseh's songs "Diamoule Mawo" which he re-titled "Yamulemao" (*Echao Pa'lante* Discos Fuentes [Colombia] 11242, 1987).

Sosseh's later ventures furthered these diasporic explorations. In Paris, in the mid-1980s, he recorded two albums with Orquesta Aragón, produced with an African public in mind (*Maestro Laba Sosseh con Orquesta Aragón*, Stock SA 3000-70; and *La Orquesta Aragón con Laba Sosseh*, LDS-2887, Tropical, Colombia, 1986). Orquesta Aragón is the most famous of all Cuban *charanga* ensembles. Their sound, with its riffing violins, light percussion, jazzy piano, and filigree wooden flute, struck West Africans in the 1950s as the epitome of modernity and sophistication. Even after the Orquesta lost its popularity at home in the 1970s, when Cubans became more excited by the jagged rhythms of songo[35] and other new sounds, its Francophone West African audience remained fanatically loyal (and remains so today). For Francophone Africans, the artistry of the ensemble sets a standard of excellence that is almost impossible for any other musicians to meet. Thus, that Aragón had consented to record with an African *sonero* caused a furor in West Africa. Many Africans regarded the album as evidence that Senegambian Latin music had come of age and that their brand of Afro-Cuban music was ready to be exported back to its point of origin. The project was presented to the public as a coming together of equals, as if Senegalese musicians had passed through a long period of musical apprenticeship and had now mastered the nuances of the Cuban sound.

Both Sosseh and Orquesta Aragón have fond memories of their collaboration that was aimed more at African listeners than Cuban or U.S. audiences.[36] Sosseh found the *charangueros* of Aragón completely professional and sympathetic, and he basked in their acceptance of him as a master of the Cuban idiom. The Cuban musicians, who had repeatedly toured Africa after the Cuban Revolution, were grateful that their mode of playing, which had gone out of style in Cuba, was

still commercially viable and aesthetically prestigious in Africa. Indeed, the releases marked the start of Orquesta Aragón marketing itself as a world music act
with more audiences in Europe and Africa than in their home country. Released
as cassettes in West Africa, where they sold well, these records were completely
overlooked in Cuba (and the United States). Neither the Cuban public nor the
government's cultural bureaucracy showed much interest in the project's diasporic
dimensions. The next time Sosseh was to have contact with Cuba, nearly twenty
years later, he would find the situation little changed.

In the late 1980s Sosseh returned to Dakar and Banjul. The combination of the
merengue craze and the rise of *salsa romántica* in New York left little room there
for his type of music (Austerlitz 1997; Washburne 2002).[37] In addition, a new
generation of salsa musicians were emerging in Senegal, musicians such as Pape
Fall whom Sosseh wanted to mentor.[38] With a minor salsa boom in Dakar, much
more work was available for salsa musicians in the city's nightclubs. Also, the re-
sort hotels of the Petit-Côte, a tourist zone about two hours from Dakar catering
to Europeans, frequently offered lucrative employment. Although Sosseh's fame
was not as extensive as it once had been, he still commanded great respect in West
Africa. He was enthusiastically welcomed home as the one Senegambian musician who had played with "immortals" such as Monguito and Orquesta Aragón.
In no time he took his place as the returning prodigal son of an Africanized Afro-
Cuban music.

Boomerang: African Salsa Comes to Havana

Not long after his homecoming, Sosseh accomplished one of the few goals of his
career that had eluded him till then. Despite his travels around the Atlantic world,
this performer, so dedicated to faithful renditions of Afro-Cuban music, had yet
to undertake a tour of Cuba itself. Through a fortuitous series of events, he was
to find himself and his Senegalese colleagues playing with their Cuban counterparts in the sacred precincts of Havana's Hotel Nacional. Before 2001 such a trip
would have been unimaginable. Senegal and Cuba had never established diplomatic relations. Occasionally ensembles such as Orquesta Aragón toured Senegal,
but it was politically sensitive for a Senegalese group to play in Cuba. Moreover,
the Cuban public was completely unaware of the popularity of their own music
in Africa and the important role played by the appropriation of Cuban culture in
the creation of African modernities in West and Central Africa in the twentieth
century. Most Cubans were indifferent to African music of any type, preferring, in
addition to their own music, U.S. jazz and soul music and Brazilian bossa nova.[39]

Léopold Senghor, the first president of an independent Senegal, abhorred Fidel
Castro and, apparently rare for a Senegalese of his generation, Afro-Cuban music
as well.[40] Notably he was a great admirer of Hispanic civilization and encouraged
the teaching of Spanish in Senegalese schools through the university level,[41] but his

promotion of *Latinité* stopped short of embracing the Cuban Revolution. His antipathy toward Castro had several roots. Senegal's neocolonial ties with France in the period after independence made it unlikely that Senegal would establish diplomatic ties with Castro's communist Cuba.[42] Furthermore, Castro's alliance with Sékou Touré of neighboring Guinea complicated matters.[43] Senghor and Touré were rivals for regional influence, and Senghor bitterly resented Cuba's military support of his enemy. Although the Senegalese public's love of Cuban music predated Castro's revolution, Senghor in 1966, on political grounds, forbade the performance of Afro-Cuban music at the first FESMAN, a huge festival of African arts and culture.[44] The rationale for his prohibition remains obscure, but many Senegalese believe it stemmed from Cold War rivalries and Senghor's discomfort with Cuba's growing presence in Africa. There were sizable demonstrations in Dakar over the ban, but the president stood firm. When Abdou Diouf succeeded Senghor in 1981, he thought it prudent to continue Senghor's anti-Castro policies, although, bowing to public pressure, he did permit Orquesta Aragón to tour Senegal numerous times.

When Abdoulaye Wade was elected president of Senegal in 2000 and his party won a majority of seats in Senegal's legislative branch in 2001, he looked for ways to inaugurate what he called a new era in Senegalese politics. Establishing diplomatic relations with Cuba was one way he could do so without arousing excessive debate, as Senegal's Cuban policy was widely regarded as a neocolonialist holdover from the Senghorian era. In 2001 the first Cuban ambassador arrived in Dakar and immediately established contact with the Senegalese-Cuban Friendship Association, an organization with many influential members.[45] In their effort to orient the diplomat to Senegalese culture, some of the association's members took the ambassador to one of Dakar's Afro-Cuban nightclubs. The ambassador was astonished to learn that his country's music had taken such deep root in Africa, and he resolved to have a Senegalese salsa group tour Cuba as a dramatic way to establish cultural exchanges between the two nations. His ministry in Havana agreed, and the financing of the trip was arranged.[46] When news of the tour reached Dakar, a frenzy of intrigue erupted in government and media circles as well as among Senegalese salsa musicians. All three groups regarded the projected trip as culturally prestigious and politically advantageous. Power struggles ensued in the Foreign Ministry over who was to control the budget for the journey and accompany the musicians to Havana. Within the highly competitive and tight-knit Senegalese salsa community, maneuvering also commenced over who was to lead and play in the touring ensemble. Sosseh remained above the fray, confident that, as the elder statesman of Senegalese Afro-Cuban music, he would play a major role in the tour.

The situation became even more heated with the arrival of Günter Gretz, the owner of a tiny but artistically distinguished German record label, Popular African Music. Obviously inspired by the pan-African salsa group Africando, Gretz saw the Cuban trip as an opportunity to carry out his own plan for uniting the

Black Atlantic musically. Using the lure of a recording contract, Gretz established business relationships with several important Senegalese salsa musicians who were unaware of the small market share of Gretz's record label. His intervention set off another round of intense infighting, and particularly harmful was the conflict between Gretz and a young *animateur* (broadcaster) with the government radio service RTS. Each sought creative control of the Senegalese salsa ensemble and would not yield to the other. With the exception of Sosseh, the group that finally traveled to Cuba was the product of a series of uneasy compromises between factions, arbitrated by the Senegalese government. The tour drew from four Dakar Latin bands—Orchestre Baobab, African Salsa, Super Cayor, and the Chez Iba house band (Shain 2009). These musicians all knew and respected one another, but their approaches to playing Afro-Cuban music differed significantly. Forging a unified ensemble from such musically disparate elements proved to be difficult.

If the tour was culturally contentious in Senegal, it turned out to be politically complicated for Cuba, as it touched on several sensitive issues for the Cuban government. The Cuban Revolution from its inception has been committed to creating what Cuban music scholar Robin Moore (2006) calls a "raceless society." The official line is that racism was endemic in the old regime but has no place in the revolutionary state. Hence to recognize and privilege Afro-Cuban culture would counter some of the Revolution's most deeply held beliefs. The Cuban state, however, recognizes that the vast majority of Cuba's poor are of African descent, and to force them to deny their cultural heritage would link the Cuban state with prerevolutionary racist policies. A further complication is that the Cuban state sometimes has found it advantageous to exploit Afro-Cuban culture for its own political and economic ends. Whereas most other forms of religious expression in officially atheist Cuba have been suppressed, the Cuban government has occasionally allowed Afro-Cuban religion to flourish as an alternative to Catholicism.[47] Similarly, although Cuba's cultural establishment clearly has been disturbed by the popularity of timba music among young Cubans, it has not hesitated to use timba to lure foreign tourists.[48] These contradictory policies demonstrate the Cuban state's ambivalence about Afro-Cuban culture, a phenomenon that it never fully can promote or repress. This ambivalence paralyzed several government ministries that were involved in planning the Senegalese visit.

The Cuban state's suspicion about timba extends to all forms of Afro-Cuban dance music. Castro considers such music irrevocably tied to the hedonistic excesses of the Batista regime that he overthrew in 1959. To counter those excesses, after the Revolution he had the Cuban state sponsor the *Nueva trova* movement with its militant folk songs; *Nueva trova* troubadours such as Silvio Rodríguez became fashionable throughout Latin America in the 1960s and 1970s. The movement's music, however, failed to catch on with the Cuban public, who preferred music people could dance to without being politically indoctrinated (Moore 2006).

By the 1980s the Cuban government grudgingly permitted Afro-Cuban music to have a higher profile domestically. Still, few officials in the government wanted to be seen encouraging music that had been branded as decadent, even if non-Cuban Africans were playing it. As a result, these officials planned few public appearances for the Senegalese.

Unaware of these contradictions and ambiguities, Sosseh and the Senegalese delegation arrived in Havana expecting a hero's welcome. Instead, they encountered administrative passivity and public indifference. The musicians waited for days in Havana for the promised schedule of performances to materialize, but nothing happened. Frustrated and bored, several of the musicians, including Sosseh, always a big consumer of alcohol, began to drink heavily and became obstreperous. After a long delay, the Senegalese finally learned that they were to play at the legendary Hotel Nacional with an all-star collection of Cuban musicians. The musicians arrived at the hotel, expecting an audience of Cuban connoisseurs, but instead they faced a horde of Canadian and Japanese tourists, bewildered at hearing Latin musicians from Africa playing old-fashioned Cuban music.[49] The few interactions between the Senegalese group and the Cuban public were equally unsatisfying, as the Cubans found the Senegalese interpretation of Cuban music odd and unsettling, even Sosseh's. They were offended by the rudimentary Spanish of some of the Senegalese singers (not including Sosseh, whose Spanish was excellent) and found it disturbing when songs were sung in Wolof. Meanwhile, the Cubans were further alienated by the ignorance among the Senegalese of how Cuban music had changed since the 1950s. The Cuban public felt little kinship with these strange visitors from overseas. Fortunately the Senegalese musicians had more positive interactions with their Cuban musical counterparts. Some of the Buena Vista Social Club stars such as Rubén González played some *descargas* with the Senegalese, and they had several opportunities to play with other Cuban artists of similar stature.[50]

Before they departed for home, the Senegalese recorded a session at Cuba's state-owned EGREM studios, an experience as troublesome as the rest of their trip. Once in the studio, Gretz clashed with the guitarist and the arranger, Yahya Fall, a close friend of Sosseh's, over the project's creative direction.[51] Fall wanted the music to have the kind of rough edge one would hear in a Dakar club. Gretz, thinking of his international public, wanted a blander sound. Ultimately Gretz prevailed. The Cuban engineering staff in the studio clearly was unimpressed and repeatedly interrupted takes to correct the Senegalese singers' Spanish. One of the singers became so annoyed that he would only sing in Wolof for the remainder of the recording session. Despite these difficulties, the resulting album has strong vocals and skilled arrangements. Sosseh sang two numbers—his famous composition from his days with Dexter Johnson, "Aminata," and a graceful rendition of "El Manisero," the song that inaugurated the history of Afro-Cuban music in

Senegal. Unfortunately Gretz's label had an extremely small budget for promotion. The international media ignored the project's release, *Los afro-salseros de Senegal en la Habana* (Popular African Music - PAM 407), and its sales have been minimal.

In 2002 Sosseh released his last important project, *El Maestro: 40 Años de Salsa* (Mélodie 00022). Whereas his two solo albums in the United States aimed to Africanize salsa, *El Maestro* sought to further Cubanize Senegalese Afro-Cuban music. Featuring such songs as "El Manisero," the album employs an electric piano to update the *charanga* sound. The ensemble work is disciplined and elegantly spare. With this project, Sosseh had come full circle, playing his Afro-Cuban repertoire from the 1960s and using only local arrangers and musicians. It received extensive airtime in Senegal, particularly during the media celebrations of Senegal's soccer triumphs in the 2002 FIFA World Cup competition, but because of shortcomings with advertising and publicity, it attracted little attention abroad. Its emphatic Latin sound underscores the Afro-Cuban foundations of much of modern Senegalese urban dance music and demonstrates its continued vitality.

A Life *in* the Hyphen

Laba Sosseh's career is replete with ironies. He began as an agent of globalization in his own society, but later in life he engaged in a kind of reverse globalization. An individual of great renown in West Africa, he mostly labored in obscurity in the United States, outside Caribbean Hispanic communities. Many who heard his music over the radio in New York and Miami most likely did not know he was Gambian. Even fewer realized that his work constituted a daring intervention in the complicated terrain of diasporic cultural politics, creating "world music" before that term had been invented. For many, living "on the hyphen"[52] induces psychological anxiety and cultural confusion because of troubling feelings of marginality and intermediacy. Sosseh was able to avoid this "nervous condition" by living *in* the hyphen. Like Léopold Senghor, who lived a very different life, choosing to spend his later years in France instead of Senegal, Sosseh was a true cosmopolitan at home in the world. For Sosseh, living in the hyphen engendered groundbreaking music and a deeper sense of his *Africanité*. Rather than caught between two cultures, his artistic modus operandi was to be African in a Cuban context and Cuban in an African context. His incessant migrations trace the reverberations of Afro-Cuban music around the Black Atlantic. His lasting accomplishment was to add his distinctive voice to that ever continuing conversation.

Notes

1. Ironically *Egypt*, the album that was honored, was an amalgam of Senegalese and Egyptian music that had little to do with Western notions of cultural prestige. But the album's message that Islam is a gentle, tolerant religion clearly resonated with the judges.

2. N'Dour plays a much different musical role in France, where he primarily plays huge arena concerts for a Senegalese immigrant audience.

3. N'Dour's career started in the late 1970s. Until the early 1990s Sosseh attracted a much more highly Western-educated audience in Senegal and had a far larger West African following than N'Dour did. In the 1990s N'Dour's personal wealth and success with prestigious overseas audiences enhanced his standing in Senegal, and he became a cultural icon in his own country. For more on music publics in Senegal, see Shain 2009.

4. Roots in Reverse interview with Laba Sosseh, July 31, 2003, Point E, Dakar.

5. For two seminal treatments of Afro-Cuban music, see Moore 1997; and Sublette 2004.

6. For further discussions on salsa, see Rondón 2004; and Flores 2000. For an influential study of gender issues in salsa, see Aparicio 1998.

7. For more on the spread of Afro-Cuban music to South America, see Wade 2000 and Waxer 2002; for its spread to Europe and Asia, see Waxer 2004.

8. For additional information on the early history of Congolese popular music, see Stewart 2000; and White 2008. For more on Boncana Maïga, see Roots in Reverse interview with Boncana Maïga, July 13, 2001, New York. Maïga is still active in African and Latin music circles. For further discussion on Salum Abdallah and Cuban Marimba, see the superb album notes for *Ngoma Iko Huku* by the noted German scholar Werner Graebner. Research on Guinean popular music, unfortunately, is rare. For more information on Balla et Ses Balladins, see the album notes on the CDs *Objectif Perfection* (Popular African Music adc 302, 1993) and *The Syliphone Years* (Sterns Music STCD 35 and 36, 2008).

9. For more on Mobutu's de-Latinization of Congolese music, see White 2008, 73–82.

10. White (2002) documents the same phenomenon in the Congo.

11. A reissue of Azpiazu's historic recordings is available on *Don Azpiazu,* Harlequin Records HQCD10. Azpiazu's recording was by no means the first of this piece. Some of the early stars of Cuban music such as Rita Montaner and Miguel Matamoros recorded superb versions of the song before Azpiazu's.

12. For more on Don Azpiazu and "El Manisero," see Roberts 1985, 76–79.

13. White (2002) and Stewart (2004) offer several variations on G. V.'s real and perceived meanings, which include "Grabation Victor" ("Victor Recording," in Spanish), "Grabado en Venezuela" (recorded in Venezuela), "Gramophone Victor," and a popular Congolese nickname "Grands Vocalistes" (great singers). White (2002) also reports that it may only be an EMI records code that lies between G. U. and G. W.

14. For an erudite assessment of the cultural significance of the G. V. Series in Africa, see Topp-Fargion 2004.

15. Roots in Reverse Interview with Baye Sy and Aminata Gaye, June 9, 2003, Dakar.

16. Most of the Cuban music played on Radio Dakar was watered-down ballroom dance versions of Cuban music marketed in the G. V. series as rumba, originally recorded for non-Hispanic dancers in the United States.

17. *Griots* (*jeli* in the Mande languages) are the hereditary poets, historians, praise singers, and musicians of the Mande cultures in West Africa. Most *jeli* of Sosseh's generation retained some adherence to their traditional functions and status. Sosseh is unusual in how little his *jeli* background figured in his artistic development and presentation of self. His bohemian lifestyle, however, and his lifelong excessive alcohol consumption were more characteristic of Senegambian *griots* than the region's Latin musicians who tend to be steady, sober individuals. For more on *griots,* see Charry 2000 and Hale 1998.

18. Roots in Reverse interview with Laba Sosseh, July 31, 2003, Point E, Dakar.

19. For more on Kassé, see Roots in Reverse interviews with Fatou Diop and Alioune Kassé, June 1, 2006, The Medina, Dakar; and Khady Ndiaye, May 31, 2006, Pikine. Madame Diop is Kassé's widow; Alioune Kassé is his son and has had an important career as a salsa and *m'balax* singer; and Ms. Ndiaye is Kassé's daughter.

20. Roots in Reverse Interview with Garang Coulibaly, May 13, 2003, HLM, Dakar.

21. Some reports indicate that Sosseh's father already was employed in Dakar and that Sosseh had established himself as a performer in both cities. See John Child's obituary of Laba Sosseh at http://www.descarga.com. Child does not indicate his source for this information.

22. Roots in Reverse Interview with Laba Sosseh, July 31, 2003, Point E, Dakar.

23. See Hayward 2000. I thank Bob White for this reference. This style of hotel music still exists in Senegal; for a description of a recent performance, see Shain 2009.

24. Senegalese music usually calls for more full-voiced singing than does Afro-Cuban music. Dakar Latin musicians claim that Youssou N'Dour, during the first phase of his career in the 1970s, gravitated toward *m'balax* music because his voice was not well suited for the Afro-Cuban sound.

25. During this period there were lively Afro-Cuban music scenes in the administrative town of Ziguinchor in Southern Senegal, the railway center of Thiès and the market town of Kaolack.

26. See Roots in Reverse Interview with Daniel Cuxac, July 20, 2004, BCEAO, Yoff.

27. Sosseh and Cuxac both had roots in southern Senegal (Casamance), which was Cuxac's birthplace and the home of Sosseh's father. Cuxac, a purist when it comes to Afro-Cuban music, is also a great admirer of Sosseh's artistry and stylistic authenticity.

28. Roots in Reverse Interview with Eddy Zervigon, July 17 2003, Maspeth, New York.

29. Africando was an African salsa group put together by the Senegalese impresario Ibrahima Sylla in the 1990s. Originally it consisted of three Senegalese singers backed up by Hispanic New York "session men." Over the years it evolved into a pan-African project with singers from all over the continent. Laba Sosseh, in 1998, recorded two songs for their album *Baloba!* (Sterns Music STCD 1082), "Ayo Nene" and "Aminata."

30. Reggae was beginning to attract Ivorian youth. In 1982 the Ivorian reggae artist Alpha Blondy released his first album, *Jah Glory,* which eclipsed Afro-Cuban music and made reggae the sound of modernity in Abidjan. For more on reggae in Ivory Coast, see Akindes 2002; and Konaté 1987.

31. Roots in Reverse Interview with Laba Sosseh, July 31, 2003, Point E, Dakar.

32. Thanks to the Senegalese guitarist and bandleader Yahya Fall, I watched Sosseh teach the younger generation of Senegalese Latin musicians several times between 2003 and 2006.

33. Senegalese in the music business told me repeatedly that this record "went gold," but I have not been able to verify this information or learn what constituted "gold status" in West Africa in the 1980s. Reportedly, in 1980, the Ivorian Minister of Agriculture presented Monguito with a gold-plated disc in recognition of his having a "gold record." Monguito made a number of records for Lassissi around that time, however, and it is not clear which album was recognized at this ceremony. According to Ariana Hernandez-Reguant, Daniel Cuxac traveled to Cuba in 1990 and 1991 to award golden record plaques to the Cuban performers Barbarito Diez and Pio Leyva (personal communication, May 26, 2008). As with Monguito, the criteria for golden-disc status remains unspecified.

34. The musicians on the album included the trésero Charlie Rodriguez, the pianist Alfredo Valdés Jr., and the renowned trumpeter Alfredo "Chocolate" Armenteros.

35. The ensemble Los Van Van developed songo that incorporated some rock elements and influences from elsewhere in the Caribbean.

36. Roots in Reverse Interview with Celso Velez and Rafael Lay Jr., of Orquesta Aragón, November 14, 2003,New Brunswick, NJ; and Roots in Reverse Interview with Laba Sosseh, July 31, 2003, Point E, Dakar.

37. For a trenchant analysis of *salsa romántica,* see Washburne 2002. This type of Latin music has proven unpopular in Africa. For a comprehensive view of merengue, see Austerlitz 1977.

38. Sosseh and Fall had played together in the Vedette band in 1960s Dakar. In 1995 Fall launched his own ensemble, African Salsa. He is regarded in Dakar as the inheritor of Sosseh's mantle and closely models his style on that of his mentor.

39. In certain sophisticated circles, however, Cubans listened to African music. The avant-garde group Mezcla was inspired to collaborate with the *Akpwon* Lázaro Ros (singer of sacred *Lucumí* songs) after hearing recordings by the Malian performer Salif Keita at a party. See Moore 2006, 218.

40. According to Timothy Mangin, a musicologist who has researched the history of jazz in Senegal, Senghor preferred jazz, having been introduced to the music in Paris by Langston Hughes (personal communication, October 18, 2007). It is likely that Senghor was predisposed to jazz because it was closely associated with French intellectuals from the 1920s through the 1960s. Although the French loved to dance to Cuban music, until recently few took it seriously as an artistic form.

41. Roots in Reverse Interview with El-Hadj Amadou N'Doye, June 19, 2003, Point E, Dakar.

42. There is a dearth of material on Senegalese-Cuban relations, reflecting the general lack of historical scholarship on the foreign policies of the newly independent African states. Much of the research in this section of the chapter is based on off-the-record conversations with Senegalese journalists and retired civil servants

43. Touré was head of state in Guinea from 1958 until his death in 1984. He and Senghor both called themselves socialists, but Touré's socialism drew from the Stalinist model whereas Senghor's was more in the French and Scandinavian tradition.

44. FESMAN (Festival mondial des arts nègres) commemorated the cultural contributions of Africans in Africa and abroad to world civilization. It explicitly promoted Senghor's *négritude* philosophy. For more on *négritude* and the cultural policies of the Senghorian state, see Harney 2004.

45. The Senegalese-Cuban Friendship Association during this period had between 150 and 200 members, and had close ties with the Cuban Embassy in Dakar. Some of the members such as Antoine dos Reis, a retired journalist, and Alioune Diop, a broadcaster, were active in Senegalese Latin music circles, but the majority of the membership was not. See Roots in Reverse Interview with Antoine dos Reis, June 6, 2003, Sacré Coeur, Dakar.

46. Roots in Reverse Interview with Antoine dos Reis, June 6, 2003, Sacré Coeur, Dakar.

47. For an informed analysis of the Cuban state's fluctuations in its policies toward Afro-Cuban religion, see Hagedorn 2001, 196–198.

48. *Timba* is a difficult term to define. Many commentators on contemporary Cuban popular culture regard it as Cuba's answer to salsa. It features harmonically and rhythmically complex arrangements, instrumental virtuosity, and frequently erotic lyrics, full of the most current street slang. Timba performers sometimes slyly criticize the failings of the Castro regime, and some such as David Calzado have had contentious relationships with government censors. For more on timba, see Hernandez-Reguant 2006.

49. A video recording of this performance shows Senegalese musicians dressed in matching tropical print shirts, a performance style that has long been out of date in Cuba. The tourists, unaware of the cultural and historical significance of the event, looked bored and unreceptive.

50. Roots in Reverse Interview with Yahya Fall, April 2, 2003, Point E, Dakar.

51. Why no Cuban artists participated in this session is unclear. Gretz may have wanted to save money, or he may have waited too long to secure the services of Cuban musicians. He claims in his album notes that members of the Senegalese delegation sought to undermine the recording session. It is doubtful, however, that any of the Senegalese present had sufficient influence to do so.

52. The phrase "on the hyphen," here and in the heading to this section, plays on the title of Gustavo Pérez Firmat's book, *Life on the Hyphen: The Cuban-American Way.*

References

Akindes, Simon. 2002. "Playing It 'Loud and Straight': Reggae, Zouglou, Mapouka, and Youth Insubordination in Côte d'Ivoire." In *Playing with Identities in Contemporary Music in Africa,* ed. Mai Palmberg and Annemette Kirkegaard, 86–104. Uppsala: Nordiska Afrikainstitutet.

Aparicio, Frances R. 1998. *Listening to Salsa: Gender, Latin Popular Music, and Puerto Rican Cultures.* Hanover, CT: Wesleyan University Press.

Attali, Jacques. 1985. *Noise: The Political Economy of Music.* Minneapolis: University of Minnesota Press.

Austerlitz, Paul. 1977. *Merengue: Dominican Music and Dominican Identity* Philadelphia: Temple University Press.

Charry, Eric. 2000. *Mande Music: Traditional and Modern Music of the Maninka and Mandinka of Western Africa.* Chicago: University of Chicago Press.

Flores, Juan. 2000. *From Bomba to Hip-Hop: Puerto Rican Culture and Latino Identity.* New York: Columbia University Press.

García Arsenio, David F. 2006. *Rodríguez and the Transnational Flows of Latin Popular Music.* Philadelphia: Temple University Press.

Gibbons, R. Arnold. 1974. "Francophone West and Equatorial Africa." In *Broadcasting in Africa: A Continental Survey of Radio and Television,* ed. Sydney W. Head, 112–113. Philadelphia: Temple University Press.

Gilroy, Paul. 1993. *The Black Atlantic: Modernity and Double-Consciousness.* Cambridge, MA: Harvard University Press.

Hagedorn, Katherine J. 2001. *Divine Utterances: The Performance of Afro-Cuban Santería.* Washington, DC: Smithsonian Institute Press.

Hale, Thomas A. 1998. *Griots and Griottes: Masters of Words and Music.* Bloomington: Indiana University Press.

Hayward, Philip, ed. 2000. *Widening the Horizon: Exoticism in Post-War Popular Music.* Sydney: Macquarie University.

Hernandez-Reguant, Ariana. 2006. "Havana's Timba: A Macho Sound for Black Sex." In *Transformation in the Cultural Production of Blackness,* ed. Kamari Maxine Clarke and Deborah Thomas, 249–279. Durham, NC: Duke University Press.

Konaté, Yacouba. 1987. *Alpha Blondy: Reggae et société en Afrique noire.* Paris: Karthala.

Larkin, Brian. 2008. *Signal and Noise: Media, Infrastructure, and Urban Culture in Nigeria.* Durham, NC: Duke University Press.

Moore, Robin D. 1997. *Nationalizing Blackness: Afrocubanismo and Artistic Revolution in Havana, 1920–1940.* Pittsburgh: University of Pittsburgh Press.

———. 2006. *Music and Revolution: Cultural Change in Socialist Cuba.* Berkeley: University of California Press.

Pérez Firmat, Gustavo. 1994. *Life on the Hyphen: The Cuban-American Way.* Austin: University of Texas Press.

Ritzer, George. 2010. *The McDonaldization of Society.* Thousand Oaks, CA: Pine Forge.

———. 1996. *The McDonaldization Thesis: Explorations and Extensions.* Thousand Oaks, CA: Sage.

Rondón, César Miguel. 2004. *El libro de la Salsa.* Bogotá: Ediciones B.

Shain, Richard M. 2009. "The Re(Public) of Salsa: Afro-Cuban Music in Fin-de-Siécle Dakar." *Africa: The Journal of the International African Institute* 79 (2): 186–206.

Stewart, Gary. 2004. *Rumba on the River: A History of the Popular Music of the Two Congos.* New York: Norton.

Storm Roberts, John. 1985. *The Latin Tinge: The Impact of Latin American Music on the United States.* New York: Tivoli.

Sublette, Ned. 2004. *Cuba and Its Music: From the First Drums to the Mambo.* Chicago: Chicago Review Press.

Topp-Fargion, Janet. 2004. Text to *Out of Cuba: Latin American Music Takes Africa by Storm,* British Library Sound Archive/Topic Records TSCD 927.

Wade, Peter. 2000. *Music, Race, and Nation: Música Tropical in Colombia.* Chicago: University of Chicago Press.

Washburne, Christopher. 2002. "Salsa romantica." In *Situating Salsa: Global Markets and Local Meaning in Latin Popular Music,* ed. Lise A. Waxer, 101–135. New York: Routledge.

Waxer, Lise A. 2002. *The City of Musical Memory: Salsa, Record Grooves, and Popular Culture in Cali, Colombia.* Middletown, CT: Wesleyan University Press.

———, ed. 2004. *Situating Salsa: Global Markets and Local Meaning in Latin Popular Music.* New York: Routledge.

White, Bob. 2002. "Congolese Rumba and Other Cosmopolitanisms." *Cahiers d'études africaines,* 168, 42-4: 663–686.

———. 2008. *Rumba Rules: The Politics of Dance Music in Mobutu's Zaire.* Durham, NC: Duke University Press.

Interviews

John Child, with Sergio George. September 18, 2007. "We Will Never Return to the Horse and Buggy." http://www.descarga.com.

Roots in Reverse Interview. Boncana Maïga. July 13, 2001, New York.

———. Garang Coulibaly, May 13, 2003, HLM, Dakar.

———. Yahya Fall, April 2, 2003, Point E, Dakar

———. Antoine dos Reis, June 6, 2003, Sacré Coeur, Dakar.

———. Baye Sy and Aminata Gaye, June 9, 2003, Dakar.

———. El-Hadj Amadou N'Doye, June 19, 2003, Point E, Dakar.

———. Laba Sosseh, July 31, 2003. Point E, Dakar.

———. Celso Velez and Rafael Lay Jr. of Orquesta Aragón, November 14, 2003. New Brunswick, NJ.

————. Eddy Zervigon, December 17, 2003, Maspeth, NY.
————. Daniel Cuxac, July 20, 2004, BCEAO, Yoff.
————. Fatou Diop and Alioune Kassé, June 1, 2006, The Medina, Dakar, and Khady Ndiaye; May 31, 2006, Pikine.

Discography

Africando *Baloba!* 2000. Sterns Music. STCD1082.
Arroyo, Joe. 1987. *Echao Pa'lante.* Discos Fuentes. DFUE 11242.
Don Azpiazu, Harlequin Records HQCD10.
La Orquesta Aragón con Laba Sosseh. 1986. LDS-2887.
Los afro-salseros de senegal en la Habana. 2001. Popular African Music 407.
Maestro Laba Sosseh con Orquesta Aragón. N.d. Stock SA, 3000-70.
La Orquesta Aragón con Laba Sosseh. 1986. Tropical LDS-2887.
Monguito El Unico and Laba Sosseh in U.S.A. 1981. Salsa Africana. Sacodisc LS-26, *Roberto Torres Presenta Laba Sosseh,* SAR 1020.
————. 1982. Salsa Africana. Sacodisc LS-26 *Laba Sosseh,* SAR 1029.
Objectif Perfection. 1993. Popular African Music adc 302.
Out of Cuba: Latin American Music Takes Africa by Storm. 2005. British Library Sound Archive/Topic Records TSCD 927.
The Syliphone Years. 2008. Sterns Music STCD 35 & 36.

Part 3.

Imagined Encounters

8

Slave Ship on the Infosea: Contaminating the System of Circulation

Barbara Browning

This chapter brings together three figures—the slave ship, the blood-borne virus, and digital information—and contemplates the ways in which they contaminate one another in the work and legacy of Fela Anikulapo-Kuti and Gilberto Gil. Contamination and its variants, contagion and infection, are risky and yet often productive terms in analyzing the relationship between political exploitation, disease, and cultural transmission.[1] Metaphorical and literal forms of "infectiousness" are often blithely yoked together in insidious and often racist ways. And yet I am, in effect, encouraging an analysis here that allows for the interpenetration of three spheres—the political, the biological, and the cultural—in the hope that these figures (the slave ship, the virus, and the digital information circuit) might also help us think through a political critique both in and of two influential artists often categorized under the rubric "world music."

Fela Anikulapo-Kuti was born in Nigeria in 1938 and died there in 1997. Without exaggeration, he was an artist who radically transformed the global understanding of African and African diasporic musics and political interventionism. The current popularity of Bill T. Jones's Broadway production *Fela!* attests to his continuing allure. *New York Times* critic Ben Brantley waxed delirious in his review of the show: "There should be dancing in the streets. When you leave the Eugene O'Neil Theater after a performance of 'Fela!' it comes as a shock that the people on the sidewalks are merely walking. Why aren't they gyrating, swaying, vibrating, in thrall to the force field that you have been living in so ecstatically for the past couple of hours?" (Brantley 2009). This rapturous embrace by mainstream audiences would surely have stunned Fela himself, who spent his life defiantly prodding and provoking not only the dominant political and cultural power-brokers in his own country but also explicitly challenging U.S. cultural domination in Africa. This is not, however, the irony examined here—although I will certainly invoke instances of Fela's political provocations. Instead, I focus on a different but equally telling irony: that of Fela's use of the figure of contagion in the context of his disinclination to directly address his own relationship to a particular pathogenic structure.

Fela died of complications from AIDS, a disease that continues to decimate many parts of sub-Saharan Africa—and a disease the very existence of which he long denied, and failed to articulate, even as he brilliantly identified the other pathologies both literal and figurative that ravaged a continent he loved fiercely. "AIDS denialism" is a complex phenomenon that is rarely analyzed with sensitivity to its full ramifications, because the stakes are so high and the threats so urgent. Fela's resistance to acknowledging his own HIV status was not a simple matter of personal denial. In his mind it was directly linked to colonial history, and to the political struggle for Africans to reassert their own cultural (political, philosophical, aesthetic, and scientific) heritage. He was certainly not the only African public figure to assert that AIDS and HIV were notions propagated by the West in an effort to implicate and constrain Africans' sexuality, and simultaneously to exploit a global market for Western pharmaceuticals. Former South African President Thabo Mbeki has been viewed as expressing related, if less explicitly stated, ideas—and has come under scathing denunciation from international observers of the pandemic.[2] Since Mbeki long set policy in a country with one of the highest rates of infection in the world, the urgency of his attending to the realities of HIV's spread, prevention, and treatment was undeniable. But, unfortunately, when he is rightly criticized for having repeatedly failed to attend to the realities of AIDS in South Africa, one subtle but extremely important point in his message becomes lost. Mbeki often stated that focusing narrowly on HIV prevention and treatment was insufficient: one must attend to the larger problem of poverty. Although Mbeki's manner of articulating this message had irrefutably catastrophic effects, the fundamental power of this insight remains important—crucial, in fact—in formulating a long-term global response to the pandemic.[3] Until the problem of the global distribution of resources (financial, informational, and medical) is addressed, no local solutions to the problem of the AIDS pandemic will make significant headway in stemming it. One way of expressing this would be to say that global poverty is a kind of superpathology within which HIV propagates as a kind of opportunistic infection.

Of course, biologically speaking, HIV is the superpathogen, the immunity-wrecking retrovirus that creates opportunities for a plethora of other infections. To call poverty a pathogen is to create a figure of speech. But what *is* the difference between literal and figurative pathology? Despite his disinclination to address

HIV at the end of his life, Fela's brilliance was in understanding that the division between literal and figurative pathologies is a false one.

Consider the lyrics of his song, "Yellow Fever," which critiques the desire of African women to aspire toward whiteness:

> Fela: *There are several kinds of fevers. The fever of malaria?*
> Chorus: *It's a sickness, a true sickness.*
> Fela: *And influenza?*
> Chorus: *It's a sickness, a true sickness.*
> Fela: *And the fever of inflation?*
> Chorus: *It's a sickness, a true sickness.*
> Fela: *And the fever of freedom?*
> Chorus: *It's a sickness, a true sickness.*
> Fela: *And yellow fever in all that?*
> Chorus: *It's a sickness, a true sickness. It's precisely the subject of this song.*

Yellow fever, of course, is a "sickness, a true sickness." But the figurative yellowing of a desire to emulate whiteness is, to Fela, also *truly* pathological—as is not only malaria and influenza but economic violence as well. And what about freedom? The lyrics imply that political consciousness can be as "catching," as "infectious," as either the blood-borne virus or cultural imperialism.

The notion of contagion or infectiousness is a powerful metaphor that has been invoked at times in seemingly benign ways, sometimes in malignant ways, and sometimes in politically productive ways to talk about African and African diasporic culture—particularly music and dance. Unfortunately the apparently benign or even celebratory assignation of African culture as "infectious" has often been accompanied by a corresponding gesture of literal fear and blaming in relation to real epidemics. The lack of a coherent global response to the AIDS/HIV crisis in sub-Saharan Africa, and the epidemiological finger-pointing at both Haiti and Africa early in the pandemic, demonstrate how devastating the fallout of this configuration can be. African political figures, activists, and artists who claim that AIDS is actually merely symptomatic of a greater global pathology of racism and discrimination are both epidemiologically and politically justified. But it *is* still important to recognize that HIV *is* "a sickness, a true sickness" and that its circulation is influenced by gender discrimination as well as racism.

Afro Beat, the cosmopolitan and insistently African musical style that Fela popularized, is almost invariably described in terms of its "infectiousness." And his political philosophy, dubbed "felism" on his posthumous official website,[4] is defined in relation to its "virulence." The lyrics of his 1976 song, "Perambulator," are said to "summarize" this politics of virulence. They warn that "perambulation"—a possible alternative term for the exploitative effects of globalization—is not necessarily progress. "Mobility"—in the forms of literal travel, Western education, or the African importation of external cultural and intellectual influences—can lead, Fela says, to *immobility*.

> See the pile that Yoruba called djedi-djedi. Doctor tries to do something about it by giving you tablets, mixtures, injections. But you are not drawn from business and your ass is always on fire. However the solution exists in African pharmacopoeia. Our doctors should do training courses with the traditional healers, because our pharmacopoeia have powerful virtues that cure all. But they don't listen to me and as well as for the pile as malaria or syphilis, we perambule to remain at the same place. They take refuge in the teaching received in the school of the White by being unaware that the latter direct their inventions above all for their personal interest, not for us! During all their schooling, they were taught all the panoply of Western science, but nothing about themselves.

There is no doubt that the suspicion of Western pharmaceutical interests and their links to exploitative global economic policies is well founded, and yet one would be hard-pressed to argue, at this moment in the AIDS pandemic, that there is not something tremendously promising, both medically *and* politically, about overturning exploitative intellectual property policies—through the distribution of generic antiretrovirals—to the global HIV-positive population.

Economic circulatory systems *are* linked to routes of literal contagion—and of healing. And the most extremely exploitative system of circulation—the trafficking of slaves—was also linked to pathological vectors. John Edgar Wideman's short story, "Fever," returns to an eighteenth-century epidemiological theory which suggested that Yellow Fever spread to the United States through the vector of Haitian slaves being transported north by slave owners fearing political foment on the island. Wideman opens his meditation on the virulent nature of the pathology of slavery in the hold of a slave ship, where an *aedes aegypti* mosquito infects a man with a blood-borne virus. It would be accurate to say that Yellow Fever simply manifests the deeper pathology of the commodification of human beings, and the slave ship as a vector of that pathology is much greater than the circulation of the mosquito. But freedom, too, is contagious—which is precisely why Haitian slaves were cast as dangerous, potentially infectious beings.

Wideman's story was published in 1989, shortly after Fela's passing. The 1990s produced a number of critical analyses of the figure of epidemia in relation to culture,[5] none of it directly addressing Fela. It was a 2003 exhibit at the New Museum in New York, curated by Trevor Schoonmaker, that first provoked me to want to consider his specific, and complicated, relationship to the metaphorical implications of infectious disease. The show, *Black President*, invited some thirty artists from around the globe to meditate on Fela's legacy.[6] Although press materials asserted that participating artists did "not all agree about Fela's legacy, philosophy or actions," the tone was certainly one of celebration, if not a kind of enshrining. Several of the show's contributors were women, some of whom self-identify as feminist artists. And yet there was a marked silence around the question of Fela's complicated sexual politics. It led to the distressing impression that there was an assumption that any explicit critique might jeopardize the question of the "legacy" of a figure that all the artists seemed to agree had so productively and beautifully spoken and musicked against the forces of colonialism and racism.

A similar silence has occurred around the current Broadway production. Fela's most insightful biographer, Michael Veal, has registered some concern regarding the disinclination of Fela's admirers to consider the complex and suspended question of the women in his life and, specifically, the fates of the twenty-seven dancers that he married in a communal wedding in 1978:

> By the end of his life, Fela's stubbornness moved him to challenge the force of death itself, despite the consequences for himself and those who shared their bodies with him . . . What is most striking about all of the discussion surrounding the circumstances of Fela's death is the absence of a sense of empathy for these women's position.

Even as Veal, thankfully, draws our attention to the disappearance of the women in Fela's life, he acknowledges that Fela's relationship to sexuality and to women was profoundly restricted by the legacy of colonial oppression. If Fela felt that his proposition of hypersexuality and access to a multiplicity of women was overturning the humiliating processes of colonization, Veal argues, instead, that it might be read as the direct result of that humiliation:

> In retrospect it is clear that he was, in the larger picture, at least partly a victim of the enduring racist legacy that holds that people of African descent are constituted by their sexuality, as well as the monumental denial among some Africans that holds that AIDS is a "white man's disease" despite its decimation of black populations around Africa and elsewhere in the world. (Veal 2000)

My own frustrations around the silences of the New Museum show, and subsequently the musical, brought into greater relief for me a musical project that I felt had addressed Fela's legacy so much more productively, specifically, the way that his political message and music continue to circulate. This was the "Red Hot + Riot" recording, a part of the Red Hot series of projects benefiting AIDS/ HIV support organizations. Femi Kuti, Fela's son, was an important participant in the project, and the family gave full copyright permission for Fela's recordings and his song catalogue. In a range of covers, samples, and remixes, the songs reproduce Fela's righteous message while *also* articulating what he himself could not or would not: the gravity of the HIV crisis in Africa. To me, the most productive critique was a remix that separated out the righteous message and allowed it to be contaminated with an equally righteous and necessary one. It makes sense, in my view, that this critical contamination was effected through music.

But I want to flash back to 1977, the year after "Perambulator" was recorded, the year when FESTAC, the Second World Black Festival of Arts and Culture, brought a number of diasporic artists to Lagos. Fela refused to perform and staged a mini-FESTAC at his Afrika Shrine. Among those in attendance was Gilberto Gil, the black Brazilian recording artist who would later serve (from 2003 to 2008) as his country's minister of culture. It was a transformative event—one might say infectious—for Gil.

For all the cosmopolitanism of Fela's music, he remained steadfastly suspicious of perambulation. For Gil, what we call "globalization" has *both* tragic and utopian resonances. The slave ship, to Gil, continues to serve as a metaphor for not only the historical but also the contemporary commodification of black people. But he simultaneously envisions the possible liberatory potential of new technologies, which might allow black artists, in particular, to critique, and contaminate, the circulation of their political and artistic productions.

Gil has been the most forceful and active artist in an initiative called Creative Commons—the brainchild of Harvard (formerly Stanford) law professor Lawrence Lessig and several colleagues, who argue that the loosening of increasingly restrictive copyright laws might actually be beneficial to artists. This may seem counterintuitive—and, indeed, some individuals have suggested that Gil's involvement in the project is evidence of a certain utopian naiveté. Black artists have long suffered from exploitative policies on the part of the recording industry (cf. Feld, this volume). The common knowledge is that more rigid copyright restrictions serve to protect the artist. And yet, for some artists, choosing to *strategically* divest themselves of *some* rights in relation to *some* of their works might be beneficial not only artistically but potentially economically.[7]

To put this very simply, envision an independent artist recording her own CD and marketing it through the Web. She might choose, through the contractual stipulations on the Creative Commons website, to make one of her songs downloadable, free of copyright infraction. This might lead to what is sometimes referred to as a "viral" marketing effect[8]—that is, the song's free circulation might encourage listeners to buy the complete CD or other copyright-protected tracks. She might choose to make another track available for sampling, if it were to be used in a not-for-profit context. She might stipulate that it could only be reproduced in its original form, or if it could be altered, if it could be used in revenue-producing contexts, and if she needed to be fully cited as the producer of the work. Of course, for my purposes in this little contaminated figural chain, of particular interest is the notion of the viral potential of loosening copyright restriction, and the links between this figure and that of the slave ship.

Certainly the terms "free" and "viral" are both polyvalent—with ramifications both figural and literal, benign and malignant. "Free" cultural expression can be understood as artistic production unfettered by restrictive legal and commercial constraints, but it can also be understood as unacknowledged and uncompensated creative labor. Historically black musicians have suffered disproportionately from a lack of attribution and compensation in the music industry. And the "viral" dissemination of information may appear to be a benignly subversive appropriation of the figure of disease to describe the ways in which music enthusiasts, Robin Hood–like, can spread the word regarding emerging artists, but it is worth remembering that it was a term coined by marketers who had a stake in figuring out how to manipulate a commercial opportunity. Positive and negative, pro- and anti-market valences attach to all these terms and concepts.

In 2004 Gil performed a benefit concert in New York with David Byrne, co-sponsored by *Wired* magazine, to promote the Creative Commons project. The songs he chose to perform were telling. A number of them were from his 1998 album *Quanta,* which explored the relation between scientific and technological advances and African spirituality. Two songs he performed struck me as entirely logical at the time, one about the tragedy of the transatlantic slave trade and the other about the utopian possibilities of the digital crossing of information across the "infosea" of the Internet. He prefaced the former song ("La Lune de Gorée") by referencing the history of slavery in the Americas, "the reason," he said, "we are here today." That meant many things—among them, that a celebration of technology's capacity to endow individuals with self-sovereignty is directly related to the historical enslavement of Africans. The lyrics of this song are by J. C. Capinan, Gil's frequent collaborator. Capinan visited Gorée, an important slaving port until nearly the end of the nineteenth century, and reported that he had been overcome with sadness entirely specific to the location and yet generalized across the globe:

Et la peau qui se trouve	And the skin which is found
Sur les corps de Gorée	On the bodies of Gorée
C'est la même peau qui couvre	Is the same skin that covers
Tous les hommes du monde	All the men of the world
Mais la peau des esclaves	But the skin of the slaves
A une douleur profonde	Has a profound pain

It is a sad song but, for Gil, it is the flip side of a celebratory samba that embraces circulation—of music, information, and viruses:

Criar meu website	To create my website
Fazer minha homepage	To make my homepage
Com quantos gigabytes	How many gigabytes
Se faz uma jangada	Does it take to make a raft

Um barco que veleje	A boat that might sail
Que veleje nesse infomar	That might sail in this infosea
Que aproveite a vazante da infomaré	That might make use of the ebb of this infotide

Ironically Gil's embrace of Creative Commons and the strategic surrendering of certain aspects of copyright was, to some extent, foiled by his own contractual obligations with Time Warner. Although he had hoped to release some of his previously recorded music, he soon learned that, as Julian Dibbell reported in *Wired*:

> Legally speaking, the decision wasn't entirely his to make. Gil retains some rights to his songs, but the rights to the actual recordings belong to Warner. Company executives in Brazil, longtime collaborators with Gil, initially gave the project their informal blessings. Soon after the plan made headlines in the US, however, Gil received a blunt message direct from the company's global headquarters: over Warner's dead corporate body. The recording rights would not be free, not even in the five-second bits and pieces typical of sampling. (Dibbell 2004)

The best he could do—until now—was to dig up a minor song he had recorded in 1998 on an independent label and make it available through Creative Commons. But he remained committed to the project, and, throughout his tenure as Minister of Culture, he regularly raised the issue of a creative rethinking of intellectual property rights.

Gil's position at the time was political, and its implications went far beyond the music industry. Notably the reason that Brazil was—and continues to be— the site of some of the most innovative thinking about intellectual property issues can be directly traced back to the vector of the blood-borne virus. As Dibbell explains, President Fernando Henrique Cardoso, in 1996, passed into law the guaranteed access of HIV-positive Brazilians to retroviral drug cocktails. The plan was a tremendous epidemiological success—rates of infection plummeted—but it presented an enormous economic strain to the government. José Serra, who was appointed Minister of Health in 1998, in Dibbell's words, "set Brazil on its path toward IP [intellectual property] independence." He told Dibbell: "I always found intellectual property boring. . . . Among economists, intellectual property isn't considered one of the noble questions" (Dibbell 2004). But given the urgency of maintaining the retroviral cocktail program, he saw its significance. Serra invoked a Brazilian law, which allowed for the overriding of patent in cases of a national health emergency, forcing the hand of the pharmaceutical industry. Major drug manufacturers cut deals with the government, and in 2007 Brazil actually carried through on its threat to import a generic version of the drug Efavirenz when the price cuts were not sufficient.

Brazil's policy on AIDS drugs has been lauded by health-care activists around the world. But its implications also extend to other forms of intellectual property. Brazil has heartily embraced the ethic of open source in diverse realms, from information technologies to banking to the entertainment industry. Dibbell has linked this ethic to the aesthetic of tropicalism, the artistic movement, initiated in the late 1960s, in which Gil himself was a major figurehead.⁹ Tropicalism drew inspiration from the "anthropophagic" movement of Brazilian modernist poets in the late 1920s—and, indeed, the cannibalizing techniques of both movements seem to resonate in the "cut and paste" era of sampled music. It is no coincidence that many contemporary recording artists cite the Brazilian tropicalists—including Gil—as a source of inspiration.

When his contract with Warner ran out recently, Gil released his new album, *Banda Larga Cordel,* and immediately signaled his intention to release extensive materials (instrumental tracks and alternative recordings) from the disc for free sharing, sampling, and modification by users. Further, during the album's tour, Gil expressly invited audience members to digitally document and share his performances. In talking about his strategies Gil argued—in an extension of Lessig's contention—that, by giving up certain rights, artists may actually gain power, particularly artists in countries like Brazil. In an economy where piracy has already decimated the recording industry, it may be time to take stock of the shifting terrain of that industry: In Gil's words: "There's a real tendency today toward the fragmentation of political power and economic advantages are being distributed across a greater number of agents." In Brazil, "independent labels already represent half of the national market, taking into consideration the consolidated ones. The major labels come in at the level of distribution, and I believe that all this in the future will be further divided with the micropulverization of enterprise and the reorganization of the market" (quoted in Marçal 2008). Although not arguing *for* piracy as a part of that process of "micropulverization," Gil is suggesting here that the music industry, and individual artists, begin to think creatively about how to navigate the circulatory patterns in that infosea.

In a recent essay, "From Hip-Hop to Flip-Flop: Black Noise in the Master-Slave Circuit," Ron Eglash (2008) recalls his surprise, and discomfort, on his first encounter, as an engineering student, with the "master-slave flip-flop circuit." At first the name struck him as an unfortunate metaphor; on further consideration, however, he saw it as a potent and perhaps even potentially emancipatory figure. The flip-flop is the fundamental mechanism in digital circuitry—the way in which binary code is generated. Eglash gives a compressed and perhaps tendentious—but fascinating—history of this mechanism. Suggesting that its origins are in sub-Saharan systems of divination, he goes on to argue that African and African diasporic cultures have both engendered and creatively reworked information technologies widely perceived to be "Western" in origin, finding liberatory potential in mechanisms often presenting themselves as replicating structures of enslavement. As Eglash concludes, "During my field work in Africa I never met a divination priest who would hesitate to engage the artificial, to express a love for the synthetic circuits of information and energy that carry our noisy signals through time and space, from one human heart to the next" (ibid.).[10]

The title track of Gil's new album returns to the notion of a sea of digital information, and it forces the question of how to navigate that sea without finding oneself back in a figural slave ship of exploitation. Combining figures of the perennially drought-stricken northeast, where improvised oral poetry and hand-printed doggerel verse continue to circulate, with images of warp-speed technological advances, Gil prophecies a sea-change—literally, a "becoming sea" of the dried-out backlands of Brazil through an influx of digital information. But he acknowledges that the first taste might be bitter and that questions of uneven access might make this a bumpy ride:

Pôs na boca, provou, cuspiu.	You put it in your mouth, tasted, spat.
É amargo, não sabe o que perdeu	It's bitter, you don't know what you're missing
Tem o gosto de fel, raiz amarga	It has a taste of bile, a bitter root
Quem não vem no cordel banda larga	Whoever doesn't come on the broadband broadside
Vai viver sem saber que mundo é o seu	Will live without knowing what world is his
Tem um gosto de fel, raiz amarga	It has a taste of bile, bitter root
Quem não vem no cordel da banda larga	Whoever doesn't come on the broadband broadside
Vai viver sem saber que mundo é o seu	Will live without knowing what world is his
Uma banda da banda é umbanda	One band of the band is Umbanda
Outra banda da banda é cristã	Another band of the band is Christian
Outra banda da banda é kabala	Another band of the band is Kaballah
Outra banda da banda é Alcoorão . . .	Another band of the band is the Koran . . .
Diabo do menino agora quer	The little devil of a boy wants
Um ipod, um computador novinho	An iPod, a brand new computer
O certo é que o sertão quer virar mar	The reality is the backlands will become a sea
O certo é que o sertão vai navegar	The reality is the backlands will navigate
No micro do menino internetinho	The microcomputer of the little internet boy

It is not a utopian vision of a world of expanding possibilities of communication. Gil has been explicit about the risks and has acknowledged the dangers of impinging on traditional means of distributing information—including the archaic forms of oral verse and hand-printed broadsides and pamphlets long associated with the impoverished and desiccated northeast of Brazil, source and target of some of the music on this album. Class stratification, as well as regional and national inequalities of access, must always be kept in mind. But the album's overwhelming message is that if the informationally deprived do not allow the infosea to irrigate their intellectual terrain, they will remain trapped in the net of the more privileged.

In the live show promoting the new album, Gil performed a number of his older songs—including "Pela Internet," cited above, as well as "Sarará Miolo," a song that resonates remarkably with Fela's "Yellow Fever." *Sarará* designates, in Brazil, a person of mixed racial heritage, with kinky but blonde hair:

Sara, sara, sara, sarará	Heal, heal, heal, sarará
Sara, sara, sara, sarará	Heal, heal, heal, sarará
Sarará miolo	Sarará flesh
Sara, sara, sara cura	Heal, heal, heal, cure
Dessa doença de branco	This sickness of the white man
Sara, sara, sara cura	Heal, heal, heal, cure
Dessa doença de branco	This sickness of the white man
De querer cabelo liso	Of wanting straight hair
Já tendo cabelo louro	When you already have blonde hair
Cabelo duro é preciso	Kinky hair is necessary
Que é para ser você, crioulo	For you to be who you are, black man

Banda Larga Cordel includes another track, "La Renaissance Africaine," that many listeners have immediately associated with Gil's earlier "La Lune de Gorée." "La Renaissance Africaine" is, again, a song about Africa sung in French. "C'est l'Afrique et sa mission," Gil sings, "clef pour la vraie construction du monde civilisé. La renaissance africaine et sa puissance, la renaissance africaine avec sa danse." It is Africa and her mission, the key to the true construction of a civilized world. The African renaissance and its power, the African renaissance with its dance. This is, of course, related to Eglash's proposition that African culture contributed to the very technologies changing the global information landscape—but, more obvious, Gil is pointing to African contributions in the form of music and dance. It was largely the work of West African recording artists singing in both African languages and in the colonial language of French that constituted the first wave of world music output—so, somewhat ironically, when Gil sings in French, he is addressing many of his African counterparts within the very market in which his own music circulates. The song, however, is also addressed to listeners in Europe and the Americas, and the message is this: as we ostensibly move "forward" in a globalized world, we cannot leave Africa behind. Access to digital technologies may be part of the consideration, but, without a doubt, even more urgent and pressing matters are at hand, namely, a horrifying increase in morbidity on the African continent in recent years owing not only to political violence but also to health issues, including, of course, the devastating impact of the AIDS pandemic. Most astonishing about Brazil's remarkably advanced debate on intellectual property issues is that, in fact, it was provoked in many ways by that very pandemic.

Intellectual property rights are related to the historical trafficking not only of black artistic production but of black people, which makes this a complex issue with no easy answers. Certainly there are contexts within which a freer circulation of life-saving medications, for example, can only be understood as righteous and just. Precisely what the freer circulation of artistic productions might mean remains to be charted. We are just starting out on this ocean, even though we have been traversing the same ocean for hundreds of years in various ways. It is a dangerous place with a pathological history of exploitation and viruses both literal and figurative. The utopian question, and I do think we need some of those right now, is whether we might stand a chance of catching a little freedom.

Notes

1. For a historical overview of the political implications of contagion stories, see Wald 2008. A seminal text on the figuring of the AIDS pandemic was Cindy Patton's *Inventing AIDS* (1990), followed by Paul Farmer's penetrating analyses (see below). Emily Martin gave an ethnographic account of cultural configurations of infection in *Flexible Bodies: The Role of Immunity in American Culture from the Days of Polio to the Age of AIDS* (1995). I took up the figure specifically in relation to world music in *Infectious Rhythm: Metaphors of Contagion and the Spread of African Culture* (1998). Subsequent analyses of other performance forms and their "infectiousness" were collected in the 2009 "Contagion" issue of *e-misférica* (6.1 [2009]), http://hemi.nyu.edu/hemi/e-misferica-61.

2. One well-publicized Harvard epidemiological study suggested that Mbeki's policies might have led directly to some 365,000 deaths. See Dugger 2008.

3. A much more fully thought out and helpful argument regarding the relationship between the AIDS pandemic and the global distribution of resources can be found in the work of Paul Farmer; see, e.g., 2005.

4. http://www.fela.net/.

5. Ibid.

6. "Black President" was a popular Fela moniker during his lifetime and was the title given to a 1981 compilation album released by EMI. The album—and the moniker—naturally received renewed attention during the presidential campaign of Barack Obama. Subsequent to his election, the hip hop artist Nas, who had previously sampled Fela's music, recorded a song with this title, this time sampling Obama's voice.

7. Lessig (2008) has elaborated on the Creative Commons strategy and other instances of more flexible thinking about copyright issues.

8. The term "viral marketing" has been in circulation for more than a decade. On the early use of the term, see Shirky 2000.

9. For more on the history of *tropicalismo,* see Dunn 2001.

10. On the relationship between Black Atlantic cultural practices and interactive technologies, see Davis 1996.

References

Brantley, Ben. 2009. "Making Music Mightier Than the Sword," *New York Times.* November 24.

Browning, Barbara. 1998. *Infectious Rhythm: Metaphors of Contagion and the Spread of African Culture* New York: Routledge.

Davis, Erik. 1996. "Roots and Wires: Polyrhythmic Cyberspace and the Black Electronic." http://www.levity.com/figment/cyberconf.html.

Dibbell, Julian. 2004. "We Pledge Allegiance to the Penguin." *Wired* 12:11.

Dugger, Celia W. 2008. "Study Cites Toll of AIDS Policy in South Africa," *New York Times,* November 25.

Dunn, Christopher. 2001. *Brutality Garden: Tropicália and the Emergence of a Brazilian Counterculture.* Chapel Hill: University of North Carolina Press.

Eglash, Ron. 2008. "From Hip-Hop to Flip-Flop: Black Noise in the Master-Slave Circuit." In *Sound Unbound,* ed. Paul D. Miller, 203–213. Cambridge, MA: MIT Press.

Farmer, Paul. 2005. *Pathologies of Power: Health, Human Rights, and the New War on the Poor.* Berkeley: University of California Press.

Lessig, Lawrence. 2008. *Remix: Making Art and Commerce Thrive in the Hybrid Economy.* New York: Penguin.

Marçal, Marcus. 2008. "Gilberto Gil quer experimentar possibilidades da tecnologia com novo disco, 'Banda Larga Cordel.'" uol.com, May 14.

Martin, Emily. 1995. *Flexible Bodies: The Role of Immunity in American Culture from the Days of Polio to the Age of AIDS.* Boston: Beacon.

Patton, Cindy. 1990. *Inventing AIDS.* New York: Routledge.

Shirky, Clay. 2000. "The Toughest Virus of All." http://www.shirky.com/writings/toughest_virus.html.

Veal, Michael. 2000. *Fela: The Life and Times of an African Musical Icon.* Philadelphia: Temple University Press.

Wald, Patricia. 2008. *Contagious: Cultures, Carriers, and the Outbreak Narrative.* Durham, NC: Duke University Press.

———. 2009. "Contagion." *e-misférica* 6.1. http://hemi.nyu.edu/hemi/e-misferica-61.

9

World Music Today

Timothy D. Taylor

A good deal has happened in the realm of "world music" since my book *Global Pop: World Music, World Markets* appeared in 1997. Although I have written much about world music since then, I have had few opportunities to step back and consider the long view of world music in the marketplace. My aim in this chapter is to lay out the nature of certain changes that have taken place in the last decade or so and to fill in some lacunae in *Global Pop* that have emerged since its publication. This chapter is less about "world music" itself than how its representations and constructions have changed in the years since 1997. The music itself, in fact, has not changed very much. To be sure, it often demonstrates an increasing familiarity with Anglo-American popular music and makes use of more sophisticated technologies and production techniques. In a more abstract and broader sense, however, it is still a category of music that includes many clever and complex amalgamations of Anglo-American popular musics with local musics worldwide.

Since *Global Pop*, world music has become somewhat better known, increasingly part of the average American's musical landscape. It is heard in the soundtracks of television programs, films, and advertising, and as background music in shops. But world music sales are still quite small, so meager, in fact, that the Recording Industry Association of America, which maintains records of sales in various categories, does not even include a world music category, instead relegating it to a category labeled "Other," which, the Association notes, includes ethnic and folk music, among other genres. Indeed, the designation of "Other" accounted for 97.1 percent of sales in 2008, the last year for which data are available as of this writing (Recording Industry Association of America 2008).

Still, world music is better represented in both recordings and print media than ever before. New sources have emerged such as the World Music Central website, containing musicians' profiles, interviews, book, CD, and concert reviews, obituaries, and other resources; the Critical World website, offering more scholarly information; dozens of Internet radio sites devoted to world music, including Pandora, which can be tailored to a listener's taste; and a surprising number of world music videos on YouTube. Print sources include *World Music* (Bohlman 2002); *Contemporary World Musicians* (Thompson 1999), an encyclopedic compendium of 404 biographies; *Rhythm Planet* (Schnabel 1998); and *Songcatchers* (Hart 2003), which lionizes artists who made field recordings of music from around the world. A glossy magazine, *The Songlines,* began publication in 1999. World music has even entered the school curriculum, with a spate of textbooks and a number of recent books targeting teachers.[1]

Yet, in most respects, the impact of world music has been minor. Significantly, however, a market for sample libraries has been growing, composed primarily of digitized bits of prerecorded music for use by composers and artists. Sample libraries contain snippets of various kinds of music that can be pasted into compositions being created on a computer, a common practice in most popular music today that is as simple as cutting and pasting text in a word-processing program. World music occupies a noticeable niche in the market for sample libraries, and through these sample libraries world music has insinuated itself into more mainstream kinds of pop and rock music, including, as noted, music used as soundtracks for film, television, and advertising, where world music has been replacing classical music in commercials for expensive goods, as I have written elsewhere (Taylor 2007, chap. 7).[2]

The ways that these sample libraries are marketed speaks to old attitudes about non-Western musics, as they are represented as exotic, strange, and evocative. A company called Killer Tracks was one of the first companies to enter the market a few years ago with the BMG Explorer Series, which the company described as follows:

> The Explorer Series draws on authentic ethnic music from around the world. Our comprehensive selection is highly evocative, conjuring up the atmosphere of exotic places, peoples and cultures. Imagine tribal dances and whirling fiestas, picture raucous traders in the medina, smell the aromas of an Indian spice market, they're all here in this global offering. This is music that appeals to all of the senses.[3]

Killer Tracks included a sample of strung-together snippets that travels all over the world, although some of the music was clearly composed, not world music at all, and other excerpts were meant simply to evoke another music but were, in fact, fabrications. With the sound of the tin whistle, which most people learned to recognize from James Horner's soundtrack to the 1997 blockbuster *Titanic,* Irish or Celtic music is signified, but this is not Irish music at all. The one-and-a-half-minute sampler included snippets featuring the Australian Aboriginal didgeridoo, the Chinese bamboo flute, Tex-Mex music, the Middle Eastern oud, and many more. In the last few years, the number of "world music" samples from Killer Tracks and other suppliers has increased dramatically, although, based on a random sampling, they are only occasionally truer to the musical traditions they purport to draw on than Killer Tracks was.

But Killer Tracks and other sample libraries that employ acoustic instruments represent the high end. Another kind of collection is frequently used in the commercial world and is simply known as "library music," which is pre-composed and stockpiled so that advertisers or advertising agencies can purchase it when the cost of commissioning original music is prohibitively high. Library music companies normally provide online searchable databases with sound samples, so that potential buyers can locate music by, for example, style, genre, or mood. One such provider is Fresh Music,[4] which sells sixteen different CDs of library "world music," for $89 per disc. One disc, *Global Village*, is described thus: "this music features ethnic rhythms and instruments made popular by such artists as Peter Gabriel and Paul Simon [and] . . . will definitely give your productions a worldly edge." Tracks from this disc, with titles such as "Global Village," "Hebridees [*sic*] Caliegh" [*sic*], and "Raja's Journey" clearly are cheaply produced by employing samples or synthesized sounds (such as the Highland pipes in the second track cited). A description of the tracks gives some idea of their intended usage:

Global Village   Time: 3:06
  Style: World (Ethnic, African)
  Use: Adventure, Light Industrial, Travel
  Category: Light Hearted, Motivational, Warm

Hebridees Caliegh   Time: 3:10
  Style: World
  Use: Ceremonial, Current Affairs, Travel
  Category: Inspirational, Pastoral, Traditional

Raja's Journey   Time: 3:08
  Style: World
  Use: Ceremonial, Educational, Light Industrial
  Category: Floating, Meditative, Pensive[5]

Although most libraries employ their own composers, some seek tracks elsewhere to complement staff compositions. Online advertisements for world music tracks are telling in their flexibility toward authenticity and their insistence on high production values:

AUTHENTIC WORLD MUSIC NEEDED BY UK MUSIC LIBRARY

Library Music Publisher with various placements in Film TV is looking for authentic-sounding World music. They're in need of various styles, such as South American, European and the Far East. Real instruments are preferred but very good synth/sampler recreations are acceptable.

PRICE: $5.00 Submission fee (per Song)

L.A. PRODUCTION MUSIC LIBRARY SEEKS WORLD MASTERS

This successful Production Music Library is looking for Orchestral masters for placement in Film, TV Advertising. They are predominantly looking for world fusion as their clients wouldn't usually require something extremely authentic—however if it is good and done in a contemporary way they would still be interested in traditional world music too. Production quality is very important here as they will not remix or re-record your tracks: they must be broadcast-quality.

PRODUCTION MUSIC LIBRARY SEEKS WORLD INSTRUMENTALS

Successful Production Music library that has been around longer than (probably) anyone reading this (!!) is looking for World-influenced instrumentals to sign to their library. Production Music libraries are like Music Publishers and Record Companies combined so they are interested in your composition and production skills. They release CD's of their composer/producers music and pitch them to companies in Film, TV, Advertising, etc. Music should lend itself to background use BUT that does not mean it can be boring.

PRICE: $5.00 Submission fee (per Song)

JAPANESE MUSIC LIBRARY SEEKS WORLD FUSION INSTRUMENTALS

Japanese Production Music Library is looking for instrumental (only) World/Ethnic Fusion tracks. They can use any influences you like (ie Asian, Latin, Celtic, etc.) but should have a contemporary production rather than 100% authentic. Also you must own both publishing & master rights to any tracks you submit. Please submit 2–4 tracks.

NB: Your song will be submitted by post on Audio CD. They will not accept email.

PRICE: $5.00 Submission fee (per Song)[6]

Elsewhere in the realm of commercial music, the importance of "world music" is now such that composers working in the advertising industry routinely state that they need to know how to compose in many different "styles" and "genres," as I have written elsewhere (Taylor 2007). The most recent book (Zager 2003) about writing commercial music speaks of this at some length, greater than I have seen in any other such book. That this subject would be treated at significant length in a recent book speaks to the significance of world music in today's commercial music landscape. After exhorting readers to learn how to compose and arrange for unusual instruments, the author, Michael Zager, writes:

> One should hire native musicians to perform a composition written in a typical folkloric style. The use of ethnic instruments requires a complete understanding of not only the technical limitations of the instruments but also of the creative playing style. There are typical rhythms, patterns, and ornamentations that are native to the playing of particular instruments. Even if a musician knows how to play the instrument, it will not sound authentic if the musician is not involved in the culture and customs of the native society. (Ibid., 24)

A vocalist who records a good deal of music for commercials told me recently, however, that she has learned how to fake various world music vocal styles. She recognizes that she does not sound as "authentic" as a traditional singer would, but given the time constraints of the advertising industry in which the music is frequently composed and recorded in as little as a day, it is far more efficient for music production companies to hire a professional commercial singer to mimic styles (Steingold 2009). One of the most successful of these, Lisa Gerrard, has invented her own language so that she is frequently employed as an all-purpose "world music" singer. The singer I interviewed told me that she is often asked to sound like Lisa Gerrard. One wonders if we now need a new language to describe this mode of production as post-postmodern, since we are speaking here not simply of simulacra of world music but imitations of those simulacra.

To return to this guidebook, Zager later attempts to educate his readership about the study of world music as a way to emphasize the importance of knowing it for the purposes of advertising:

> *Ethnomusicology* is the study of non-Western cultures. George Harrison, of the Beatles, did more to promote the synthesis of ethnic instruments in traditional pop music than any other musicians. He studied the sitar (a guitar-like instrument) with the world-renowned Indian classical sitar player Ravi Shankar. He then proceeded to use the sitar on the Beatles albums *Rubber Soul, Sgt. Pepper's Lonely Hearts Club Band,* and several others. This was the beginning of what is now known as World Music. *Billboard,* the leading music magazine, has a contemporary World Music chart that is printed every week. (Zager 2003, 25)

"Authenticity" in these situations clearly is extremely fluid and negotiable. Most important is not that the music "is" authentic in a way that it can be traced to real people playing music in traditional ways but that it merely signifies this kind of authenticity. High production values clearly matter more than music that is clearly linked to traditional musical practices. All that is necessary today is to have some kind of "root" musical signifier of musical roots, for example, the tin whistle for Irish music or didgeridoo for Australian aboriginal music. Christoph Borkowsky Akbar, director of Piranha Records says that,

> Styles such as the Cuban *son* or Balkan Gypsy music became so successful because they are a perfect answer to this need, forever renewing themselves without losing their authenticity in the international arena. . . . All you need [for the next big thing] is a strong musical tradition with musicians who understand how to adapt to new times and strange audiences, as well as record labels who understand how to communicate between these musicians and the global markets. (Quoted in Henderson 2002, 40)

Despite the growing number of world music sounds, or sounds that signify "world music," the music industry's usual racism, xenophobia, and Euro- and Americo-centrism remain. The *Billboard* charts and Grammy Award winners have scarcely changed since I wrote *Global Pop*. Musicians whose music sounds more like Anglo-American pop are at a great advantage. And even if they're not popular musicians, they can do well if they are American or European. Italian tenor Andrea Bocelli was considered a world music act by *Billboard* magazine and was proclaimed *Billboard*'s top-selling world music artist in 1998 and 1999 (Henderson 1998, 1999). The Grammy Awards, since *Global Pop* was published, have continued along the lines I wrote about more than a decade ago. The winners since *Global Pop* are:

Year	Artist	Album	Country
1996	The Chieftains	*Santiago*	Ireland
1997	Milton Nascimento	*Nascimento*	Brazil
1998	Gilberto Gil	*Quanta Live*	Brazil
1999	Caetano Veloso	*Livro*	Brazil
2000	Joao Gilberto	*João Voz e Violão*	Brazil
2001	Ravi Shankar	*Full Circle—Carnegie Hall 2000*	India
2002	Rubén Blades	*Mundo*	Panama

Immediately obvious are the presence of perennial favorites, the Chieftains and Ravi Shankar. The number of Brazilian musicians is also striking, and it is possible to include Rubén Blades in this list if we expand "Brazilian" to something broader, such as "Latin." I am pleased that these musicians have received mainstream recognition, but at the same time there are Latin Grammy Awards for their music, which makes one wonder: Where are the musicians from elsewhere? With the exception of Ravi Shankar, all the awardees are from Europe or the Americas.

Perhaps finally recognizing this geographical bias, the National Academy of Recording Arts and Sciences, which oversees Grammy Awards, instituted several changes in the "Best World Music Album" category, announcing these changes in 2003 as follows:

> World music is now represented by two categories in its own field: Best Traditional World Music Album and Best Contemporary World Music Album. The Traditional World Music category will include recordings of international non-Western classical music and international non-American and non-British traditional folk music, as well as international cross-cultural music based on the above criteria. The Contemporary World Music category will include recordings of world/beat, world/jazz (with a higher percentage of world than jazz), world/pop and cross-cultural music with contemporary production techniques. ("Academy Elects New National Officers" 2003)

The first nominees in these new categories showed a much better spread than in the past. The "Best Traditional World Music Album" brought in musicians and recordings that were scarcely recognized previously such as mountain music from Puerto Rico, Indian ghazals, and Tibetan chanting, the eventual winner; the "Best Contemporary World Music Album" nominees include musicians who have always been well represented on the nominee list such as Caetano Veloso and the winner Cape Verdean chanteuse Cesaria Evora. All the winners following the change in policy are listed in Table 1. Certainly all are worthy recipients, but, nonetheless, the selection was rather cautious: all are well-known musicians or genres.

This bifurcation of the Grammy world music category demonstrates the new importance of musical sounds that are not heard as "authentic" or "pure" but partake freely of Anglo-American musical sounds and styles. Elsewhere I have written of the shift in preference away from the kind of world music that was valorized by the industry—music the West thought of as "authentic" in the sense of being "pure" or unspoiled—to music that is heard as "hybrid" (Taylor 2007; Frith 2000). The "purer" musics did not sell very well; what sold, and continues to sell, are musics that are more palatable, closer to the classic Bhabhaesque formulation of difference and the Other, with the Other being *almost the same, but not quite* (Bhabha 1994, 86; emphasis in original). Critics who once excoriated certain musicians for not being "authentic" enough and for caving in to Anglo-American

Table 1.

Year	Award	Artist	Album	Country
2003	Best Traditional World Music Album	The Monks of Sherab Ling Monastery	*Sacred Tibetan Chant*	Tibet
2003	Best Contemporary World Music Album	Cesaria Evora	*Voz D'Amor*	Cape Verde
2004	Best Traditional World Music Album	Ladysmith Black Mambazo	*Raise Your Spirit High*	South Africa
2004	Best Contemporary World Music Album	Youssou N'Dour	*Egypt*	Senegal
2005	Best Traditional World Music Album	Ali Farka Toure and Toumani Diabate	*In the Heart of the Moon*	Mali
2005	Best Contemporary World Music Album	Gilberto Gil	*Eletracústico*	Brazil
2006	Best Traditional World Music Album	The Soweto Gospel Choir	*Blessed*	South Africa
2006	Best Contemporary World Music Album	The Klezmatics	*Wonder Wheel*	United States/ Jewish
2007	Best Traditional World Music Album	The Soweto Gospel Choir	*African Spirit*	South Africa
2007	Best Contemporary World Music Album	Angélique Kidjo	*Djin Djin*	Benin/United States
2008	Best Traditional World Music Album	Ladysmith Black Mambazo	*Ilembe: Honoring Shaka Zulu*	South Africa
2008	Best Contemporary World Music Album	Mickey Hart, Zakir Hussain, Sikiru Adepoju, and Giovanni Hidalgo	*Global Drum Project*	Various
2009	Best Traditional World Music Album	Mamadou Diabate	*Douga Mansa*	Mali
2009	Best Contemporary World Music Album	Béla Fleck	*Throw Down Your Heart: Tales from the Acoustic Planet, Vol. 3, Africa Sessions*	United States/ Africa
2010	Best Traditional World Music	Ali Farka Touré and Toumani Diabaté	*Ali and Toumani*	Mali
2010	Best Contemporary World Music Album	Béla Fleck	*Throw Down Your Heart, Africa Sessions Par 2: Unreleased Tracks*	United States/ Africa

popular music sounds and styles reversed themselves and began to praise those very same musicians for their hybrids, which became a new form of authenticity.

The Problem of Cultural Imperialism

Even as world music climbs the ladder of mainstream awareness, many Americans are cognizant that their popular culture is popular around the world. In the popular press, with the increasingly salient coverage of the phenomena of globalization, transnationalism, and other views that exclaim "we're all one world now," a good deal of coverage has been based on the realization that American popular culture travels farther and more quickly than ever before. Although academics have not, by and large, adopted a theory of homogenization with the alacrity of the popular press (Pieterse 1994; Barber 1995), the mainstream American press now routinely uses the phrase "cultural homogenization" (occasionally when discussing music); and the word "McDonaldization" has entered the public lexicon as well (Ritzer 1993, 1996; Alfino, Caputo, and Wynyard 1998). Fears of the demise of local cultures and musics are registered in such endeavors as the Endangered Music project of the American Folklife Center at the Library of Congress. In short, the death of the local is thought to be occurring with the rise of the global, which has a decidedly American accent (Hannerz 1996; Lash and Urry 1994; Wilson and Dissanyake 1996; Guilbault 1993).

The rise of the global is sometimes true, at least and, perhaps most noticeably, in the case of music. Young people around the world dream of becoming the next pop star like their American export equivalents. Electronic dance musics, unlike all other popular musics, do not have lyrics that might limit their audiences, and they are being produced and danced to around the world. Goa, or psychedelic, trance, for example, is produced in Europe, Israel, India, South Africa, and North America, and it is usually difficult to tell where a particular track was made.[7]

In the last few decades governments worldwide have been complaining more and more vociferously about what is seen as the onslaught of American popular culture.[8] Governments in Canada, France, Israel, New Zealand, and South Africa have imposed quotas for ensuring that domestic musics receive adequate radio airtime; other countries are considering such quotas (Farnsworth 1994; Greenberg 1998; Lee 1974; Pfanner 2005; Shuker and Pickering 1994). Canada is perhaps the most outspoken as of this writing; in the late 1990s the heritage minister convened two international conferences on American cultural imperialism—which it describes as the replacement of non-Canadian forms with American forms—and is aggressively pursuing ways of limiting the influence of American popular culture on Canadian culture.[9] Cultural imperialism has received some coverage in the American press as well (Cowen 2007; Garten 1998; "Uncle Sam is Pop Culture to the World" 1989).

Most scholars who examined the cultural imperialism concept with respect to music, however, ultimately rejected it as inadequate to explain how musics intermingle (see Martin, this volume).[10] It was too "top-down" a model, with its assumption of the wicked West imposing its sounds on the unsuspecting masses of a so-called Third World that was assumed to have neither the knowledge nor the agency to protect itself from foreign assault. Cultural imperialism also was too rigid a model to explain the myriad and complicated ways that cultural forms can mix. I am arguing here that if people take cultural imperialism to be real, we must take it seriously ethnographically, and it is possible to do this without adopting it wholesale as an analytical framework.

Furthermore, fears of the global homogenization of music tend to oversimplify. A music that sounds as though it has been polluted by Western musical styles can, nonetheless, occupy the same social space and fulfill the same social function as a more "traditional" music that is being supplanted by newer music. In other words, if one views music not simply as a formalistic-stylistic entity and understands it instead as an activity serving certain functions in particular cultures, it might not be so easy to conclude that Western music is wiping out local musics.

Consider, for example, *gita gisalo*, a guitar music of the Bosavi people of Papaua, New Guinea, recently anthologized by Steven Feld (2001). In the liner notes to that anthology, Feld writes that the guitar and ukuleles were introduced to the Bosavi area in the mid-1970s, around the same time as the appearance of cassette players and cassettes of Western popular musics. These two novelties fueled musical experimentation, and by the 1980s and 1990s some string bands were fairly proficient. According to Feld, the song, "My Father, My Heart," by the Kemuli String Band, continues the tradition of using ceremonial song poetics to evoke memories of the dead, in this case the father of the composer and singer Oska. The most significant feature here is the use of the syllable *ya-*, which, Feld says, represents the sound of the crying voice. When the singers utter this syllable, "they simultaneously imitate the vocal break of the crying voice," which "makes Bosavi listeners think of the sound of the sung-weeping of funerary laments for the recently deceased" (Feld 2001, 32).

The sounds that appear to be "Western" to Western ears are coupled with sounds and devices that sound Bosavi to Bosavi ears. Assuming that Western cultural forms somehow wipe out or overpower the forms of other cultures is no less Euro- and America-centric than most writings on globalization. Thus there appears to be a problem with theories that are too abstract to capture what goes on in certain cases; for example, it is fruitless to theorize that cultural "gray out" is or is not occurring without referring to specific cases. If one thinks in these terms, it becomes clear that instances arise where Western forms replace or seriously imperil other forms; there are also cases of resistance, and many more cases where sounds from different cultures coexist. If general theorization is possible, one could argue that, overall, global cultural production is becoming more diverse, not less, although this diversity does not necessarily mean that some musics are not disappearing at the same time. It may be that the global popularity and influence of certain American and European sounds will come to mean that even as new musics crop up around the world, they will be less different than they used to be in some places, in a process Scott Lash (1990) described as "de-differentiation," which he sees as symptomatic of contemporary times. But to theorize that wholesale homogenization is, or is not, occurring is difficult, if not impossible, to do without reference to the myriad practices in real places and in real time, as some have begun to do (Diehl 2002; Luvaas 2009; Meintjes 2003; Wallach 2008; White 2008).

World Music and Social Class

One feature of world music that has become clearer since *Global Pop* was published is the nature of its audience. Record labels frequently leave cards in the CD jewel cases that solicit information from consumers, and labels sometimes make this information known. For example, Bob Haddad, president and producer for the now defunct Music of the World, an independent record label based in Chapel Hill, North Carolina, said that the cards consumers returned "show that the buyers of purer ethnic music tend to be well-educated, well-travelled [*sic*], 25 and over—often between 35 and 60 years old—and might speak several languages" (quoted in Henderson 1997, 52). This is a group, in other words, with high educational capital and, presumably, fairly high incomes. One record company executive, commenting on a radio station in Los Angeles that was in the process of changing from so-called easy listening to "contemporary rock artists and singer-songwriters with a smattering of folk, soul, blues, reggae and world music" was a little more blunt: "The demographic it appeals to is one that advertisers find very appealing for their education and financial status. Even if the station only gets a certain level of success, those people are the ones that advertisers really want to get to" (Puig and Hochman 1994, 24). Another record company representative said that "we discovered that the demographics of the people buying Irish albums were the same as for those buying reggae and world beat. Not the same individuals, necessarily, but the same demographic—mostly white, college-educated adults looking for something different."[11]

But this segment of the middle class cannot necessarily be seen as an index of "world music." I believe, in fact, that there is a new kind of capital, in Pierre Bourdieu's (1984) sense of cultural capital, that is increasingly deemed necessary in this moment of hype over globalization. In an article on the use of world music in television advertisements (Taylor 2007), I called this new capital "global informational capital," referring to the increasing importance in developed countries of possessing a kind of capital that stands in for real knowledge of the world in the current so-called information age.

The importance of global informational capital needs to be understood in part by examining the recent emphasis in the business world on globalization and, more generally, on discourses of globalization in the public domain, for it is now commonly believed that today everyone lives in an information, or global, economy.

Classicalization of World Music

Because of the music industry's realization of the high cultural and educational capital of the world music audience and the rising importance of global informational capital, world music is encroaching on the space once held by classical music; indeed, world music is replacing classical music in certain ways and is becoming increasingly "classicalized."

Considering the former point first, classical music in the United States brings in little revenue for record labels and is slowly losing audiences. Orchestras and opera companies are failing, and the prestige of classical music is waning. Further, major labels release fewer classical albums than ever before, and world music is coming to occupy that slot. For example, the major record retailers, at least in New York City, increasingly sequester world music from the rest of the shop, just as classical sections are separated in such stores. One of these shops in Times Square eliminated its classical section entirely, and world music now occupies the noise-proofed portion of this store.[12] Another major retailer in New York City also noise-proofed the world music portion of its store and even has a separate entrance so patrons can walk directly to that area. This segregation of world music in stores is similar to the kind of protection from other customers and sounds that classical music listeners expect.

Treating world music as one would classical music is not only occurring in the United States. In the United Kingdom *Gramophone*, the venerable British classical recording review magazine, began a new spin-off magazine, *The Songlines*, to my knowledge, *Gramophone's* only non-classical magazine. *The Songlines*, according to its editor, offers more serious and in-depth coverage of world music compared to its competitors such as *Folk Roots* in the United Kingdom or *Rhythm Music* in the United States (quoted in Broughton 1998). Although this seems to be true, these more in-depth articles are fairly brief, sometimes only a page. Significantly the magazine was originally the size of a journal, less than 9½ inches, which emphasized its status as a connoisseur's journal and not a slick commercial magazine, though that is what it subsequently became (Taylor 2007). Another development is that BBC Radio 3, which until fairly recently was the classical station, began to air world music under the direction of Roger Wright, who began as controller in 1998. The record label Naxos, which occupied the low-budget classical niche, has now branched out into world music.

More than simply filling in the gap left by a waning classical music niche, world music has begun to mix with classical music sounds. It is now possible to hear classicalized world music performances such as Jonathan Elias's *The Prayer Cycle*, released in 1999, featuring singers as diverse as Alanis Morissette and Nusrat Fateh Ali Kahn (Elias 1999). The result is a mixture of world music, classical, and new age styles, an increasingly common sound (see Parney 1999). It is not a coincidence that Jonathan Elias heads one of the biggest advertising music companies, Elias Arts. To give some idea of the sound of this work, and its somewhat forced eclecticism, the sixth movement of nine, "Innocence," features a chorus that sings in Swahili, Alanis Morissette in Hungarian, and Salif Keita in Bambara. I should also note that this recording was released on the Sony Classical label, another sign of the classicalization of world music—or, in this case, the "worldification" of classical music—as the label seeks to broaden what may be included in the classical category.

Conclusions

Sales data clearly indicate that, although world music is not commercially important to the music industry, as it does not provide much revenue, it nonetheless has seeped into the broader musical soundscape of the contemporary West, largely through samples and usages in broadcasting. In a sense, the digital world has digitized, atomized, world music so that it is broken up and disseminated everywhere, though not always in ways easily recognized by listeners. This process could only have taken place after world music—which is, after all, a vast collection of wildly different musics from all over the planet—had been reduced to a "style" or "genre" so it could be disciplined, managed, and discursively constructed. The music and marketing industries could then dissect and disseminate it for their profit-driven ends, marking their triumph over this vast collection of musics—at least for now.

Notes

I thank Steven Feld for the many conversations we have had on this subject over the years, which have helped shape and clarify my thinking. I also thank Bob White for his helpful and insightful comments, and Marissa Steingold for her comments on the travails of a singer in the world of commercial music. Thanks are also due to the audience at the British Forum for Ethnomusicology, where this chapter was presented on April 19, 2009. And, as ever, I thank Sherry B. Ortner.

1. Books for teachers include Anderson and Moore 1997; Anderson and Campbell 1996 [1989]; Campbell 1996, 2001; Campbell, Drummond, and Dunbar-Hall 2005; Floyd 1996; Leith-Philipp 1995; Reimer 2002; and Volk 1998. Textbooks include Alves 2005; Bakan 2007; Miller and Shahriari 2005; and Nettl et al. 2007.

2. On the sampling of world music, see Théberge 2003. see

3. http://www.killertracks.com/frontdoor/ourmusic.cfm.

4. http://www.freshmusic.com.

5. http://www.freshmusic.com.

6. http://www.themusicbroker.net.

7. For more on Goa/psychedelic trance, see Taylor 2001.

8. European fears of Americanization are not new, however. See Kuisel 1993; and Pells 1997.

9. This conference was widely reported around the world but was scarcely noted in the U.S. press. For an overview, see Cobb 1998.

10. For example, Goodwin and Gore 1990; Laing 1986; and Robinson et al. 1991. For an excellent overview and critique of the discourse of cultural imperialism, see Tomlinson 1991.

11. Some retailers and label executives refer to this group as "cultural creatives," a term that originated in an *American Demographics* magazine article in 1997 that was used to describe a group of thirty-five year olds and above who are well educated, financially solvent, and curious about other cultures and traveling (Ray 1997). See also Ray and Anderson 2000. For a discussion of this group with respect to world music, see Fries 1999.

12. I thank Jason Oakes for bringing this to my attention.

References

"Academy Elects New National Officers." 2003. http://www.grammy.com/news/academy/2003/0605trustees.aspx.

Alfino, Mark, John S. Caputo, and Robin Wynyard, eds. 1998. *McDonaldization Revisited: Critical Essays on Consumer Culture*. Westport, CT: Praeger.

Alves, William. 2005. *Music of the Peoples of the World*. New York: Schirmer.

Anderson, William M., and Marvelene C. Moore, eds. 1997. *Making Connections: Multicultural Music and the National Standards*. Reston, VA: National Association for Music Education.

Anderson, William M., and Patricia Shehan Campbell, eds. 1996 [1989]. *Multicultural Perspectives in Music Education*. Reston, VA: National Association for Music Education.

Bakan, Michael B. 2007. *World Music: Traditions and Transformations*. New York: McGraw-Hill.

Barber, B. R. 1995. *Jihad vs. McWorld*. New York: Random House.

Bhabha, Homi K. 1994. *The Location of Culture*. London: Routledge.

Bohlman, Philip V. 2002. *World Music: A Very Short Introduction*. New York: Oxford University Press.

Bourdieu, Pierre. 1984. *Distinction: A Social Critique of the Judgement of Taste*. Translated by Richard Nice. Cambridge, MA: Harvard University Press.

Broughton, Simon. 1998. Personal communication, November 6, Maastricht, the Netherlands.

Campbell, Patricia Shehan, ed. 1996. *Music in Cultural Context: Eight Views on World Music Education*. Reston, VA: National Association for Music Education.

———. 2001. *Lessons from the World*. New York: McGraw-Hill.

Campbell, Patricia Shehan, John Drummond, and Peter Dunbar-Hall, eds. 2005. *Cultural Diversity in Music Education: Directions and Challenges for the 21st Century*. Queensland: Australian Academic Press.

Cobb, Chris. 1998. "Culture Ministers Meet to Fight U.S. Dominance," *Ottawa Citizen*, June 29, A-5.

Cowen, Tyler. 2007. "For Some Developing Countries, America's Popular Culture Is Resistible." *New York Times*, C-3.

Diehl, Keila. 2002. *Echoes from Dharamsala: Music in the Life of a Tibetan Refugee Community*. Berkeley: University of California Press.

Farnsworth, Clyde H. 1994. "The Border War over Country Music." *New York Times,* October 30, F-7.

Feld, Steven. 2001. Liner notes to *Bosavi: Rainforest Music from Papua New Guinea*. Smithsonian Folkways Anthologies CD 40487.

Floyd, Malcolm, ed. 1996. *World Musics in Education*. Hants, U.K.: Scolar.

Fries, Laura. 1999. "World Music Goes Coast to Coast." *Billboard,* September 25, 94.

Frith, Simon. 2000. "The Discourse of World Music." In *Western Music and Its Others: Difference, Representation, and Appropriation in Music,* ed. Georgina Born and David Hesmondhalgh. Berkeley: University of California Press.

Garten, Jeffrey E. 1998. "'Cultural Imperialism' Is no Joke." *Business Week,* November 30, 26.

Goodwin, Andrew, and Joe Gore. 1990. "World Beat and the Cultural Imperialism Debate." *Socialist Review* 20 (July–September): 63–80.

Greenberg, Joel. 1998. "Israel Battles New Foreign Foe: Music." *New York Times,* December 20, 10.

Guilbault, Jocelyne. 1993. "On Redefining the 'Local' through World Music." *World of Music* 32:33–47.

Hannerz, Ulf. 1996. *Transnational Connections: Culture, People, Places*. New York: Routledge.

Hart, Mickey. 2003. *Songcatchers: In Search of the World's Music*. Washington, DC: National Geographic.

Henderson, Richard. 1997. "What in the World Is It?" *Billboard,* June 28, 52.

———. 1998-1999. "The Year in World Music." *Billboard,* December 26, 1998–January 2, YE-91.

———. 2000. "The Year in World Music." *Billboard,* December 25, 1999–January 1, YE-94.

———. 2002. "World Music Knows No Borders." *Billboard,* October 26, 40.

Kuisel, Richard F. 1993. *Seducing the French: The Dilemma of Americanization*. Berkeley: University of California Press.

Laing, Dave. 1986. "The Music Industry and the 'Cultural Imperialism' Thesis." *Media, Culture and Society* 8 (July): 331–341.

Lash, Scott. 1990. *Sociology of Postmodernism*. London: Routledge.

Lash, Scott, and John Urry. 1994. *Economies of Signs and Space*. Thousand Oaks, CA: Sage.

Lee, Dennis. 1974. "Cadence, Country, Silence: Writing in Colonial Space." *Boundary 2* 3 (fall): 151–168.

Leith-Philipp, Margo. 1995. *Teaching Musics of the World*. Affalterbach, Germany: Philipp Verlag.

Luvaas, Brent. 2009 "Dislocating Sounds: The Deterritorialization of Indonesian Indie Pop." *Cultural Anthropology* 24 (May): 246–279.

Malm, Krister. 1993. "Music on the Move: Traditions and Mass Media." *Ethnomusicology* 37 (Fall): 339–352.

Malm, Krister, and Roger Wallis. 1992. *Media Policy and Music Activity*. London: Routledge.

Meintjes, Louise. 2003. *Sound of Africa! Making Music Zulu in a South African Studio*. Durham, NC: Duke University Press.

Miller, Terry E., and Andrew Shahriari. 2005. *World Music: A Global Journey*. New York: Routledge.

Mitchell, Rick. 1992. "American Tastes Move to World Beat." *Houston Chronicle*, January 26, 8.

Nettl, Bruno, Thomas Turino, Isabel Wong, Charles Capwell, Philip Bohlman, and Timothy Rommen. 2007. *Excursions in World Music*. 5th ed. Englewood Cliffs, NJ: Prentice Hall.

Parney, Lisa Leigh. 1999. "Songs of 'Prayer Cycle' Seek Universal Themes." *Christian Science Monitor*, April 23, 20.

Pells, Richard H. 1997. *Not Like Us: How Europeans Have Loved, Hated, and Transformed American Culture since World War II*. New York: Basic Books.

Pfanner, Eric. 2005. "Some Industry Advice to German Musicians: Never Mind the English Lessons." *New York* Times, July 25, C-8.

Pieterse, Jan Nederveen. 1994. "Globalisation as Hybridisation." *International Sociology* 9 (June): 161–184.

Pratt, Mary Louise. 1992. *Imperial Eyes: Travel Writing and Transculturation*. New York: Routledge.

Puig, Claudia, and Steve Hochman. 1994. "New Station Aims to Give Pop Fans a Choice." *Los Angeles Times* July 1, 4-24.

Ray, Paul H. 1997. "The Emerging Culture." *American Demographics* 19 (February): 28–34.

Ray, Paul H., and Sherry Ruth Anderson. 2000. *The Cultural Creatives: How 50 Million People Are Changing the World*. New York: Harmony Books.

Recording Industry Association of America. 2008. "2007 Consumer Profile." http://76 .74.24.142/8EF388DA-8FD3-7A4E-C208-CDF1ADE8B179.pdf.

Reimer, Bennett, ed. 2002. *World Musics and Music Education: Facing the Issues*. Reston, VA: National Association for Music Education.

Ritzer, George. 1993. *The McDonaldization of Society*. Thousand Oaks, CA: Pine Forge.

———. 1996. *The McDonaldization Thesis: Explorations and Extensions*. Thousand Oaks, CA: Sage.

Robinson, Deanna Campbell, et al. 1991. *Music at the Margins: Popular Music and Global Cultural Diversity*. Newbury Park, CA: Sage.

Schnabel, Tom. 1998. *Rhythm Planet: The Great World Music Makers*. New York: Universe.

Shuker, Roy, and Michael Pickering. 1994. "Kiwi Rock: Popular Music and Cultural Identity in New Zealand." *Popular Music* 13 (October): 261–278.

Steingold, Marissa. 2009. Interview by author, February 27.

Taylor, Timothy D. 1997. *Global Pop: World Music, World Markets*. New York: Routledge.

———. 2001. *Strange Sounds: Music, Technology, and Culture*. New York: Routledge.

———. 2007. *Beyond Exoticism: Western Music and the World*. Durham, NC: Duke University Press.

Théberge, Paul. 2003. "'Ethnic Sounds': The Economy and Discourse of World Music Sampling." In *Music and Technoculture*, ed. René T. A. Lysloff and Leslie C. Gay, Jr., 93–108. Middletown, CT: Wesleyan University Press.

Thompson, Clifford, ed. 1999. *Contemporary World Musicians*. Chicago: Fitzroy Dearborn.

Tomlinson, John. 1991. *Cultural Imperialism: A Critical Introduction*. Baltimore: Johns Hopkins University Press.

"Uncle Sam Is Pop Culture to the World." 1989. *U.S. News and World Report*, August 7, 9.

Volk, Terese M. 1998. *Music, Education, and Multiculturalism: Foundations and Principles.* New York: Oxford University Press.

Wallach, Jeremy. 2008. *Modern Noise, Fluid Genres: Popular Music in Indonesia, 1997–2001.* Madison: University of Wisconsin Press.

Wallis, Roger, and Krister Malm. 1984. *Big Sounds from Small Peoples: The Music Industry in Small Countries.* London: Constable.

White, Bob W. 2008. *Rumba Rules: The Politics of Dance Music in Mobutu's Zaire.* Durham, NC: Duke University Press.

Wilson, Rob, and Wimal Dissanyake, eds. 1996. *Global/Local: Cultural Production and the Transnational Imaginary.* Durham, NC: Duke University Press.

Zager, Michael. 2003. *Writing Music for Television and Radio Commercials: A Manual for Composers and Students.* Lanham, MD: Scarecrow.

Discography

Bosavi: Rainforest Music from Papua New Guinea. 2001. Smithsonian Folkways Anthologies CD 40487.

Elias, Jonathan. 1999. *The Prayer Cycle.* Sony Classical, SK 60569.

10

The Promise of World Music:
Strategies for Non-Essentialist Listening

Bob W. White

Sound is the same for all the world
Everybody has a heart
Everybody gets a feeling
Let's play! Sound box!
Rock, reggae, jazz, mbalax
All around the world . . . the same
Pachanga, soul music, rhythm and blues . . . the same
La samba, la rumba, cha-cha-cha . . . the same
Sound is the same for all the world
Everybody has a heart
Everybody gets a feeling
Mbaqanga, ziglibiti, high life music . . . the same
Merengue, funk, Chinese music . . . the same
Bossa nova, soul makossa, rap music . . . the same
Come on people, dance
Everybody in the world has a culture
Believe what you believe
Respect your customs
Everybody must do what the heart says
Don't cause trouble; Treat people well
Be sociable; Exchange ideas
Music is the same the world over
Musicians, too, are cut from the same cloth
We're aiming to entertain you

—Youssou N'dour, "The Same," Sony/Columbia, 1992

One question has yet to be asked regarding the relatively recent phenomenon of world music: What can music teach us about other cultures? If we take Youssou N'dour's singsong text at face value, the answer would be "not very much," since we have known for some time that "everybody has a culture." In this chapter I show that the promotion and consumption of world music is a series of essentializing practices that actually hide behind a rhetoric of non-essentialism. For those who consume or promote this type of cultural commodity, world music represents a promise that comes from the desire to heal the wounds of a colonial past and, increasingly, a neoliberal present. Unfortunately, however, the cosmopolitanism in the consumption of world music is often one step away from essentialism, as Western consumers identify with a musical culture that is either poorly defined or not defined at all. In the first part of the chapter I analyze essentialist strategies in the promotion and consumption of this emerging genre of music. The second part of my analysis focuses on the relationship between world music and the expression of a cosmopolitan lifestyle that seeks to increase the social status of the Self by consuming the music of the Other. Finally, I discuss several important moments of anti-essentialist critique and propose a series of listening strategies whose main objective is to make the encounter with other peoples' music more complex by going beyond the simple act of listening.

The Figures of World Music

Music is often presented as a form of cultural expression capable of bringing cultures closer together and teaching about tolerance, a kind of promise to respect and honor cultural diversity. Steven Feld (2000) argues that discourses about "world music" tend to take one of two forms. The first, which he refers to as a discourse of *anxiety,* is critical not only of globalization but also of its composite elements: capital, modernity, and technology. The second is a discourse of *celebration* whose focus is either the genius of the human spirit (using such concepts as resistance, appropriation, and agency) or the universal potential of humanity, perhaps most fully embodied in the millennial expression "global village." Taking Feld's observations as a starting point, I will explore the discursive patterns that enable promoters of world music to bring this form of music to potential consumers. The promotion of world music rests on a number of motifs, or *figures,* that are not always explicit but work together to reinforce a community of taste around this category of music. In this section I analyze three figures of language—universality, hybridity, and solidarity; each one mediates the relationship between the artisans of world music and their potential fans.[1]

FIGURE 1: MUSIC AS A UNIVERSAL LANGUAGE
Given its capacity to represent reality without recourse to language, music is often perceived as a language in itself.[2] Music is thus seen as a universal form of com-

munication free from linguistic mediation that enables contact between human beings by virtue of its ability to act directly upon the senses, as in these examples:

> Music in all its forms is a vital necessity, a hyphen that brings together generations and cultures from the most traditional to the most contemporary. Music is a universal language that should make a contribution against the spirals of hate, exclusion and violence that divide men and threaten the cohesion of our societies. It is a celebration of social harmony and tolerance. Musical celebration expresses, in the space of an evening, the will of all to live together, with curiosity, generosity and sharing. It is in this spirit that I say to all: make music! (Donnedieu de Vabres 2004)

> The Real World "Recording Week" first demonstrated this philosophy in 1991 when Real World Studios threw open its doors for one week to 75 international artists and producers from over 20 countries. Not only were several albums by individual artists recorded, but also the accumulation of so many creative minds in one place inevitably led to the start of exciting new musical dialogues. The result is a triumphant celebration of music as the global language of emotion. (Real World Records 2008)

From this perspective, the capacity of music to communicate outside of language somehow reduces the time and distance that separate different types of moderns and primitives, as suggested in these examples:

> Since the dawn of time people all over the world have wrapped a piece of skin around a hollowed out log and have been keeping the beat. If you're in the jungle, grab a couple of sticks and tap them together. In the middle of the city, a trash can lid will do. In Tibet the Damaru drum is made out of two halves of a human skull. The two pieces are joined together, covered with skin and a beater on a length of rope is used to produce the sound. ("Drumming" 2008)[3]

> But it is her trip to Cuba that was the most important. It is there that she found the memory of humanity through a music in which she recognized the dialects and idiomatic expressions that were the result of slavery as far away as her native country of Benin, from which she left in exile to escape the censorship of a totalitarian state before finally becoming a resident in France and the USA. The primary theme of "Oyaya" (that means "joy" in Yoruba) is the reunification of humans through music and its history. This joy, expressed by an exceptional voice, is the cement between the subtle links that unify ancestral music and contemporary melodies. (Kidjo 2008; my translation)

Harmony is a metaphor for bringing people together in new forms of community:

> [The Artist] Nick Page lives and breathes a philosophy of musical and cultural inclusion. Every song he selects for his "Power Singing" workshops bears the hallmark of his approach: energy and power. He teaches the melodies bit by bit to audiences comprised of both avid and reluctant singers of all ages. Before he is done, they are unified in voice and heart, rolling in harmonies, true believers in the power of music to intensify the bonds of the human community. (Page 2008)

This sense of community (which sometimes takes the form of a communion) is made possible by music's refusal to see the differences that separate human beings:

> Many people have asked us how we arrived at our company name "One World Rhythm." The answer to our company identity is as old as music itself. Music transcends cultural and religious boundaries. Music sees beyond gender and age. Music knows no monetary system or economic class. And music can take our hearts and imaginations to distant lands and enchanted locales. (One World Rhythm 2008)

The capacity of music to bring people together increases our awareness of racism and creates possibilities for imagining new ways of organizing society:

> Equally important, the festivals have also allowed many different audiences to gain an insight into cultures other than their own through the enjoyment of music. Music is a universal language, it draws people together and proves, as well as anything, the stupidity of racism. As an organisation, WOMAD now works in many different ways, but our aims are always the same—at festivals, performance events, through recorded releases and through educational projects, we aim to excite, to inform, and to create awareness of the worth and potential of a multicultural society. (WOMAD Foundation 2007)

But if for some people music represents a bridge between different cultures, for others—especially those of us writing about world music from within the walls of the academy, such as the renowned ethnomusicologist Bernard Lortat-Jacob—this bridge is fragile and dangerous:

> The musical tower of Babel truly exists, contrary to what the apostles of "world music" would have us believe, and in their image, several rising stars

of traditional music. The "world music" ideology presents itself as something universal. This is why it is false, or even dangerous. (Lortat-Jacob 2000; my translation)

World music, from this vantage point, risks sacrificing difference on the altar of the Universal. One of the best examples of this sacrifice comes to us from Putumayo, today one of the world's most visible independent world music labels, with more than one hundred titles and fifteen million products sold since 1993.[4] In 1999 Putumayo launched a public school-based educational program whose main objective was to "illustrate music's capacity to deepen our understanding of the world through positive, shared experiences" (Putumayo World Music 1999, 5). This program, titled "World Playground," consists of a teaching guide with songs from a dozen different cultural contexts (some regional, others national), a map of the world, and a "passport" students fill out as they progress through a musical journey of cultural diversity.[5] The activity book presents general information about the different countries (languages, ethnic groups, important dates, foods, animals, climate, and indigenous musical instruments), but entries are generally limited to one page or the length of an encyclopedia entry. In addition to information about the country, a short biography of the artist representing the country is also included, as well as a summary of the content of the song that artist contributes to the accompanying CD. Lyrics from all the songs are transcribed and translated into English at the end of the booklet.

"World Playground" strongly emphasizes the "celebration of diversity," but clearly Putumayo's presentation of diversity is quite limited. The production style, the choice of information, and the illustrations (brightly colorful, in art naïf style, and always by the same artist) work together to create the impression of a historical equivalence between the different countries represented in the series. This equivalence functions not only with regard to the different country profiles (each one has a national dish, a national monument, and a national holiday) but also in terms of sound, since, as the introduction to the passport explains, music teaches us about other cultures ("Listen closely to the music! It will tell you a lot about the people, places and cultures of the world"). But what exactly does music teach us? Bob Marley's mother sings, "Don't worry, bout a thing, cause every little thing, gonna be alright." Manu Chao becomes the King of Bongo ("Deep down in the jungle I started banging my first bongo"), and the blues singer Eric Bibb sings about the importance of turning obstacles into "stepping stones." Clearly we are far from the problems of poverty, inequality, and injustice that form the foundations of alternative rock music, blues, and reggae. This erasure, which combines a diluted version of universal humanism with the culture of "fun," is echoed in the titles of other albums produced by Putumayo: *World Party, World Groove, World Lounge,* and a collection of intercultural collaborations titled *One World, Many*

Cultures.[6] Thus the globe is presented as nothing but a huge cultural playground, with music providing unlimited access to a world of play.

FIGURE 2: HYBRIDITY AS A FORM OF AUTHENTICITY

Tim Taylor (1997), one of the first authors to document the centrality of authenticity in the phenomenon of world music, has also observed that discourses of authenticity are constantly shifting: "It appears, in other words, that world musicians may not be expected to be authentic anymore in the sense of being untouched by the sounds of the West; now it is their very hybridity that allows them to be constructed as authentic" (2007, 144).[7] This hybridity generally expresses itself as an opposition between tradition and modernity, but the temporal metaphor can also be accompanied by a metaphor of mixing over space:

> On *Ama*, her third album for Real World Records, Yungchen again brings that voice to songs infused with the quiet spiritual power of Tibetan Buddhism, but with a decidedly 21st century global feel. Trumpet, strings, African kora, Middle Eastern percussion and the even, sweet tones of a National Steel guitar are delicately woven around Yungchen's magical voice. With guest appearances by the British singer Joy Askew and the incomparable Annie Lennox, *Ama* becomes that rare destination where East really does happily meet West. No translators, or politicians, required. (Lhamo 2008)

The hybrid nature of the music is made possible by collaborative methods (a topic discussed below) that convey an air of conviviality and reciprocity to the practice of making music:

> Whilst there is a tendency for people to pull together this diverse range of releases under the banner "world music," the reality of the Real World output extends beyond this categorization. We find that great music is enjoyable to listen to irrespective of the nationality of artists creating it. Indeed, many of the most exciting sounds that you will discover on our label are the result of collaborations between musicians from many different countries. (Real World Records 2007)

> "Assembly," the result of their combined labours, merges the poetry and grace of Wagogo melodies with science-fiction funk, the shape-shifting sound of a digitally enhanced roadhouse band. Shimmering thumb piano melodies and the many voices of Hukwe—some high-pitched and keening, others of seismic depth and resonance—are woven within dense rhythmic laminates of sternum-shaking beats and insistent grooves, gilded with the signature tone of Brook's own invention, the infinite guitar. (Zawose and Brook 2008)

This invocation of hybrid identity reflects not only the cultural situation in which many world music artists find themselves, but it is also an integral aspect of record companies' promotional strategies. In the words of Steven Feld: "invoking hybridity as one's own identity position, one then is licensed to claim the full spatiotemporal terrain of that identity as an artistic palette" (1996, 2). In certain cases of musical hybridity, sounds and styles are piled on top of one another and the result is a frenetic mix in which the hybrid—not its quality but its mere presence—is more important than any of its constitutive elements:

> Ozomatli belong to a new breed of global music hoodlum alongside the likes of Manu Chao and Los De Abajo. They all play a kind of hi-octane pan-Latino dance music which mixes elements like ska, samba, salsa, punk, hip hop to varying degrees, and, in Ozomatli's case, funk, Tex Mex, swing and soul as well. On stage, they rely mainly on live instruments, old style, and mash all their influences together with rocket-propelled abandon, new style. (Ozomatli 2008)

Promotional language describes a world in which influences circulate freely without constraints, frontiers, or filters. In this context, cultural hybridity is not only a state of mind but also a source of artistic inspiration:

> Cultures constantly blend and influence each other. Nowhere is this occurrence more apparent and celebrated than in World Music. (Putumayo 1999)

In the context of world music, hybridity is either presented as a space of liminality between two worlds (neither here nor there but in between) that can just as easily be emancipatory or tragic[8] or as a source of potential strength since cultural hybrids can free themselves from the chains of tradition by adding on successive layers of strategic identity. In a fascinating debate on recent critiques of hybridity, Jan Nederveen Pieterse argues that "hybridity is a journey into the riddles of recognition. Take any exercise in social mapping and it is the hybrids that are missing" (Pieterse 2001, 220). This point is well taken, but the case of world music suggests that discourses of hybridity (at least regarding the products of culture) are not as marginal as they may once have been. Pieterse refers to the "world music model of hybridity" as an example of how the *longue durée* of hybridity has been ignored in recent critiques, but this dismissal signals a certain discomfort with the observation that hybridity increasingly makes good marketing sense (ibid.).[9] For fans of world music, cultural hybridity is valued not only because it combines desirable aspects of several identities (thus representing the possibility of having the "best of all worlds") but also because it is the protagonist of an epic myth of the future: a world without racism, without hate, and with a multitude of colors living together in harmony and style.

FIGURE 3: CONSUMPTION AS A GESTURE OF SOLIDARITY

For many consumers of world music, buying a CD constitutes a gesture of solidarity between the consumer and the artist, who represents (or at least stands for) people struggling for economic and political survival. In this way, participating in the world music phenomenon can be seen as a political and social gesture that enables consumers to project their desire for global social change and express their support, albeit symbolically, for people who struggle every day with the injustice of poverty and underdevelopment. The promotion of world music has always relied on the presence of a certain number of artists who use music as a platform to speak out against poverty and injustice. The best example of this is probably the reggae superstar Bob Marley. Marley is well known for having sung about peace and love, but his words (and those of reggae in general) also include a great deal of material that exposes the social and racial inequalities within and between post-industrial societies.[10]

Since Marley, a number of reggae artists have become known as rebel celebrities (for example, Côte d'Ivoire's Tiken Jah Fakoly), but reggae is not alone. Thomas Mapfumo carefully built a name for himself in his home country of Zimbabwe through a musical style called *chimurenga* (the Shona word for "struggle"), whose sound is inspired by the traditional mbira (thumb piano) and whose lyrics criticize the abuse of political power, both inside and outside Zimbabwe. According to the promotional material from his record company, Mapfumo continued trying to return to Zimbabwe until 2005, a time when he considered that his life was truly in danger. As made clear in the following excerpt, that his album, *Rise Up*, was banned by the official radio station in Zimbabwe confers a certain moral authority to his work:

> Today, the firey, militant voice has matured into a powerful call to arms, devoid of anger, solemn in its intimate understanding of the human cost of war. The music is as powerful and pure as ever. From the opening bars it slips into a poised, relaxed groove, with its unfailing hooks, its hypnotic harmonising refrains and the stately grace and moral authority of the great Mapfumo. (WOMAD 2008)

Mapfumo continues to integrate messages of protest and calls for solidarity into his live performance, though it is not exactly clear what form this "support" should take:

> You know if you gonna' see something wrong, you must be able to stand up and say "this is wrong." So . . . what is happening in Zimbabwe now is not the right thing, it is the wrong thing. And we would like you to support the Zimbabwean people to reliberate themselves.[11]

Coming out of the alternative rock scene in France in the 1980s, Manu Chao, former leader of the group Mano Negra, launched his solo career with a more Latin-sounding music than his previous work,[12] but his reputation as a musical activist and engaged humanist remain at the center of his public and media personality:

> His social engagement is today more humanist than political (even though he tries to keep his private life separate from his public battles), which is a perfect reflection of his music, with its diverse influences. His lyrics speak of love and education and his messages are more akin to ethical activism than political slogans. His battles are infused with everyday life and independent of the language he uses, they always have a universal value. With a measure of obstinacy, he deconstructs and reconstructs the work, with the use of electric formulas, going back up the mountain after each fall. "Giving up is permanent suicide." (Mondomix 2008; my translation)

Chao has close links with the Zapatista movement in Mexico, often participates in anti-globalization events, and is involved in labor movements in several countries where he tours. Thomas Mapfumo and Manu Chao exemplify how political activism is used in the promotion of world music, and they are far from being the exception. The image of the "rebel" is often accompanied by a story of exile, partly because this creates sympathy for the artist because of his or her experiences as an economic or political refugee, as in the case of Maryam Mursal or Geoffrey Oryema.[13] Enjoying the music of exiled artists does not only mean one likes the music; it also demonstrates solidarity with their political cause and sympathy for their suffering.

In the context of increasingly global "commercial activism" (Mallet 2002, 849), it is not surprising that a record company such as Real World would devote a portion of its media apparatus to what one might term "global civic education." The section of the Real World website titled "Exposure" includes a listing of human rights organizations that have partnership agreements with the record company. One of these organizations, Witness (co-founded by Real World owner Peter Gabriel), supplies local human rights organizations with video cameras to document human rights violations and abuses. In addition to direct action and education, Real World also emphasizes fair-trade–style philanthropy. In a short text printed on a number of the company's products, Putumayo claims to have contributed more than $500,000 to nonprofit organizations. With the company promising to donate a portion of the proceeds from the sale of the CD to a particular nonprofit, effectively making philanthropy part of the packaging and enabling consumers to support artists who are like-minded in their humanitarian leanings.[14]

A discourse of solidarity is evident in the interactions between musicians, and stories of cross-cultural musical collaboration are an important part of the evolution of world music as a genre. Tim Taylor (2007) described how collaboration became an important source of cultural capital for the most visible stars of the world music scene, especially Paul Simon, Peter Gabriel, David Byrne, and Ry Cooder. Although the trope of collaboration certainly has the potential to "smooth over" the exploitation of non-Western musicians (ibid., 127), I argue that talking about the collaborative nature of a cross-cultural music project acts more as a guarantee of ethical behavior than a cover-up, enabling artists to distance themselves from the accusations and criticism that plagued Paul Simon's 1986 Grammy award-winning *Graceland*.[15] Taylor's discussion of collaboration in the work of Bill Laswell is a good example of this phenomenon. Laswell, who seems to have a clear sense of his role as a cultural mediator ("You get obsessed with the idea of being a catalyst" [Snowden 1994]), plays heavily on the importance of collaboration in his work ("You have to look directly into the idea of collaboration with people" [Sherrard n.d.]). But, as Taylor points out, Laswell makes every effort to distance himself from tourists, anthropologists, and ethnomusicologists. This gesture of distancing himself says just as much about the creative process in cross-cultural collaborations as it does about the expectations of Western consumers, many of whom want to believe that human beings can work together in spite of their cultural, social, and economic differences (White and Yoka 2010a).

Although one cannot deny that many Western artists have shown themselves to be cavalier and negligent, if not outright exploitative, in their use of sounds from non-Western countries (see Feld 1996, 2000, and this volume; Meintjes 1990), more important is the structural and discursive formations that reproduce the conditions for solidarity that are determined by actors and institutions in Western countries. To understand the solidarity motif in world music, we first need to understand the politics of cross-cultural collaboration. In analytical terms, this means we must focus not on the intentions of individual artists but on the dynamics between artists, companies, and audiences. At the same time we need to form a clear picture of what actually happens when artists of different cultural and socioeconomic backgrounds meet if we are understand exactly how exploitative relationships are enacted and reproduced. As I argue in the introduction to this volume, this is quite possibly the most urgent need for the critical study of music in the context of globalization, especially given the astonishing lack of research on the co-production of knowledge in anthropological writing and practice.[16]

Consumer Cosmopolitanism

World music stands out from other categories of music primarily because of its capacity to render explicit the link between music and cultural identity. Indeed, world music sells itself on this basis, sending consumers the message that this music is not merely music but a manifestation of deeply held cultural values and traditions that, in many cases, are at risk of disappearing. Thus the underlying suggestion of cultural content enables listeners to connect with world music artists, not because they share the same cultural background or values but because one of their goals in listening to world music is to connect with a culture different from their own.[17] Obviously there is nothing unusual about identifying with the music one consumes. Indeed, identification, in some sense, is the basis of music's status as a commodity, because without it record companies would have no way to conceive of and target different music markets. Unique about world music is that its consumers identify with people who are radically different from them, and it is this very difference that fuels their desire for the products and branding of world music.[18]

The typical consumer of world music is harder to identify now than twenty years ago (Romer 2007) but, contrary to most popular music, he or she is not between the ages of eighteen and twenty-five. In the words of music producer and writer Joe Boyd: "The primary audience for what we call world music is not youthful: it is the middle-class, middle-aged, coffee-table-record audience that buys Buena Vista Social Club" (quoted in Denselow 2004). Tim Taylor confirms this observation and discusses the importance of Western consumers to possess "a kind of capital that stands in for real knowledge of the world in this cultural moment of globalization" (Taylor, 2007, and this volume). In terms of marketing, consumers targeted by a medium-sized label such as Putumayo are probably similar to consumers of world music in general: "A large portion of [our] target audience consists of 'cultural creatives,' a sociological and lifestyle term for 50 million North Americans and millions more around the world."[19] With this description, Putumayo seems to be targeting baby-boomers, a generation, although growing old, that continues to represent a key demographic in various sectors of consumer marketing. Within this group, marketers are especially interested in those baby-boomers—also known as "bobos" (short for "bourgeois bohemians"; see Brooks 2000)—who enjoy listening to world music as they sit in a café reading a book and sipping a cup of coffee. Indeed, here is how Dan Storper described the relationship between "world music" and coffee in the liner notes to *Music from the Coffee Lands* (Putumayo 1997), the label's second best-selling CD:

> For some reason I don't fully understand, I've always loved the flavor of coffee. It began with ice cream as a kid. Along the way, my tastes developed from instant coffee to fresh ground to cappuccino, my current addiction. I never really thought about the connection of coffee to music until I'd started Putumayo Music and began to consider the music I enjoyed hearing while sipping coffee and reading in cafés. As you travel through this collection, we hope you'll consider the multi-cultural connections that music and coffee share.

The rest of the liner notes speaks primarily about the artists, without explicitly linking the music, the country, and coffee production. The real connection, however, is the marketing, because people who buy world music also buy other luxury items such as expensive coffee.[20] In another CD from the same series, the liner notes link music and other luxury items more directly:

> The music of Taffetas, a collaboration between Swiss and West African musicians, symbolizes the connection between the tropical climates where cacao is grown and the mostly northern countries that transform it into a delicious treat . . . The Swiss are reputed to eat more chocolate per capita than anywhere else in the world, 25 pounds per person per year. (Putumayo 2004)

The connection not made in this text, however, is the one between world music and the history of capitalism, which, through the extraction of natural and agricultural resources from the southern nations, has made it possible for certain people to eat chocolate while others struggle to put basic food items on the table. The history of the role played by luxury items in the emergence of industrial capitalist economies is well known (see, for example, Mintz 1986), and it can easily be argued that world music is a part of this extractive tradition. According to Steven Feld (1988), culture industries from the West "tend to draw upon and incorporate African and Afro-American materials, products, and ideas but stabilize them at the levels of labor, talent, or 'influences,' levels at which they can be continually manipulated for export and recirculation in made-over forms." As with other luxury products, promotional language speaks to those who know how to appreciate the "good things in life" and how to distinguish between "good" and "superb":

> Before Real World, only with great determination, or a lot of travelling, was it possible to access music by artists working outside Western Europe and North America. Now, you can stroll into high street stores and find CDs of music from every continent, many of them bearing the Real World colour bar logo. There's an enormous variety of styles, moods and genres on CDs that bear this logo, but they all have one thing in common—the quality of the recording and the production is superb. (Gabriel 2008)

Keir Keightley (2004) demonstrates that the idea of travel has long been part of the promotion of exotic music, and, in fact, the promotional language of world music draws considerably from metaphors of travel. The *Rough Guide to World Music*, generally considered the most important publication of this new genre, is organized by region and by country. It contains considerable information related to what has been referred to as "sonic tourism" (Taylor 1997). In a fascinating discussion about the use of world music in public commercial space, Anahid Kassabian (2004) argues that the presence of world music in cafés and restaurants can be seen as a form of "distributed tourism," where the distinction between "here" and "there" is not actually erased—as in Baudrillard's notion of simulacrum—but is simultaneous: "In this sense, then, 'here' becomes false, virtual, the simulacrum, the Starbucks shop, while 'there' maintains an innocent, untainted relationship to authenticity, easily pictured by Putumayo's cover art." Thus what is being sold with world music is not just the music but a particular lifestyle that responds to consumers' need to perceive themselves as "citizens of the world," rootless without being uprooted.[21]

In recent years various branches of the human sciences have expressed much interest in the subject of cosmopolitanism, and this is not the first time in history that the topic has been considered good food for thought (Cheah and Robbins 1998). Indeed, the subject of cosmopolitanism has demonstrated an amazing resiliency—just as cosmopolitans themselves have done—although scholars at the end of the 1990s, already weary of the vague language of globalization, began desperately searching for a new theoretical paradigm, and cosmopolitanism seemed as good as any.[22] If we agree with Kwame Anthony Appiah (2006) that the slogan of cosmopolitanism can be summarized as "universality plus difference," then what exactly is the nature of that difference? Appiah's analysis suggests that it is not the difference that matters per se as much as the cosmopolitan's ability to honor it. According to his analysis, the pluralism so dear to cosmopolitans is based on two different "strands" or ethical propositions: (1) that we have obligations to others, even (or perhaps especially) if they are strangers; and (2) that we take seriously the value of human life and, by extension, human lives (ibid., xv). These two propositions fit nicely with the cosmopolitan discourses of world music.

If we take seriously the promotional language of world music, consumers of cosmopolitanism, especially those who accept the ideology of world music without any critical reflection, believe that music is capable of helping us build a better world, not only because it breaks down the barriers that separate us or because it values difference, but also because it speaks out against injustice. The quest for this type of music places the consumer symbolically on the side of the victims of history or, as some critics of cosmopolitanism might suggest, completely outside history. I contend that we see this posture as a promise to act as a "citizen of the world," one that oversees the principles of cultural diversity, respect, and tolerance. At the same time, however, by assuming this posture, consumers of world music imagine themselves in a position of superiority in relation to the provincialism of their compatriots. In this sense consumer cosmopolitans are not very much different from cosmopolitans elsewhere:

> *Joe Boyd: We can't forget, though, that this is a marketing concept. I would bet that there are people who, when they first went to Womad, went to hear Sunny Ade or Nusrat. If they had been asked, "Would you like to hear some English Folk Music?" they would have said, "Ugh, you must be joking!" But over*

the years, because of their exposure to world music, their ears have been opened to the idea of music that comes out of a tradition. It's a marketing crossover.

Charlie Gillet: I don't fit into that model. I've been listening to this music and it makes me feel nauseous.

Joe Boyd: Charlie is a typical self-hating Englishman!

Charlie Gillet: I'm the least self-hating person I know. You're trying to say that I hate my own culture, but I have no affinity whatever with it. I grew up listening to Little Richard and Gene Vincent.

Joe Boyd: Whether you want to admit it or not, you are an Englishman, and that is English culture.

Charlie Gillet: No, I'm a man of the world. I mean, that is what this whole thing is about, isn't it? (Denselow 2004, 1)

Essentialism and Other People's Music

The term "essentialism" refers to an overemphasis on traits or characteristics (permanent, discernable, and verifiable) that describe the nature or "essence" of a thing, person, or culture. The most well-known critiques of essentialism are generally associated with the scholarship of post-colonial studies, which was influenced not only by the publication of Edward Said's *Orientalism* in 1978 but also by the work of the Subaltern Studies Group, a collective of South Asian scholars whose critique of Eurocentric social theory beginning in the early 1980s attempted to elaborate a new language for explaining history in non-Western terms.[23] Since these early critiques of Western sources of knowledge about the Other, discussions of essentialism have become increasingly common in the humanities and social sciences. In the most well-known variations on this theme—Spivak's (1993) notion of "strategic essentialism," Gilroy's (1993) discussion of "double consciousness," and Bhabha's (1994) "third space"—there is a strong emphasis on the historical experiences of colonialism and slavery, but there is also a sense in which the institutions of Western domination and knowledge production are unable to fully encapsulate either the agency or identity of colonized peoples. Anti-essentialist critiques are not only claims about history and cultural identity but also about cultural complexity.

Anthropologists have long been struggling with the question of essentialism. Franz Boas, the German-born anthropologist often referred to as the "father of American anthropology," is most often credited with promoting a four-field approach to the study of human cultures (ethnology, archaeology, physical anthropology, and ethnolinguistics), and many North American anthropology departments continue to function with some version of the four-field model.[24] But underlying this methodological orientation was a political conviction to fight against two of the most enduring and emblematic essentialisms of the era: evolution and race. Boas's early work with the Bureau of American Ethnology led him to criticize the evolutionary bias of nineteenth-century museum display, arguing that museums should not be organized according the arbitrary assignment of evolutionary stages but instead according to cultural areas. In his later work Boas conducted research with children of American immigrants as part of his larger intellectual project to discredit the scientific racism of the eugenics movement (Baker 2004). Despite Boas's sustained efforts to historicize culture and demystify race, the generation of scholars that followed him (many of whom were his students) were apparently more committed to the concept of culture than race, and the result was the consolidation not only of a concept but of a discipline.[25]

Not until much later would anthropology return to the question of essentialism, especially with the publication of two edited volumes (Hymes 1969; Asad 1973) that in many ways foreshadowed the "crisis of representation" in American anthropology in the 1980s. The articles in these volumes were critical not only of anthropology's involvement in the elaboration of colonial models of governance, but they also cried out for new methodologies and conceptual frameworks that would enable anthropologists to talk about culture "within a frame of reference that includes ourselves" (Hymes 1969, 11). Some of these ideas were later echoed in the work of Johannes Fabian (1983), whose trenchant critique called attention to the propensity of ethnographic writing to erase a shared frame of historical reference, and Lila Abu-Lughod (1991), whose commitment to the practice of "writing against culture" proposed a forceful critique of the essentialism inherent in the anthropological notion of culture.[26]

The material in this chapter discusses the practices of consumers who, despite their best intentions, fall into the trap of essentialism. These practices must be seen as part of a long history of primitivism (Feld 2000), exoticism (Taylor 2007; Jules-Rosette 2007), and othering (Born and Hesmondhalgh 2000) that are by no means limited to the domain of musical expression (Torgovnick 1990). But in what sense is the essentialism of world music different from other essentialisms? One distinction between world music and other cultural products is the way world music speaks out loud about cultural identity (White 2000). Even more so than other cultural commodities, world music references a geographical region, a linguistic identity, and a cultural history. Indeed, promoters of world music depend on this in order to sell their products. Second, and more important, the essentialism of world music differs from other essentialisms in that the former's preference for a culturally marked product acts as a form of positive prejudice. Positive prejudice can clearly be negative in social and political terms, as it subjects the complexity of the Other to the needs and whims of the Self. Love can be every bit as essentialist as hate, and a number of world music artists (among them Salif Keita and Youssou N'dour) have expressed frustration with the label "world music" because of its potential to reinforce essentialist ideas that limit artistic creativity and cultural experimentation.

Although I do believe that world music tends to reinforce some of the most subtle and problematic forms of essentialism, I do not believe that all world music is bad or even that all consumers of world music are bad. On the contrary, my motivation to write this chapter comes partly from the fact that I myself am a fan of world music and that I have noticed myself falling unconsciously into the essentializing practices of consumption described above. Despite all the problems with this category of music, there are projects and practices that attempt to repel the essentialism inherent in the evolution of this genre. In 1988 David Byrne's label, Luaka Bop, produced the CD *Cuba Classics 2: Dancing With the Enemy*, a fascinating compilation of popular dance music from Cuba in the 1960s and 1970s.[27] The album is not only a critique of American foreign policy toward Cuba but is also a rare occasion to gain an understanding of the dynamics between popular culture and authoritarian regimes of power (Averill 1997; White 2008).[28] Listening to this compilation and reading the liner notes, we discover a variety of styles and sounds not generally associated with Caribbean or Latin American music. Here we get a sense of how Cubans during the peak of the Cold War were listening to music that is in dialogue with popular music from abroad, highlighting the complexity of Cuba's economic and political isolation.[29] Byrne's comments from the liner notes underline a central paradox of globalization, namely, that despite the impact of "African derived musics" in Western society and culture, we still fail to see people of African descent as having histories or philosophies:

> Little did the colonizers and slave traders suspect that musics (and therefore the philosophies) of their victims would soon spread across the globe like wildfire. The Africans, through their musics, have conquered the minds of the children of their oppressors. Even Republicans dance to what once were African beats. The minds of whites, like my own, have been confounded and confused. We have experienced some of our most joyous, most ecstatic moments through African derived musics, and yet we have been brainwashed to believe that the originators of these attitudes and grooves are somehow more "primitive" than ourselves. So, our experience tells us one thing and our Official Culture tells us the opposite.

This excerpt bursts the bubble of primitivist discourses about Africa. Not only does it show that people of non-African descent are capable of experiencing transcendent moments of joy through music of African origin, but it also suggests that the cognitive dissonance caused by this listening experience ("our experience tells us one thing and our Official Culture tells us the opposite") can act as a catalyst for formalizing knowledge about politics and history.

Another interesting example comes from the independent record label Crammed Discs.[30] This Brussels-based record company, which covers various types of new and emerging popular music from across the globe, has an impressive repertoire of world music artists, including, especially, breakout "traditional" groups such as

Taraf de Haidouks and the Congolese thumb piano sensation Konono N°1, whose first album was produced, in 2004, as part of Vincent Kenis's *Congotronics* series. The second album in the series is a compilation of urban traditional music in Kinshasa, including several groups that play what is referred to locally as "la musique tradi-moderne." Producing two albums—where one presents a certain genre of music and the other a particular group within that genre—is a new approach in marketing non-Western music and creates an unexpected effect on listeners. Such a presentation runs counter to Western narratives about artistic genius and star quality (Taylor 2007, 137), as it encourages consumers to analyze the product in a specific way, going back and forth between the genius of Konono N°1 and the realization that the group's genius is actually part of a larger category of cultural production and creativity.

The ethnographic style of the information in the liner notes (a trademark of Kenis' productions) and the visual content of the videos included with the CD work together to give listeners a nuanced view of the relationship between the music and its social context. In the accompanying images, different groups of musicians are portrayed in different performative settings (festival stages in Europe, home recording sessions, popular bars, courtyards, and shopping centers in Kinshasa) and in different types of garb (ranging from a folklore style to the urban everyday). The short descriptions of the bands emphasize that the musicians in these groups are clearly urban in their lifestyle and outlook, but the notes also provide valuable information about the differences between the regions and subregions that serve as a constant source of renewal and inspiration for traditional groups in an urban setting (White 2008). This ethnographic style of production, which combines elements of ethnomusicology, documentary film, and music journalism, also has a strong historical component, giving listeners cues about the complex dynamics between popular culture, politics, and history:

> Bolia We Ndenge come from the Lake Mai Ndombe. Only a century ago, the whole region was still *Domaine de la Couronne,* i.e. a giant labor camp for the personal benefit of King Leopold II. At one point, to calm discontent, the *force publique* gave accordions to local chiefs; the idea might have been suggested by Stanley, an accordion aficionado himself. See the movie [included with CD] for an evocation by Bolia We Ndenge of this important moment in the history of world music; the accordion and *force publique* uniform are genuine vintage items. The accordion became very popular in Congo until it was supplanted by the guitar in the 1950s.

Information of this type, simple yet suggestive, encourages listeners to look for aspects in the music, such as its content and form, that might provide insight about individual experiences and cultural complexity in the region. Descriptions of the production process include subtle references to Congo's economic and political decline, without bombarding listeners with clichés about the region's deterioration under Mobutu:

> Kisanzi Congo's line-up is similar to Konono's, and they also come from the Bacongo province (specifically the Mbeko region). But whereas Konono's electric likembes use raw power to carry their message, Kisanzi Congo rely more on virtuosity and adopt a freer form. We recorded this piece in a deserted shopping mall in the center of Kinshasa, formerly called *Galerie des Trois Z* ("Zaire—our country, our river, our currency").

Simple descriptions—for example, the stylistic difference between a group that plays with raw power and one that relies more heavily on careful virtuosity—enable listeners to see musical groups and their members as individuals with different sensibilities, resources, and objectives (cf. *Cuban Classics 2*). The very fact that the producer provides information about the production of the album ("We recorded this piece in a deserted shopping mall") demystifies his authority and enables listeners to imagine the terms and conditions of a relationship characterized by unequal access to resources: although the producer is not rich, he can always leave the region. Both these projects (the *Cuban Classics* series and the *Congotronics* series) are good examples of artistic and cultural mediation in the constantly evolving category of world music (cf. Hernandez-Reguant, this volume). In addition to experimenting with different ways of presenting the context of non-Western musical styles to local audiences, the producers of these projects focused on styles that are clearly important to audiences at home, taking a chance on their intuition that foreign audiences might also be moved by the music and curious about the conditions under which it has emerged.

Strategies for Non-Essentialist Listening

The analysis presented thus far has attempted to describe the ideological foundations of the category of world music through a close reading of the promotion and consumption of this emerging cultural commodity. But the postmodernist strategy employed here (discourse analysis, critique of representation, textual analysis of cultural products) is fraught with dangers. A convincing case can be made against this type of armchair ethnography that benefits from the increased availability of cultural products and performances from developing economies as a source of information about politics, aesthetics, or experience. This situation, by no means novel, requires us to develop new kinds of methodologies to understand how consumers make use of and interpret cultural products such as music (White and Yoka 2010a). To avoid these traps, I have constructed my analysis in a specific way. First, readers are not to misconstrue the material presented here as an interpretation of the listening experience of non-Western music by various types of "locals." My intention, in other words, is not to understand how Western consumers of non-Western music somehow "get it wrong" in relation to a pure, authentic understanding by those in the music's country of origin. Furthermore, by no means am I presenting an ethnographic description of those who promote and consume non-Western music in the West. Instead, my analysis is limited to what the various types of consumers and specialists say about world music as a commercial phenomenon and how these utterances are informed by and play into various strategies of promotion and marketing.

It is not sufficient, in my view, to deconstruct discourses and representations of world music or even to criticize the abusive practices of artists or industry specialists; neither of these strategies bear on the practices of promotion and consumption that are crucial to the reproduction of world music as a category of knowledge about cultural or racial difference. Instead, if our theoretical work is to be truly critical, we need to provide models that apply the principles of intellectual curiosity, systematic research, and self-reflexive listening.[31] Following this line of thinking, the sections below offer strategies that can be applied by promoters and consumers alike to give new meaning to the promise of world music. As an experiment in applied cultural criticism, these recommendations and warnings—some of which require the exertion of additional time and energy—are intended to help the intellectually curious to combat the most problematic aspects of musical essentialism.[32]

QUESTION THE NOTION OF MUSIC AS A UNIVERSAL LANGUAGE

We often invoke the idea of the universal when we cannot describe why we enjoy certain types of music. Universalist discourses attempt to explain this affinity, but affinities can have more to do with individual tastes and desires than with the inherent qualities of the Other or his or her music; running toward the Other can actually be a way of running away from the Self. *Question the status of "universals" in music. First, are they universal? Second, are they about music or about values?*

BE MORE SPECIFIC ABOUT WHAT IS MEANT BY "HYBRID"

Hybridity is a real phenomenon, especially in the context of world music production, but the notion of hybridity is often used as a promotional strategy for artists or styles of music without any explanation about what is actually being combined and to what effect. In order to describe hybridity, it is necessary to distinguish between the different musical and cultural components and to understand how they have been adapted to new social and cultural contexts. The clichés of hybridity—mixing, melting, and blending—tell us little about the music and also little about the Other, and they often conflate different forms of hybridity (biological, religious, linguistic, artistic, racial, etc.).[33] *Try to describe exactly what is being mixed and to determine if certain elements of the mix are dominant over others.*

BE AWARE OF CLICHÉS

Clichés inevitably find their way into the promotional language of world music, in announcements, reviews, liner notes, and so on. They are also commonly heard in lyrics, as world music artists often neglect song lyrics in response to Western consumers' remarks about the sound or rhythm of the music. Certain exotic descriptions of the music such as "sensual," "bewitching," and "tropical" should indicate to listeners that the promotion of the music is geared to reducing the complexity of the artist to a series of positive stereotypes having to do with sexuality, witchcraft, and tourists' desire. *Seek out and avoid clichés by comparing the promotional content of music to that of other styles or regions.*

BE SKEPTICAL OF BINARY OPPOSITIONS

Binary oppositions (hot/cold, body/mind, us/them) often signal ideologically driven language. Dividing the world into a series of binary opposites can also serve the purposes of different types of rhetoric, not all of them politically driven. As with other aspects of essentialism, these mechanisms reduce the complexity of a culture by defining that culture primarily in terms of what it is not. *Identify binary oppositions and try to invoke entirely different models for explaining the function or meaning of cultural practices and beliefs.*

STRIVE FOR A BALANCE BETWEEN SIMILARITIES AND DIFFERENCES

The tension between similarity and difference, which is central to anthropological inquiry, can be mobilized in the analysis of cultural products but must be balanced. For example, placing too much emphasis on similarities oversimplifies the Other and tends to erase problems having to do with power, inequality, and ideology. On the other hand, overemphasizing differences can obscure the presence of the Self and naturalize traits or characteristics that may have nothing to do with the Other as an individual. *Compile a list of characteristics of a particular world music project or artist and ask a friend, colleague, or family member to compare the number and type of similarities and differences.*

DON'T BE AFRAID TO TALK ABOUT SOUND

One does not need formal training in music to talk about the way music sounds. We can describe what we hear in music in simple, everyday language that would readily reveal possible prejudgments, preconceived notions, and cultural stereotypes. Technical jargon, however, can be counterproductive, since specialized language and conceptual tools tend to operate on the basis of exclusion. Once these evaluations become explicit, they can be used to verify and explore distinctions between the ways that foreign listeners and locals hear the music. *Familiarize yourself with the descriptive terms for sound and song structure—such as "timbre," "melody," "harmony," "rhythm," and "lyrics"—in order to form a basis of comparison with other songs and genres.*

PAY ATTENTION TO GENRE

The question of genre is complex in the analysis of world music, because world music itself is an amalgam of different already existing national and ethnic genres. Instead of one all-encompassing genre evolving into a series of smaller, more specialized genres, world music represents a process of generalization. By insisting on individual artists independent of the musical genres that have contributed to their sensibility and sound, music promoters play to the whims of the "star system." Certain artists promote themselves as being part of a national sound or genre, when, in fact, they are completely unknown in their country of origin (White 2000). *Given this phenomenon, listeners have much to gain by learning to compare not only artists within the same genre but also different genres of music.*

TRY TO UNDERSTAND THE LYRICS

A significant number of world music artists sing in their native language. While this is a positive aspect of world music from many perspectives, we do not have to know the language of the lyrics to understand the song's basic message (and here I am not referring to the supposed "universality" of music as a language; see above). Song lyrics do not necessarily give us access to the worldview of the Other but rather to the way that the Other represents him- or herself. In this sense, language is a renewable resource of information about culture (by means of proverbs, idiomatic expressions, recurring themes, etc.). Be alert to the use of colonial languages (which usually signals a message intended for Western audiences), to the use of figurative language (where multiple meanings are mobilized through irony, metaphor, or satire), and to the use of clichés (see above). *If the liner notes do not include translations of the lyrics, find someone who knows that language and can provide you with a sense of the song's meaning.*

SPEAK WITH REAL HUMAN BEINGS

Why should we accept the information that a record company decides to print on a website or in the liner notes of a CD? After all, music companies—even small, well-intentioned, independent labels—are not selling culture or society but are selling CDs. *Try to befriend someone who comes from the country that interests you and exchange ideas with that person not only about the music itself but also about the role music plays in that particular society.* You might ask the following questions: What do people in your country think about this artist? Is this music popular at home? What other kinds of music are popular? What kind of people listen to this type of music? An excellent way to make such a contact, especially if one does not live in a large, urban area, is through country-based Web initiatives such as listserves, blogs, and Web-based news forums.

FIND OUT MORE ABOUT A COUNTRY'S CULTURE, POLITICS, AND HISTORY

Understanding a country's music alone is not enough to gain an understanding of the cultural, social, and political context of that country. Learning about the context surrounding the music will provide you with images and ideas intrinsic to the culture of the artist and will likely have a positive impact on your listening experience. Knowing more about the culture of a particular music style (its social organization, language, religious beliefs, and values) can make your listening experience more immediate and vivid. Being aware of a country's history (its periods of conflict and insecurity, sources of cultural heritage, mythology of national heroes, and political figures) enables one to understand textual, sonic, and visual references. *By understanding the political dynamics of a country or region, we can better understand why artists might want or be forced to leave their country of origin.*

QUESTION YOUR TASTES

Ask yourself why you are attracted to certain styles of music but indifferent or even repulsed by others. Have you been influenced by the tastes of your associates or your family? Are your likes and dislikes linked to cultural stereotypes attached to the music? *Compare your listening history to that of a friend, colleague, or family member in order to highlight the key elements of your patterns of preference.*

The desire to encounter the Other through world music is fraught with risks, especially if that desire is the Self's primary objective. People have multiple reasons for wanting to meet the Other (education, information, services, wealth, etc.), but regardless of the objectives, inter-cultural encounters inevitably lead to the desire to learn more about the personal, social, and cultural complexity of people different from us. How many of us have discovered a musical genre in all its historical and stylistic complexity after having discovered a hit song or an international star of that genre? World music is not a problem per se; it becomes a problem, however, when the listener-consumer makes claims about the world through music without attempting to go beyond the simple projection of a personal listening utopia. If there is one promise we should make to the Other, it is not to love his or her music; with the seemingly endless supply of musics available today, that would be much too simple. The promise we *should* make is to exert every effort to allow ourselves to become destabilized by what lies behind the music, for behind every musical genre, every artist, every song lies a history, an interplay of politics and culture, a "structure of feeling."[34] Music can be a window into this complexity, but it can also be a brick wall. It can tell us something about other people, but this requires a certain degree of personal and historical effort. To paraphrase the French historian Marc Bloch speaking on the subject of history, music does not explain things, it has to be explained.

Notes

This chapter was first presented in Paris, in May 2007, at an interdisciplinary conference, "Nouveaux Essentialismes," organized by the Institut de Recherche pour le Développement (IRD). I am grateful to the organizers and to Julien Mallet for the invitation. I also thank Tim Taylor, Richard Shain, and Denis-Constant Martin for their extremely helpful comments on an earlier version of this chapter. Some of the analysis in the final two sections has benefited from conversations with Nicole Bernier. I am also grateful to the Social Sciences and Humanities Research Council of Canada for its support of Critical World, the intellectual home for the research in the chapter.

1. Drawing from a particular tradition of discourse analysis, I focus more on what is said about reality than reality itself. From a methodological viewpoint, I have been primarily influenced by two sources: the sociolinguistics of John Gumperz and the "cultural models" approach to discourse analysis. See Holland and Quinn 1987.

2. For a critique of the idea of music as a universal language, see Tagg 1993.

3. According to Yahoo.com, which hosts Associated Content: "Associated Content from Yahoo!™ is an open publishing platform that enables anyone to earn money by sharing their knowledge with an online audience of millions."

4. Putumayo boasts that fifty of its collections have sold more than one hundred thousand copies each, and several have surpassed three hundred thousand in sales. In the United States alone Putumayo is distributed in more than thirty-five hundred "non-traditional" music retailers such as coffee shops, health food stores, museums, bookstores, and gift shops.

5. The accompanying CD is Putumayo's third best-selling album (Zwerlin 1998).

6. Putumayo's slogan is "Guaranteed to make you feel good."

7. Denis-Constant Martin writes: "World music sells, to a large extent, because of the discourses and the images that are associated with it; but it also sells because of the music itself, and if it were not for the music, discourses of authenticity, for instance, would not be possible" (personal communication). See also Brennan 2001.

8. Cf. Homi Bhabha's notion of "third space" (1994).

9. Pieterse is responding primarily to Jonathan Friedman (1997, 1999), who has criticized the notion of hybridity on a number of counts, not only that hybridity is only meaningful as a critique of essentialism but also that it stands for the privilege of an international cosmopolitan elite, an argument that resonates with my discussion of "consumer cosmopolitanism" below. Much like Pieterse, Kraidy (2005) notes that the history of thinking on hybridity is expansive and requires a more careful historiography. Following in the footsteps of the most oft-cited discussions of this topic (Appadurai, Bhabha, Canclini, Hall), both authors attempt to recuperate the idea of hybridity as something that can be useful empirically, theoretically, and normatively (Pieterse 2001, 238).

10. Although reggae music is not generally classified as world music (either because it predates world music or surpasses it in terms of production and global coverage), Bob Marley's music may be seen as a kind of transition between what Marc-Antoine Lapierre refers to as "musique mondialisée" and "musique du monde." See http://www.criticalworld.net/projet.php?id=78&type=0.

11. Excerpt from a concert. See http://www.realworldrecords.com/thomasmapfumo/index.lasso?section=media.

12. See Manu Chao's 1989 album *Clandestino*.

13. Journalist Jina Moore (2007) argues similarly in a recent article, where she quotes the owner of the World Music label: "People interested in world music are looking for that kind of meaning . . . They want to be connecting with other cultures, enjoying music that has more spirit and soul to it than just another rock band trying to create hits."

212 | Bob W. White

14. For example, were 15 million CDs sold at $20 each, the resulting amount of approximately $300 million, divided by the company's philanthropic contributions ($0.5 million), would represent approximately .0016 percent of their sales. Since Putumayo began operating with two employees in 1993, the privately held company has grown to a team of seventy, selling 1.5 million records in 2009, an increase of 24 percent from the previous year. Its annual revenue is $15 million—$9.5 million from the United States and $4.5 million from Europe. The company does not reveal its annual profit, only reporting that it has been profitable "for the past few years," but its costs are obviously reduced since compilations mean cheaper contracts with artists. In the words of Dan Storper, executive director and founder of Putumayo World Music: "Doing a compilation is like dating, while signing an artist is like getting married" (quoted in Zwerlin 1998).

15. On the *Graceland* debate, see Feld 1988; Hamm 1995; and Meintjes 1990.

16. Phil Hayward (1999) has attempted to do this for the music of the Australian rock group Not Drowning, Waving and for their musical collaborators in Papua New Guinea. Louise Meintjes (2003), in her recent ethnography of recording studios, explores how sounds and meanings are created as the result of a kind of forced cross-cultural collaboration in contemporary South Africa. Both these monographs, however, discuss examples of collaboration that cannot be considered successful either in political or cross-cultural terms. In fact, as Meintjes's analysis suggests, the metaphor of mediation is probably more appropriate than that of collaboration. For an extended discussion of the question of collaboration in ethnographic research, see White and Yoka (2010b).

17. Since the writings of Adorno and Horkheimer (1979) on the culture industry, we are accustomed to questioning the standardization of culture that results from mass marketing and mass consumption. What differs today, however, is the way that cultural industries (now plural and considerably more neutral than in the Frankfurt school reading) use "difference" as a means of selling the idea of difference (see Erlmann 1996).

18. In recent years anthropology has paid increasing attention to the question of consumption, especially following the publication of Grant McCracken's influential *Culture and Consumption* (1990), which, in many ways, set the agenda for the ethnographic study of consumption in Western societies and laid out the first substantive critiques of an antimaterialist bias in the human sciences (an argument he makes even more forcefully in his 2005 follow-up to this book, *Culture and Consumption II*). Another leading figure in the anthropology of consumption, Daniel Miller, published his first monograph on this subject in 1987. *Material Culture and Mass Consumption* presents an analysis of the relationship between people and things in the writing of four social theorists (Hegel, Marx, Munn, and Simmel), with a special emphasis on the question of objectification. Miller has maintained a brisk pace in his publishing in the last twenty years, including a number of ethnographies and edited volumes on topics as varied as modernity, capitalism, shopping, Christmas, cars, saris, and cell phones. For a good example of this approach, see Miller 2001. Taylor (2007) presents an overview of recent consumption literature outside anthropology. His discussion emphasizes trends in Western consumerism over time, especially the changing perception of workers from producers to consumers and the importance of consumption as a form of self-fashioning (cf. my discussion of "consumer cosmopolitan" [White 2002]).

19. http://www.putumayo.com/en/about_us.php.

20. Some Putumayo products also include recipes, for example, for peanut sauces or chocolate cakes without flour.

21. Contrary to much of the recent literature on cosmopolitanism, rootedness cosmopolitan practices seem to be endemic, at least in sub-Saharan Africa. White (2000) de-

scribes one such example of this rootedness through the appropriation of Afro-Cuban music in the Congo. For another similar example, see Shain 2002, and this volume). Martin's (2008) analysis of popular music and jazz in postwar South Africa performs a similar operation, and the work of both Shain and Martin calls attention to the fact that world music is just as much about circulation and agency as it is about the globalization of asymmetrical power relations.

22. In his recent book Appiah explains that he decided to use the "rubric" of cosmopolitanism as his focus, as he found "globalization" and "multiculturalism" inadequate (2006, xiii). Elsewhere I have argued that, unlike "globalization" or "modernity," cosmopolitanism is not something that happens to people but something that people do (White 2000); given this observation, Appiah's theoretical justification reads like something of a non sequitur.

23. The Subaltern Studies Group (SSG) used Gramsci's notion of subaltern to get around the opposition and elitism inherent in standard Marxist readings of history, although, as several observers have noted, SSG's engagement with European social theory and philosophy is a complex subject in itself. For a good overview of this argument and a discussion of the impact of Subaltern Studies on the fields of history, anthropology and literature, see Prakash 1994.

24. The predominance of the four-field model has recently been called into question owing to a number of bitter conflicts and highly visible departmental splits. For a critique of the four-field model, see Segal and Yanagisako 2005.

25. According to Kamala Visweswaran, "The paradox of the Boasian legacy is that it was the cultural anthropologists among his students who most strongly affirmed the biological existence of race in order to clearly distinguish culture from it" (1998, 74). For another discussion of Boas's ambiguous legacy with regard to race and culture, see Mullings 2005.

26. For a recent reconsideration of the question of essentialism in anthropology, see Fischer 1999. The article argues for a return to the notion of "cultural logic" and includes a number of interesting responses to Fischer's polemic on the relative values of culturalist and constructivist approaches to knowledge.

27. For more on this project, see Hernandez-Reguant, this volume.

28. David Byrne, among the most well-known artist-producers of world music, has also made a number of important recordings with non-Western artists. Byrne and his longtime collaborator, Brian Eno, are the topic of Steven Feld's contribution to this volume. For an expanded version of Byrne's political views on world music, see his article "I Hate World Music," available at http://www.luakabop.com/david_byrne/cmp/worldmusic.html.

29. Deborah Pacini Hernandez (1998) explains that, despite the ongoing tensions between Cuba and the United States, *Dancing with the Enemy* was not the first postrevolutionary Cuban recording to be distributed in the United States. Her article discusses the period in the 1990s when an increase in exchange and travel between the two countries opened up new possibilities for Cuban musicians, although not all Cubans since this period coincided with the emergence of a market for world music and a preference for artists of Afro-Cuban descent.

30. http://www.crammed.be.

31. One inspiration for the formulation of these strategies is the philosophical hermeneutics of Hans-Georg Gadamer. According to Gadamer (1996), understanding is necessarily situated (especially in relation to the past, in what he refers to as the "efficiency of history"), and knowledge is co-produced. In this model, prejudice, rather than being seen

as an obstacle, becomes a resource for reworking knowledge about truth. Different types of unverified knowledge about Others (prejudice, preconceptions, historical consciousness) are articulated through the use of an "inner ear," a sensibility that enables us to listen to ourselves listening to others. Following a model of non–goal-oriented behavior, the Self and the Other engage in a series of questions and answers, followed by restatements and verifications, and from this back-and-forth motion emerges a temporary common language that serves both parties in their quest for understanding.

32. David Jenneman (2007) has written a fascinating account of Adorno's mostly failed attempts to use popular culture as part of a larger critical pedagogy through music, film, and radio after his arrival in the United States. In many ways Jenneman's analysis unsettles the conventional wisdom about Adorno's relationship to popular culture and mass media.

33. Amselle (2001) offers a fascinating discussion of the biological nature of the hybridity metaphor.

34. For an ethnographic discussion of Raymond Williams's notion of "structure of feeling" in the context of audience-based research in the Democratic Republic of Congo, see White 2010.

References

Abu-Lughod, Lila. 1991. "Writing against Culture." In *Recapturing Anthropology: Working in the Present*, ed. Richard Fox, 137–162. Santa Fe, NM: School of American Research Press.

Adorno, T., and M. Horkheimer. 1979. "The Culture Industry: Enlightenment as Mass Deception." In *Dialectics of Enlightenment*, ed. T. Adorno and M. Horkheimer, 94–136. London: Verso.

Amselle. 2001. Jean-Loup. *Branchements. Anthropologie de l'universalité des cultures.* Paris, Flammarion.

Appiah, Kwame Anthony. 2006. *Cosmopolitanism: Ethics in a World of Strangers.* New York: Norton.

Asad, Talal, ed. 1973. *Anthropology and the Colonial Encounter.* London: Ithaca.

Averill, Gage. 1997. *A Day for the Hunter, A Day for the Prey: Popular Music and Power in Haiti.* Chicago: University of Chicago Press.

Baker, Lee D. 2004. "Franz Boas Out of the Ivory Tower." *Anthropological Theory* 4 (1): 29–51.

Bhabha, H. K. 1994. *The Location of Culture.* New York: Routledge.

Born, Georgina, and David Hesmondhalgh, eds. 2000. *Western Music and Its Others: Difference, Representation, and Appropriation in Music.* Berkeley: University of California Press.

Brennan, Timothy. 2001. "World Music Does Not Exist." *Discourse* 23, no.1 (winter): 44–62.

Brooks, David. 2000. *Bobos in Paradise: The New Upper Class and How They Got There.* New York: Simon and Schuster.

Byrne, David. 1999. "I Hate World Music." *New York Times,* October 3.

Cheah, Pheng, and Bruce Robbins, eds. 1998. *Cosmopolitics: Thinking and Feeling Beyond the Nation.* Minneapolis: University of Minnesota Press.

Denselow, Robin. 2004. "We Created World Music." *The Guardian,* June 29. http://arts.guardian.co.uk/features/story/0,11710,1249391,00.html.

Donnedieu de Vabres, Renaud. 2004. Former French Minister of Culture and Communication, June 11.

"Drumming: The Universal Language." 2008. http://www.associatedcontent.com/article/7618/drumming_the_universal_language.html.

Elrmann, Veit. 1996. "The Esthetics of the Global Imagination: Reflections on World Music in the 1990s." *Public Culture* 8:467–487.

———. 1999. *Music, Modernity, and the Global Imagination: South Africa and the West.* New York: Oxford University Press.

Fabian, Johannes. 1983. *Time and the Other: How Anthropology Makes Its Object.* New York: Columbia University Press.

Feld, Steven. 1988. "Notes on World Beat." *Public Culture* 1:31–37.

———. 1996. "Pygmy POP: a Genealogy of Schizophonic Mimesis." *Yearbook for Traditional Music,* 28:1–35.

———. 2000. "A Sweet Lullaby for World Music." *Public Culture* 12 (1): 145–172.

Fischer, Edward F. 1999. "Cultural Logic and Maya Identity: Rethinking Constructivism and Essentialism." *Current Anthropology* 40, no. 4 (August–October): 473–499.

Friedman, Jonathan. 1997. "Global Crises, the Struggle for Cultural Identity and Intellectual Porkbarelling: Cosmopolitans vs. Locals, Ethnics, and Nationals in an Era of De-Hegemonisation." In *Debating Cultural Hybridity,* ed. P. Werbner and T. Modood, 70–89. London: Zed.

———. 1999. "The Hybridization of Roots and the Abhorrence of the Bush." In *Spaces of Culture: City—Nation—World,* ed, M. Featherstone and S. Lash, 230–256. London: Sage.

Gabriel, Peter. 2008. http://gab-news.blogspot.com/2005_05_22_archive.html.

Gadamer, Hans-Georg. 1996. *Vérité et Méthode: les grandes lignes d'une herméneutique philosophique.* Paris: Éditions du Seuil.

Gilroy, Paul. 1993. *The Black Atlantic: Modernity and Double Consciousness.* Cambridge, MA: Harvard University Press.

Hamm, Charles. 1995. *Putting Popular Music in Its Place.* New York: Cambridge University Press.

Hayward, Philip. 1999. *Widening the Horizon : Exoticism in Post-War Popular Music.* Sydney : John Libbey.

Hesmondhalgh, David. 2002. *The Cultural Industries.* London: Sage.

Holland, Dorothy, and Naomi Quinn, eds. 1987. *Cultural Models in Language and Thought.* Cambridge: Cambridge University Press.

Hymes, Dell, ed. 1969. *Reinventing Anthropology.* New York: Vintage Books.

Jenneman, David. 2007. *Adorno in America.* St. Paul: University of Minnesota Press.

Jones, Andrew F. 2001. *Yellow Music: Media Culture and Colonial Modernity in the Chinese Age.* Durham, NC : Duke University Press.

Jules-Rosette, Bennetta. 2007. *Josephine Baker in Art and Life: The Icon and the Image.* Urbana: University of Illinois Press.

Kassabian, Anahid. 2004. "Would You Like Some World Music with Your Latte? Starbucks, Putumayo, and Distributed Tourism." *Twentieth-Century Music* 1, no. 2: 209–223.

Keightley, Keir. 2004. "Adventures in Sound: Audio Technology and the Virtual Global." Presentation given at the symposium "Critical Worlds I," University of Montreal, November.

Kidjo, Angelique. 2008. http://ayemusic.free.fr/accueil.html.

Kraidy, Marwan M. 2005. *Hybridity, or the Cultural Logic of Globalization*. Philadelphia: Temple University Press.

Lhamo, Yungchen. 2008. http://www.yungchenlhamo.com/discography.html.

Lortat-Jacob, Bernard. 2000. Musiques du monde: Le point de vue d'un ethnomusicologue. *Transcultural Music Review*, no. 5. http://www.sibetrans.com/trans/trans5/lortat.htm.

Mallet, Julien. 2002. World Music : Une question d'ethnomusicologie ? *Cahiers d'études africaines*. 42 (4): 168: 831–852.

Martin, Denis-Constant. 2002. Les "musiques du monde": imaginaires contradictoires de la globalization. In *Sur la piste des OPNI (Objets politiques non-identifiés)*, ed., Denis-Constant Martin, 398–430. Paris: Karthala.

———. 2008. *Our Kind of Jazz:* Musique et identité en Afrique du sud. *Critique Internationale* 38 (January–March): 91–110.

McCracken, Grant. 1990. *Culture and Consumption: New Approaches to the Symbolic Character of Consumer Goods and Activities*. Bloomington: Indiana University Press.

———. 2005. *Culture and Consumption II: Markets, Meaning, and Brand Management*. Bloomington: Indiana University Press.

Meintjes, Louise. 1990. "Paul Simon's *Graceland,* South Africa, and the Mediation of Musical Meaning." *Ethnomusicology* (winter): 37–73.

———. 2003. *The Sound of Africa! Making Music Zulu in a South African Studio*. Durham, NC: Duke University Press.

Miller, Daniel. 1987. *Material Culture and Mass Consumption*. Oxford: Blackwell.

———. 2001. *The Internet: An Ethnographic Approach*. Oxford: Berg.

Mintz, Sidney. 1986. *Sweetness and Power: The Place of Sugar in Modern History*. New York: Penguin.

Mondomix. 2008. Music review. http://manu_chao.mondomix.com/fr/portrait263.htm.

Moore, Jina. 2007. "To Shift Records, World-Music Artists Sell Exotic Back Stories." *Christian Science Monitor,* October 5.

Mullings, Leith. 2005. "Interrogating Racism: Toward an Antiracist Anthropology." *Annual Review of Anthropology* 34:667–693.

Ozomatli. 2008. http://realworldrecords.com/ozomatli/.

One World Rhythm. 2008. http://www.topblogarea.com/sitedetails_2106.html.

Pacini Hernandez, Deborah. 1998. "Dancing with the Enemy: Cuban Popular Music, Race, Authenticity, and the World-Music Landscape." *Latin American Perspectives*. 25 (3): 110–125.

Page, Nick. 2008. Promotional material. http://worldmusicpress.com/new.htm.

Pieterse, Jan Nederveen. 2001. "Hybridity, So What? The Anti-Hybridity Backlash and the Riddles of Recognition." *Theory, Culture, and Society*, 18 (2–3): 219–245.

Prakash, Gyan. 1994. "Subaltern Studies as Postcolonial Criticism." *American Historical Review*, 99 (5): 1475–1490.

Putumayo World Music. 1997. CD liner notes. *A Putumayo Blend: Music from the Coffee Lands*. Putu 135–2.

———. 1999. *World Playground Multicultural Activity Kit*. With activities and CD. New York.

———. 2004. *Music from the Chocolate Lands*. Putu 230-2 [note: the acronym went from "Putu" to "Put"]

Real World Records. 2007. http://realworldrecords.com.

———. 2008. http://realworldrecords.com/about/text.html.

Romer, Megan. 2007. "Top 10 World Music Myths." http://worldmusic.about.com/od/worldmusic101/tp/WorldMusicMyths.htm.

Said, Edward W. 1978. *Orientalism*. New York: Vintage Books.

Segal, Daniel A., and Sylvia J. Yanagisako. 2005. *Unwrapping the Sacred Bundle: Reflections on the Disciplining of Anthropology*. Durham, NC: Duke University Press.

Shain, Richard. 2002. "Roots in Reverse: Cubanismo in Twentieth-Century Senegalese Music." *International Journal of African Historical Studies* 35 (1) : 83–101.

Sherrard, Geoffroy. N.d. "The Illustrious Industrious Bill Laswell." http://www.sherrard.org/glow/Laswell/laswell1.html (accessed June 1, 2011).

Snowden, Don. 1994. "Material: A Musical Meeting Ground: 'Hallucination Engine,' the seventh album from the Bill Laswell group, explores an unusual range of genres with artists from around the globe. *Los Angeles Times*, February 26. http://articles.latimes.com/1994-02-26/entertainment/ca-27581_1_hallucination-engine (accessed June 1, 2011).

Spivak, Gayatri. 1993. *Outside in the Teaching Machine*. London: Routledge.

Tagg, Philip. 1993. "'Universal' Music and the Case of Death." *Critical Quarterly* 35 (2): 54–85.

Taylor, Timothy. 1997. *Global Pop: World Music, World Markets*. New York: Routledge.

———. 2007. *Beyond Exoticism: Western Music and the World*. Durham, NC: Duke University Press.

Torgovnick, Marianna. 1990. *Gone Primitive: Savage Intellects, Modern Lives*. Chicago: University of Chicago Press.

Visweswaran, Kamala. 1998. "Race and the Culture of Anthropology." *American Anthropologist*, 100 (1): 70–83.

White, Bob W. 2000. *Soukouss* or Sell-out? Congolese Popular Dance Music on the World Market. In *Commodities and Globalization: Anthropological Perspectives*, ed. A. Haugerud, M. P. Stone, and P. D. Little, 33–58. New York: Rowman and Littlefield.

———. 2002. "Congolese Rumba and Other Cosmopolitanisms." *Cahiers d'études africaines* 42 (4), 168: 663–686.

———. 2008. *Rumba Rules: The Politics of Dance Music in Mobutu's Zaire*. Durham, NC: Duke University Press.

———. 2010. "Écouter ensemble, penser tout haut: musique populaire et prise de conscience politique au Congo-Zaïre." In *Musique et société à Kinshasa: Une ethnographie de l'écoute*, ed, Bob W. White and Lye M. Yoka, 211–238. Paris: L'Harmattan.

White, Bob W., and Lye M. Yoka. 2010a. "La démarche ethnographique et la 'collaboration.'" In *Musique populaire et société à Kinshasa: Une ethnographie de l'écoute*, ed. Bob W. White and Lye M. Yoka, 15–61. Paris: L'Harmattan.

———, eds. 2010b. *Musique populaire et société à Kinshasa: Une ethnographie de l'écoute*. Paris: L'Harmattan.

WOMAD (World of Music Arts and Dance) Foundation. 2007. http://www.womad.org.

———. 2008. http://womadshop.com/detail/284.

Zawose, Hukwe, and Michael Brook. 2008. http://realworldrecords.com/assembly/.

Zwerlin, Mike. 1998. "Putumayo and the Secrets of World Music." *International Herald Tribune*. February 24.

Contributors

Barbara Browning is Associate Professor, Performance Studies, New York University.

Steven Feld is Distinguished Professor of Anthropology and Music, University of New Mexico, and Professor II, Institute of Music Research, University of Oslo.

Philip Hayward is Director of Research Training at Southern Cross University, Lismore, Australia, and Adjunct Professor at Pattimura University, Ambon, Indonesia.

Ariana Hernandez-Reguant is Associate Professor, Department of Communication, University of California, San Diego.

Denis-Constant Martin is Outstanding Senior Research Fellow, Les Afriques dans le monde, Centre de recherches pluridisciplinaires et comparatistes, Sciences Politiques, Université de Bordeaux.

Rafael José de Menezes Bastos is Associate Professor, Department of Anthropology, Universidade Federal de Santa Catarina, Brazil.

Daniel Noveck is Researcher, Department of Anthropology, Smithsonian Institution, Washington, D.C.

Richard M. Shain is Associate Professor, School of Liberal Arts, Philadelphia University.

Timothy D. Taylor is Professor, Departments of Ethnomusicology and Musicology, University of California, Los Angeles.

Bob W. White is Associate Professor, Department of Anthropology, University of Montreal, Canada, and is author of *Rumba Rules: The Politics of Dance Music in Mobutu's Zaire.*

Index

Activism, 75, 161, 167, 197
Adorno, Theodor W., 80, 212n17, 214n32
Advertising, 11, 150, 172–176, 182–184; commercials, 76
Aesthetics, 7, 10, 43, 46–50, 80, 104, 117, 127–128, 146, 160, 206; aesthetic autonomy, 43, 48–50; aesthetic laughter, 84; aesthetic pluralism, 40; aesthetic space, 49; aesthetic-philosophical, 78; aesthetics of tropicalism, 167
African American artists, 21–24, 34n4; in churches, 23, 28; *juba*, 21
African American music, 21, 26–27, 29–30, 32, 35n19; plantation songs, 22. *See also* Negro spirituals
African American music, 21, 26–27, 29–30, 32, 35n19; plantation songs, 22. *See also* Negro spirituals
African music, 10, 33, 46, 111, 116–117, 122, 130n16, 146–147, 150n1, 151nn2,3,8,13,14, 152nn19,20,21,23,30,

153n39, 160–165, 200; African Afro-Cuban music, 125, 139–140, 145, 150, 151nn9,10, 152nn24,25,27, 154n49 (*see also* Africando); African instruments, 20, 27; African labels, 115; African musical forms, 29, 32. *See also* Black culture; *Griot*
Africando, 115, 143, 147, 152n29
Agency, 52, 86n11, 136, 181, 190, 202, 212n21
Alternative, 54, 64, 79, 116, 144, 148, 161, 167, 193, 197
Altruism, 112, 124
Amazon, 5, 10, 75–76, 85, 86n8
Amazon.com, 43
Ambient music, 42, 45
American music, 3, 27–29, 55, 114, 129n1, 172, 178
Amerindians, 20, 76, 84, 85
Anglophone, 61, 117, 138, 139, 140
Anikulapo-Kuti, Fela, 8, 11, 159–164, 169, 170n6

221

Myth, 48, 78–80, 85n6, 86n8, 195; mythical figure, 54, mythical thought, 78, 79; mythology, 195

Narrative(s), 8, 11, 41–42, 86n8, 94, 95, 108, 123, 125–128; quest narrative, 48; Western narrative, 205

National: national authenticity, 117; national ballet, 129n3; national boundaries, 4, 141; national census, 60, 72n7; national cultural context, 193; national culture, 71, 117, 138; national discourse, 58; national divisions, 8, 141, 169; national economy, 54; national genre, 209; national identity, 6, 55–57; national industry, 76; national market, 167; national music, 56, 61, 70–71, 77, 80, 115, 126, 140, 194; national music contests, 60, 73n14; national press, 84; national politics, 55; national public sphere, 72n2, 77; national sovereignty, 76; national symbol, 193, 210; nationalization, 114; pan-national, 60; state-owned industry, 113 (*see also* Radio)

Native, 19, 20, 24, 35n10, 54, 78, 82, 93, 106, 176, 209

N'dour, Youssou, 136, 151nn2,3, 152n24, 179, 189, 190, 203

Negotiations, 6, 54, 94, 103, 106–107, 113, 130n20, 177

Negro spirituals, 23, 28, 30, 31; African American spirituals, 42, 49; negro songs, 21, 29, 35n19

Neoliberalism, 190

Network, 4, 53, 66, 67, 69, 71, 111, 123, 130n10, 144

New York Times, 45, 47, 117, 119, 126, 136, 159

Nightclub, 58, 72n8, 116, 130n10, 205; African nightclub, 139–142, 144, 146, 147, 149; salsa club circuit, 136, 144

Non-western, 3, 52, 137, 176, 198, 202; non-western engagement, 72; non-western music, 1, 4, 6, 7, 11, 111, 118, 128, 135, 136, 173, 178, 198, 205–207, 213n28

Nostalgia, 50, 96, 123; cultural politics of nostalgia, 8, 42; imperialist nostalgia, 47, 108

Opposition, 5, 31, 57, 77, 194, 213n23; binary opposition, 208

Oppression, 32, 33, 35n18, 163, 204; systems of oppression, 17

Orality, 58, 168–169; oral history projects, 56

Oriental, 25, 32, 78; orientalism, 81, 127, 202

Other (the), 11, 19, 34n2, 78–79, 83–84, 94, 108, 190, 202–203, 207–210, 213n31; Bhabha formulation, 178; commercialization of, 33; cultural others, 107; as music category, 178; othering, 20

Ownership, 32, 41, 50

Pacific culture, 63–69, 181

Pacifism, 81

Pan-African, 20, 31, 140, 147, 152n29; pan-Africanism of exile, 20, 29

Pan-Americanism, 117, 144

Partnership, 101, 109n11, 143, 197

Peer-to-peer sharing, 66–67

Performance, 10, 22, 29, 42, 55, 56, 58, 67, 70, 123, 125, 152n23, 159, 167, 170n1, 192, 206; cultural performance, 9, 54; dance performance, 93, 95, 101; during celebrations, 24–26, 34nn9,10, 57, 60; folkloric performance, 10, 101; local performance, 57, 58; museum performance, 100, 101; of music, 2, 5, 29, 61, 69, 71, 130n10, 139, 141, 147, 149, 154n49, 184, 196

Philanthropy, 83, 99, 197, 212n14

Phonographs, 1, 76, 78–80, 85n6, 142

Piracy, 62–63, 66–67, 167

Pleasure, 7, 10, 20, 33, 41, 49, 50, 82, 144

Pluralism, 4, 40, 201

Policy, 147, 153n47, 164; on AIDS, 160, 167, 170n2; cultural policies, 153n44; economic policies, 162; foreign policies, 115, 121, 147, 153nn42,47, 204; of racial segregation, 24, 148

Politics, 6, 46–50, 112, 204, 205, 206, 209, 210; Cold War politics, 111; of

Reggae, 2, 17, 18, 23, 56, 61–63, 65, 68–69, 82, 152n30, 182, 189, 193, 196, 211n10
Regimes of value, 41, 50, 107
Relationships, 6, 9, 18, 35n10, 41, 56, 75–78, 107, 114, 127, 159–163, 170nn3,10, 190, 199, 201, 205, 212n18, 214n32; business relationships, 148; contentious relationship, 86n11, 153n48; dyadic relationship, 135; exploitative relationships, 198; Norawa relationship, 106; Relationship, 32–33, 35n18; unequal relationship, 206
Religious, 21, 34n5, 42–44, 68, 95, 141, 207, 210; politico-religious establishment, 78–79; religious awakenings, 20, 23; religious boundaries, 148; religious colonial art, 100; religious experience, 40, 47; religious expression, 148; religious gatherings, 34n5; religious institutions, 78–79; religious music, 21–31, 95 (see also Spiritual music); religious practice, 41, 44, 49, 54; religious sounds, 42, 50
Repertoires, 22, 25–30, 60, 69, 72n9, 121, 123, 138, 140, 150, 204; creole repertoire, 25–26; imported repertoire, 24–25; local repertoire, 57
Representation, 12, 47, 83, 84, 107–108, 172, 206, 207; crisis of, 203
Resignification, 41–42, 49–50
Resistance, 17, 42, 56, 68, 72n1, 100, 138, 160, 181, 190
Resonance, 96–97, 164, 194; symbolic resonance, 97
Rights, 164, 166, 175; civil rights, 81; Copyright and Related Rights Act, 66; indigenous rights movement, 10, 75; intellectual property rights, 166–170; human rights, 82, 197
Ritual, 46, 77, 85, 94, 95; ritual dissociation, 109n16; ritual knowledge, 83
Rock music, 6, 10, 17, 18, 42, 49, 56, 61–63, 75, 80–82, 101–102, 109, 114, 125, 139, 141, 153n35, 173, 182, 189, 193, 197, 211–212; Spanish rock, 121
Rolling Stone, 45

Roots, 63, 81, 82, 97, 117, 137, 138, 147, 152n27, 177; folk roots, 183; grassroots, 70; rootedness, 212n21
Royalty, 41, 66, 68, 117

Salsa, 114–115, 121, 129nn4,5, 130n16, 136–138, 141–150, 151n6, 152nn19,29, 153nn37,38,48, 195
Saussure, Ferdinand de, 81, 85n4
Schismogenesis, 42
Schizophonia, 9, 40–42, 49–50
Schools: art school, 42; music school, 97, 99–100, 105–106
Shamanism, 77, 83
Simon, Paul, 3, 118, 174, 198
Simulacrum, 49, 81, 176, 201
Skepticism, 7, 84, 208
Slave, 17–33, 34nn5,9, 14, 48, 162, 165, 167; Indonesian slaves, 25; musical practices of slaves, 17, 20–23, 24, 26–30, 33; slave ship, 7, 11, 159, 162, 164, 168; slave trade, 2, 8, 11, 19, 53, 162, 165, 204; social death of, 20, 32; strategies of, 20. See also Jim Crow; South Africa
Slavery, 6, 8, 9, 10, 17–32, 162, 165, 191, 202
Social class, 2, 82, 127, 136, 169, 182, 192, 199; class struggle, 86n11; middle class, 112, 136, 182, 199; working-class, 82, 136
Social life, 2, 20, 24–25, 41, 50, 107
Socialism, 81, 112, 114, 119, 128, 153n43; socialist bureaucracy, 112–113
Solidarity, 19, 114, 118, 124, 127, 190, 196–198
Song contests, 60, 67, 73n14
Sosseh, Laba, 10, 11, 135 150, 151nn4,17,18, 152nn21,22,27,31,32,33, 153n38, 154n49
Soul music, 18, 22, 23, 25, 67, 141, 146, 182, 189, 195
Sounds: as ethnic commodity, 40–42; found sound, 42; fusion sound, 111, 121; global sounds, 46; hybrid sound, 118; musical sound, 7, 178; religious sounds, 41, 42, 50; sonic circulation, 42; sonic tourism, 200; Sounds Maga-

ing, 159; of globalization, 1, 2; misunderstandings, 6, 7, 19; model of
understanding, 77
Universal, 5, 33, 78, 79, 135, 190, 193,
197, 207; *kathoton,* 78, 80; universal
language, 2, 78, 190–192, 207, 211n2;
universal value, 107, 197
Universality, 79, 97, 190, 201, 209

Value, 6, 10, 42, 52, 58, 71, 81, 94, 100,
107, 190, 195, 207, 210, 213n26; category of, 83; central value, 79; cultural
value, 96, 100, 198–199; explanatory
value, 77; production value, 64, 174,
177; universal value, 107, 197; value of
music, 35n19; worlds of value, 96, 97.
See also Regimes of value
Video, 5, 12, 37, 44, 64, 66, 70, 133, 154,
173, 197, 205
Violence, 17–18, 26, 191; economic violence, 161; of encounter, 32–33; language of, 6; political violence, 170
Violin, 10, 21, 25, 70, 94–100, 103–108,
108n1, 145
Viral marketing, 164–165, 171n8

War, 196; Civil War, 21, 23, 27; Cold
War, 81, 111, 113–114, 121, 147, 204;
interwar, 2; postwar, 9, 57, 139; World
War II, 2, 54, 55, 57, 59, 97, 139
Weber, Max, 78
West, 5, 7, 8, 11, 41, 76, 78, 80–84, 116,
135, 160, 178, 181, 184, 194, 200

West Africa, 24, 113–115, 125, 129n6,
135–150, 151n17, 152n33, 169, 200
Western audiences, 7, 10, 11, 118, 127,
151n3, 181, 209
Western music, 2, 3, 8, 10, 18, 27, 42,
46–47, 50, 61, 65, 68, 69, 72nn4,8,10,
76, 83, 85n6, 135, 181; history of,
78–81; non-western music, 1, 4, 6,
135, 205, 207; Western instruments,
59; Western musicians, 76, 112, 128,
130n18, 198
Westernization, 55
Westernness, 80–81
World beat, 42, 178, 182
World Music, 8, 17–18, 33, 40–42, 46–
47, 50, 65, 70, 94, 107–108, 118, 120,
122–126, 128, 130n18, 146, 150, 159,
169, 170n1, 172–180, 182–184, 185n11,
189–201, 203–210, 211nn7,10,13,
212nn14,21, 213nn28,29; classicalization of, 183–184; conceptualizations
of, 4, 10–12, 40–41, 135–137; history
of, 2–4, 70; world music industry, 7,
9, 50, 53, 111–113, 115–117, 125, 128;
world music networks, 130n10
World system, 55, 76, 78

Yoruba, 48, 162, 191
Youth, 21–23, 48, 58–60, 64, 68, 120,
128, 129n4, 141, 148, 152n30, 180,
199; young musicians, 65, 69, 124,
137, 140, 144, 152n32; youth protests, 82

Tracking Globalization

Illicit Flows and Criminal Things: States, Borders, and the Other
Side of Globalization
Edited by Willem van Schendel and Itty Abraham

Globalizing Tobacco Control: Anti-Smoking Campaigns in California,
France, and Japan
Roddey Reid

Generations and Globalization: Youth, Age, and Family in the New
World Economy
Edited by Jennifer Cole and Deborah Durham

Youth and the City in the Global South
*Karen Transberg Hansen in collaboration with Anne Line Dalsgaard,
Katherine Gough, Ulla Ambrosius Madsen, Karen Valentin, and
Norbert Wildermuth*

Made in Mexico: Zapotec Weavers and the Global Ethnic Art Market
W. Warner Wood